Not Your

Mother's Divorce

Not Your Mother's Divorce

A Practical,
Girlfriend-to-Girlfriend Guide
to Surviving the End of an Early Marriage

Kay Moffett and
Sarah Touborg

BROADWAY BOOKS

New York

PRINTED IN THE UNITED STATES OF AMERICA

BROADWAY BOOKS and its logo, a letter B bisected on the diagonal, are
trademarks of Random House, Inc.

"The Book of Love," written by Stephin Merritt, © 1999 by Stephin Merritt
and published by Gay and Loud (ASCAP). Reprinted with permission.

Visit our website at www.broadwaybooks.com

First edition published 2003

Library of Congress Cataloging-in-Publication Data

Moffett, Kay.
Not your mother's divorce : a practical, girlfriend-to-girlfriend guide to
surviving the end of an early marriage / Kay Moffett & Sarah Touborg.
          p. cm.
    1. Divorce—Psychological aspects. 2. Young women—Conduct of life.
    3. Young women—Life skills guide. 4. Young women—Psychology.
              I. Touborg, Sarah. II. Title.
                HQ814M64 2003
                  306.89—dc22
                  2003058531

ISBN 0-7679-1350-7

1 3 5 7 9 10 8 6 4 2

"*I don't believe it. That's my ex-wife.*"

Contents

How This Book Was Born   1

Chapter One: Where Did Our Love Go?   7

Chapter Two: Suddenly Single   33

Chapter Three: "There's Something I Have to Tell You . . ."
*Sharing Your News and Getting the Support You Need from
Friends, Family, and Work*   56

Chapter Four: Losing a Bed, a Bank Account, and a Roommate
Physical and Financial Separation   76

Chapter Five: Untying the Knot
The Legal Process   108

Chapter Six: In the Company of a Vivid Ghost
Encounters with Your Ex   136

Chapter Seven: Here Comes the Divorcée
Single in Society   160

Chapter Eight: The Dating Scene—Take Two   184

Chapter Nine: Retying the Knot—Or Not   216

Chapter Ten: When Life Hands You Limes,
    Make Mojitos   236

Books for Consultation & Consolation   246

Acknowledgments   251

Index   253

Not Your
Mother's Divorce

How This Book Was Born

> The book of love is long and boring and
> written very long ago. It's full of flowers
> and heart-shaped boxes and things we're all
> too young to know.
>
> —The Magnetic Fields,
> *69 Love Songs*

When we, your fearless authors, first met in college, divorce was far from our minds. We were roommates and English majors who bonded over our mutual love of literature and, specifically, doomed women writers of the twentieth century. We spent many hours discussing (and procrastinating work on) our senior theses—Sarah's on the tortured Virginia Woolf and Kay's on the equally tortured pair of poets Anne Sexton and Sylvia Plath. At that time, the world often seemed overwhelming with all of its interesting options: The Great American Novel with that cute new professor or Victorian poetry with the dowdy and world-renowned expert? The pasta bar or the salad bar? The bookbag or the knapsack? The two of us were notorious for our indecisiveness. Perhaps most mystifying of all, we were particularly stumped by which parties to go to on

Saturday nights. In fact, sometimes we would spend so much time debating the pros and cons of various events, that by the time we had devised an itinerary for the evening, the parties were practically over and we happily hung out drinking wine in our room.

After college, Sarah went to England to study steamy seventeenth-century poetry, and Kay began teaching public school in New York City. Soon after Sarah's return, we both developed crushes on, and eventually full-blown relationships with, men who were in the same fields as we were, with similar interests and ambitions. With age and growing confidence, we were both becoming more decisive. In fact, we both decided that these guys were the ones for us and married them about five years out of college and barely four months apart. In December 1995, Sarah and T. had a winter wonderland wedding in Central Park. In March 1996, Kay and F. had a funky, flamingo-filled wedding in Florida.

During our first years of being married, now living on different coasts (Sarah in New York working in book publishing, and Kay in San Francisco getting a graduate degree), we would on occasion confess to each other on the phone, "This is hard work!" But we'd typically reassure ourselves that we'd just hit some early stumbling blocks in the lifelong project known as marriage. Both children of divorce, we were determined to make our marriages work—*we* could do this thing that our parents couldn't, and we wanted to do it well.

When Sarah and T. landed in counseling less than a year into their marriage, Sarah believed that "if I just work hard enough at this, we can work through 'the kinks' " (as she'd euphemistically labeled their frequent fights). T.'s temper was unlike anything she'd ever experienced, and counseling was not, in fact, doing much to help get to the root of their issues as a couple. However, when one day T. exclaimed in a session, "The problem is, you just haven't read enough Faulkner!" something shifted in Sarah. (She wished afterward that she'd retorted, "And you just haven't read enough Shakespeare!"). The preposterous accusation was her wake-up call to realizing, with immense sadness and disappointment, that T. was searching for something much deeper in himself that Sarah couldn't possibly offer.

T. moved out a few weeks after the Faulkner incident, and though it took Sarah quite some time to accept his decision to leave the marriage, she realized, though she initially hated to admit it, that she was much, much happier on her own. The period following T.'s moving out felt incredibly scary and uncertain, but it also brought some unexpected opportunities. In particular, it was a chance to renew and deepen female friendships and family ties. Dating, for the first time as a true adult, was unnerving at times, but also proved to be an exhilarating and important part of the recovery process.

At about the time that Sarah was getting divorced, Kay began going through a period of intense self-exploration (she lived in San Francisco, after all). Over a three-year period of figuring herself out and growing into her own skin, she not only began to question her career choice, but also her marriage to F. Kay and F.'s lives had become so closely intertwined during their early years together, with practically all the same friends and interests, that she eventually wanted more independence from him, which didn't suit his needs. Kay also realized that they had quite different sensibilities, worldviews, and future aspirations. While they got along well on a daily basis, on a deep level they didn't see the world in the same way and often didn't connect about some of the ideas and emotions that mattered most to each of them.

What was difficult was that Kay and F. were strong communicators and cared about each other very much, so while there were major differences between them that they couldn't reconcile, they remained close in many ways. It was excruciatingly difficult for Kay to make the decision to leave F., with whom she had spent most of her twenties and who was effectively her best friend. But something inside of her knew the fit was wrong for the long term. She fought this feeling for a few years, but not listening to her heart only made her grow depressed. After a great deal of angst and torturous reflection, Kay decided to separate from F. He resisted her decision vehemently at first, but soon came to feel it was the right move, partly because he met someone with whom he felt he was more compatible. This development wasn't easy for Kay, but she came to accept it, and eventually she and F. decided to divorce.

Both of us, during the darker days of our respective divorces, scoured the shelves at bookstores for something to help us make sense of things and found nothing that spoke to us. All the books were geared toward older women with children. Many assumed the woman had been left by the man for another woman or that the husband was something of a scoundrel, which wasn't the case for either of us. Plus, they all seemed overly earnest and borderline cheesy, with titles and covers neither of us could envision handing the cashier. However, we definitely felt the need for some seasoned counsel, which we were able to get only from each other and the few other divorcées we had each gotten to know.

The fall after Sarah and T. had separated, she planned a trip to the Bay Area to reconnect with Kay and their beloved college roommates. During a spirited dinner reunion, Sarah described the book she wanted to write, something which would put to good use the wry new perspectives and amusing anecdotes she was collecting through the difficult and unexpected process of her separation and divorce. Our friends all encouraged Sarah to write the book and promised we'd buy it.

A year after her separation, Kay was feeling antsy, like she wanted to do something creative with all the pain, wisdom, and newfound joy that had come from the experience, but she didn't know exactly what. Fortuitously, Sarah emailed her around this time and said, "I'm thinking of finally writing that book about divorce. Do you want to write it with me?" It was pure telepathy and cosmic alignment; Kay didn't have to think twice before agreeing and writing back, "YYYYYEEEEESSSSS!!!!!!" And, thus, this book was born.

A month later, we met up in Palm Springs with an old college roommate, Liddy, for a semi-spontaneous girls' weekend of sun, fun, and copious gabbing. At a café one morning, we began sketching out the book, with Liddy deftly facilitating and summarizing the discussion along the way (we now refer to her as the "midwife"). A few lattes later, we had a list of ten chapters in front of us: everything we had wanted to read about and be consoled about during the divorce but had had to figure out largely on our own.

Eventually, we interviewed thirty other women in order to broaden our understanding of young divorcées' experiences beyond our own particular circumstances. We did not choose these women according to a statistically random sampling, rather our research was anecdotal and qualitative, based on conversations with women in our wider social network. We either knew our interviewees as friends or acquaintances or found them through friends, relatives, and work. The vast majority of these women had married under thirty and divorced under thirty-five, and the remaining few had married under thirty-five and divorced under forty. None had children. All had attended college and had careers of some sort or another. Many lived on the East and West Coasts, like ourselves; however some lived in the middle of the country. The women spanned the gamut in terms of coming from working-class, middle-class, and upper-class backgrounds, and though the majority were of European American background, several were of East Asian, South Asian, or Latin American descent.*

Being college-educated career women like ourselves, another thing that many of these women had in common was high

---

*All of the marriages were straight, although one woman we interviewed discovered during her marriage that she was gay.

achievement—some might even say overachievement. We all had a desire to excel in the realms of both work and love and wanted to make a good life for ourselves. None of us was especially rebellious, although some of us had some wild periods or wild sides. But, for the most part, we had built somewhat conventionally successful lives, with good educations, blossoming careers, strong groups of friends, and what we had hoped would be happy marriages.

Now remarried, Sarah feels oddly thankful for the painful dissolution of her early marriage and the reservoirs of self-knowledge and self-confidence she had no idea it would bring. And, as painful as her breakup was, Kay has only grown more happy and fulfilled since. She has dated several men and learned tremendous amounts about herself in the process, and she feels quite certain that she will one day retie the knot with someone very wonderful. We know that if you're just beginning the process, you may feel daunted by what lies ahead, but we assure you: you *will* come out the other side. If you're anything like the women you'll meet in this book, you'll not only endure the experience, you'll actually become a stronger and happier person because of it.

In the first chapter, we'll explore what drove us and many of these women to marry and divorce, and in the following nine chapters, we'll share our collective advice, anecdotes, and encouragement for surviving and thriving after the end of an early marriage. We aim to provide you with the book we didn't have: a book about, by, and for the young, childless divorcée. We hope the two of us and all the other divorcées whose voices appear in this book can serve as older sisters, walking ahead a little bit and showing the way home.

CHAPTER ONE

Where Did Our Love Go?

> There are no events but thoughts and the
> heart's hard turning, the heart's slow
> learning where to love and whom. The rest
> is merely gossip, and tales for other times.
>
> —Annie Dillard,
>
> *Holy the Firm*

Where *did* our love go? This is the million-dollar question. The question you ask yourself over and over again. The question others want to ask you when they hear the news, even if only the bold ones actually blurt it out. It's the black box at the wreckage site that no one can find and everyone's hunting for. We dedicate this first chapter to this question because it's the first one on everyone's minds, including yours. If you want to get straight to the nitty-gritty of the practical steps you can take to move on, feel free to skip ahead to chapter 2. But for those of you who want to take a closer look at why a marriage can end or what forces may have been at work in your own situation, this chapter is designed to give you some preliminary insight.

There are many ways that your marriage may have ended. Countless ways. There might be Another Man or Another Woman. There may have been an infidelity of a different sort, say concerning finances. Maybe one of you began to question your sexuality. Perhaps somebody had substance abuse issues. Or maybe it was less dramatic: you just outgrew each other over time, having met when you were younger and changed significantly, for example, in a so-called quarter-life crisis. One of you may have recognized the shift in your marriage first, or maybe it dawned on both of you around the same time in a moment of truth. It may have slapped you in the face or it may have crept up on you slowly like a dull ache.

Let's be realistic: getting married is always about taking a leap of faith, acting on a well-informed hunch, and like any other choice in life, the decision may not work out the way you had hoped. The statistics are there for all to see: approximately half of the married world (at least in this country, and Great Britain is close behind) gets divorced. Consider the many peers you have in Hollywood: Drew Barrymore, Angelina Jolie, Nicole Kidman, Jennifer Lopez, Julia Roberts, Meg Ryan—the list goes on.

What's more, divorce is occurring earlier and earlier in marriage, with 25 percent of divorces taking place after only two years, according to Pamela Paul, author of *The Starter Marriage and the Future of Matrimony*. Paul also found that in 2000, over four million twenty- to thirty-four-year-olds reported their status as "divorced." The trend is being documented everywhere. In April 2001, *Jane* published an article entitled "Young, Hot, Divorced"; on July 12, 2001, the *New York Times* Home section ran an article called "Just Divorced, Gone Shopping," about the joys of retail therapy for the newly divorced at places like IKEA; and Paul published *The Starter Marriage* in 2002, about the growing trend of young, childless divorces. The point being you are not alone, and you are not a bad or freakish person. In fact, you are in excellent company.

Until now, divorce was most likely something that happened to *other* people, people like your parents' friends or your friends' parents. But this is not your mother's (or mother's generation's) divorce. Partly because that older generation paved the way, there is much more acceptance and far less stigma than there ever has been toward divorce. In our postfeminist era, women have much greater social, economic, and political freedom, and this means that, despite the difficulty of the situation, you have many more choices and opportunities than your sisters of yesteryear.

People will likely say to you, "Well, at least you didn't have children." And, in many ways, things *are* simply easier for you than for women who are older and/or have children and are facing the same challenge. There's less to disentangle, and without offspring you really can leave your ex and your relationship with him in the dust if you so choose. The reality is you still have a huge portion of your adult life ahead of you and, as daunting as it may sound, you have a chance to wipe the slate clean and start over.

However, even though you may not have to worry about bambinos, you are likely still undergoing an enormous and painful life change. You are probably trying to make sense of What Went Wrong, and this soul-searching will take a while. Don't worry about trying to solve the riddle right away—you won't be able to figure it out all at once. Some puzzle pieces will come easily, others will fall into place later. But one good place to start is to think about what brought you and your ex to the altar in the first place.

Tying the Knot at Quarter-Life

Despite the fact that there is much more freedom than ever before to marry older, say in your early to mid-thirties, the vast majority of divorcées we spoke with got married in their twenties. They did so despite the fact that dating for long periods of time and extended cohabitation are often precursors to marriage nowadays, and that waiting until your thirties to have children is also common practice, especially among college-educated professional women. So, why did we and the divorcées in this book marry fairly young for our generation? And how does that relate to why we divorced?

Nuptially Obsessed:
Marriage as National Pastime

Despite the wave of feminist feeling and progress in the seventies and eighties, we live in a country that is matrimonially obsessed. In *The Starter Marriage*, Paul suggests that we Gen-Xers, those born between 1965 and 1978, are drawn to marry early because of all the social and personal tumult we saw in our parents' "me" generation. Generally liberal-minded folk, we Gen-Xers seem to have embraced a new kind of traditionalism as a way of finding security in an increasingly uncertain world. These yearnings for stability are bolstered by the bridal mania in pop culture and the seductive commercialization of marital romance and commitment, from charming movies like *Four Weddings and a Funeral* to *Martha Stewart Weddings* and *InStyle*'s regular features on the weddings of Hollywood stars. Not to mention *Bride's, Bridal Guide, Elegant Bride, Modern Bride*, and *Wedding Style* magazines, which call out to women with the promise of the fantasy long before they actually decide to walk down the aisle.

Not only is it hip and glamorous to get married—not only do you get the ring, the princess gown, and the fabulous parties—it's also supposed to be the path of goodness. We get bombarded with all sorts of lovely moral messages about the institution, perhaps from our families but also from the radical and not-so-radical right in this country, who sponsor publicity campaigns about the virtues of marriage, push promarriage/antidivorce legislation, and want us all betrothed by age twenty. Even liberals such as Sylvia Ann Hewlett, founder and chair of the National Parents' Association, encourage us to marry young and put off our career until later. In her recent book, *Creating a Life: Professional Women and the Quest for Children*, Hewlett advises young women to give "urgent priority" to finding a marriage partner in their twenties and have their first baby before thirty-five. In addition to the pundits, our national government also makes clear its preference for married people over nonmarrieds by giving the nuptially connected serious tax breaks. We're seeped in the cult of marriage, and we don't even realize it. You get married. That's what you *do*.

Europe, on the other hand, while being in many ways more old-fashioned, is less fixated on marriage. Many Europeans cohabitate for decades and have several children without getting married. The *New York Times* ran an article on the topic on March 24, 2002, citing the following figures: in Iceland, 62 percent of all births were to unwed parents in 1999, in Norway the statistic was 49 percent, in France 41 percent, in Britain 38 percent, and in Ireland, where divorce only became legal seven years ago, the number was 31 percent, a figure on a par with the United States. The Europeans quoted in the article maintained that in Europe there's little social distinction made between being married and cohabitating, or between children born out of wedlock and those born within a marriage. The *Times* attributed this more laissez-faire view of marriage to changing attitudes toward religion and the state and a growing belief that "when—and whether—to marry are increasingly seen as deeply personal choices free from the traditional moral judgments of community, family or church."

In America, however, getting married is still a central part of leading a "good life" and being successful. Even for Americans who are less religious and less typically traditional in their values, it's de rigueur to marry if you want to have "made it" in life. And, for more religious folk, it's also part of being "good" in the eyes of the big man in the sky. But, regardless of who you are, in much of America today you're considered only a partial success if you're a highly accomplished, professional (straight) man or woman but have never married. And couples who stay together a long time but never marry are constantly questioned about why they don't "make it official," as if they are somehow less of a couple or less committed to each other if they don't sign a legal document and throw an extravagant party called a wedding.

It makes sense, then, that those of us who are eager to be successful and attain the good life would get married earlier rather than later. The young divorcées in our book, including ourselves, were generally high-achievers, college grads who pursued careers, so it's not surprising we felt drawn to wed when we found someone appropriate and the time felt right. Just like we wanted to get good grades, get a good job, and start building a career we would be proud of, we wanted to attain the traditional markers of success in our personal lives. And while goals are important in life and can help you attain what you want, they can also sometimes become ends unto themselves, driving you into decisions somewhat quickly and perhaps blinding you to what you *really* need and want.

Broad cultural and generational trends, then, set the backdrop for the individual stories of those of us women who marry—and divorce—relatively young. However, each of us has our own very particular story which encompasses both these subtle internalized societal pressures and a unique personal and familial history that explains why we married when and who we did.

Leaping Before Looking:
The Aspirations of a Young Heart

Even with this larger context in mind, young divorcées can often feel that their decision-making around their marriage was somewhat faulty—that they either hadn't thought the choice through very well or used dubious reasons for tying the knot. Often the decision-making involved unconscious desires and needs that only came to the surface after the relationship ended. While some women knew they were making a mistake the day they said their vows, most of the women we spoke with did not have this inkling of doubt. Rather, they thought at the time, as the people they were at the time, that they were making the right choice for themselves. Looking back on the experience, the young divorcées we talked to gave a variety of explanations for why they made the decision to marry.

First and Only Love

Some women marry the first man they have a real relationship with, their first real love. These women are often somewhat late bloomers in the romantic arena, even though they've already achieved success academically and perhaps professionally. Sydney, for instance, hadn't had much experience with guys and met her ex-husband in college. The way she felt with him opened up a whole new way of being to her: "To be so loved and adored by him was, in a way, the attraction." Looking back, she's not sure she was ever deeply in love with him, but she loved being loved and having a steady boyfriend, so when he asked her to marry him a couple of years later, she felt nervous but also felt she "had better say yes."

Mehta, too, had had little experience with men when, at age twenty-one, she met the man who would become her husband in the office where she worked while finishing college. He was somewhat older and worldly wise, and she admired his extensive knowledge and intellect. He made her feel special, which she had never felt before. Because he was all she had ever known romantically and because she wanted to be married by a certain age, largely due to pressure from her parents, they tied the knot.

Tanya remarks about her ex-husband, "He was my first real love, it was the first totally mutual love I'd ever had after casual things and some unrequited things in college, and we had a strong spiritual connection as well." She met him in Ecuador and when they moved to the United States and he needed a green card, she didn't think twice about marrying him.

Some women marry the first man they have a substantial relationship with, the only serious romantic love they have ever known, partly because he is the only thing they can imagine. Divorcées who fit into this category often say that they didn't contemplate the decision much, it just seemed like the next natural thing to do.

Shelter from the Storm

Some young women turn to marriage as source of safety, a harbor from a chaotic upbringing or a confusing adult world. Miranda, for instance, married K. because she felt she could really trust him versus some of the caregivers in her upbringing. She felt he would never leave her and would take care of her. On the flip side, Rachel had a very protected upbringing and was scared of wandering out into the world beyond her hometown. She was also professionally lost and perplexed about her calling in life. When her boyfriend moved to a big city and asked her to marry him, she agreed, partly because he was an anchor to hold on to and a safe way for her to leave her comfort zone and explore new places.

Looking back, these women all felt they made the decision to marry based largely on fear and that, for this reason, the decision came back to haunt them. In Miranda's words, "The truth is, when I got married the first time [she has since remarried], it was from weakness . . . I think I met up with a person whose weaknesses fit like a puzzle piece with mine, so that he propped me up in my weak places. But I don't think that's a way to grow."

All in the Family

We're all familiar with the familial pressures to get married: Aunt Mary who asks you every Thanksgiving when you're going to bring home a husband, your grandmother who warns you about waiting too long to find a man, and so on. But the pressures also come in less direct and more subtle ways. It's the average age of getting married in your family, it's all your cousins' wedding invitations arriving every other week, it's your mother telling you about relative so-and-so and neighbor so-and-so and how they had a lovely ceremony on a beautiful blue day in May. And, if you have siblings, you may also feel a bit of sibling rivalry around beating them to the altar, or at least not lagging too far behind. For decades, you are marinated in all these messages about what is supposed to happen when you're approximately a certain age, and so you start to make this expectation a reality without perhaps being fully conscious of why you are so eager to commit yourself to someone for life.

In Leslie's family, everyone had married young and she had always thought she would. When her then-boyfriend proposed to her when she was twenty-four, after nine months of dating, she was euphoric and said yes. She had come from a high-achieving, perfectionist family, and the timing fit her idea (and her parents' idea) of how her life should unfold. Looking back, she sees she was very developed intellectually and socially but not emotionally, which is why she "made the unsophisticated decision to get married to a guy who was really not right" for her. Getting divorced was the first thing she did that let her parents down, and she thinks it was "the adolescent rebellion" she'd never had before.

Some women experience a more overt external push to get married. Cindy, for instance, said she felt "forced" into her wedding. She and M. had been together a few years, she was twenty-five and everyone kept saying, "When are you going to get married? What's holding you up?" Her parents were very traditional and wanted her to get married before moving in with M., and his parents had never had a wedding and they really wanted one, so the two families orchestrated a lavish ceremony and celebration. She says she didn't enjoy the wedding for one second and felt panicky and stressed the whole time. Once she moved in with M., she discovered he had major substance abuse issues that led to the downfall of their relationship.

Our family's expectations for us regarding marriage can obviously play a large role in when and whom we decide to marry, which is not necessarily a problem. The women above, however, felt that they had followed their family's wishes somewhat unwittingly, without stepping outside the familial blueprint for their lives and making sure it was what *they* wanted.

"He Fit the Fairy Tale"

As we grow up, we develop notions of what our perfect man or soulmate will be like—partially from our families, partially from our social context, and partially from our unique personalities. When we meet a guy who feels like a human embodiment of those traits, we can think we've found "The One." Sometimes, because he fits our ideal, we have trouble seeing the real him and assessing the real relationship we're in with him.

Sydney feels that she received strong conditioning from her grandmother and parents about meeting the guy she would marry in college. From a young age, she remembers hearing stories about "a Cinderella environment" at college, and when she met her ex-husband there, "he fit the fairy tale." She had gotten clear messages about the kind of man she should marry—from a good family, with a good job—and he "totally fit the resume of what my family wanted for me." Sydney leapt at the opportunity to marry her college beau because his part had been written into her script long ago, and like a good girl, she was playing her part of marrying him. She later discovered she was never really in love with him and they weren't especially compatible. Our friend Dawn had very similar notions when she went off to college of finding herself an "alpha male varsity athlete" to marry. She dated the captain of the football team throughout college, tied the knot with him soon after they graduated, and got divorced from him after ten fairly miserable years of marriage.

Romance, weddings, and marriage bring out the idealist in everyone. Sarah remembers her own mother's wedding mania, which belied the fact that she'd gone through a terrible divorce herself. There was something strangely resilient and enduring about the fairy tale of a gorgeous, frothy wedding of the kind she loved to imagine for Sarah and her sisters. Talking about Sarah's wedding became a point of connection for Sarah and her mother, even though her mother always secretly harbored doubts about T.'s suitability for Sarah. These ideals—of the perfect man, of the perfect day—can cloud your perception of things. You are so focused on how things should be (and have existed in your mind for so long), that you have trouble looking at the perhaps confusing and disappointing reality that this person may not be right for you or this wedding day really shouldn't be happening.

"Everyone's Doing It!"

We all like to think peer pressure ceased to exist when we left our high school hallways and vowed never to return. However, young divorcées frequently report having felt a keen pressure to get married because all their friends were and it was what you did when you hit a certain age. The thick, creamy envelopes with raised lettering cram your mailbox week after week, and you start to wonder why you and your boyfriend aren't getting married. The pressure is as much external as internal, in that getting married by a certain age can become a personal goal for many women (and men) based to a large extent on their social context.

Both Gina and Elizabeth had been with their boyfriends for several years when they began to feel it was time to get married. Gina says she and E. had a tumultuous relationship, breaking up and getting back together numerous times, but at the five- to six-year point, she felt it was time to get married. Everyone else was tying the knot and, she says, "We were in this zone where everyone kept asking, when are you guys going to get married?" She thought their relationship would improve and everything would get better once they wed, which she now considers rationalization and faulty thinking.

Similarly, Elizabeth began to raise the marriage question at the three- to four-year mark in her relationship with her ex, feeling that she was now in her late twenties and it was time to get married. In both Gina's and Elizabeth's cases, they initiated the idea of marriage and cajoled the guy into it, but looking back, they both think they were responding to a lot of external pressures as opposed to a strong feeling about the rightness of the relationship.

Maeve admitted that she married her ex largely because she was one of the only women she knew at that point in her life (she was thirty-two) who wasn't married, and she started to feel "serious social pressure." An old guy friend who had carried a torch for her since high school emerged and wanted to marry her, and she agreed without being at all sure about him. A short time after they eloped to Florida, she realized she had married someone she didn't really love but thought would make a good partner.

Friends and your wider social network, like your family, can infiltrate your thinking and inform your decision-making in ways you don't even realize, and pretty soon you're swept up in planning a wedding and entering a marriage with someone you're not totally convinced about or who's not totally convinced about you.

A Curious Kind of Rebellion

Gen-Xers are the first generation with large numbers of divorcing parents. We found that those people who were children of divorce had an especially strong yearning for familial stability after a childhood of instability. They had a desire to prove themselves "better" than their parents, more capable of a normal, happy marriage and family life than the generation before them. This overcompensation characterized both of us. For instance, we both felt some underlying instinct to make up for the mistakes of our parents and succeed where they hadn't. We never said this to anyone, probably not even to ourselves, but it was there, percolating underneath the conscious decision-making. As we spoke with other children of divorce, we heard a similar tune of wanting to settle down and create the kind of marriage and home life we had missed out on as children—even if we had little idea of what such a healthy, happy situation looked like.

A Stamp of Legitimacy

One final pattern that emerged among the women we spoke with was a drive to marry in order to gain some legitimacy in society and to have the personal realm of their lives figured out. In many cases, getting married for this reason can be forcing something that hasn't yet run its natural course. Isabel, for instance, who later came out as a lesbian, got married to a man she was very ambivalent about in order to finally "settle" the question of her sexuality and be acceptable in society's eyes. Needless to say, the move didn't settle the issue at all. Erin had just emerged from a rocky relationship, and her parents were also getting divorced, so when her new boyfriend asked her to marry him after two months of torrid romance, she felt getting married would settle her life down and help her return to a life that made sense, both in her eyes and others'. Unfortunately, their marriage did nothing of the sort—in fact, it ended up being something of a disaster. For many, getting married can seem like the perfect way to of legitimize yourself as a normal, well-adjusted adult and put yourself in a category that others can easily understand and condone.

Divorcing at Third-Life

In retrospect, it's easy to see the road to divorce for many of us, as the reasons or readiness for getting married were often flawed in the first place. However, many people have entered marriage for some of the same largely unconscious reasons, have encountered serious stumbling blocks, and yet remained together—to different degrees of happiness and unhappiness. So what are the particular social forces and situations that cause so many of us to get divorced at a relatively young age?

Not Your Mother's Divorce

Ours is the first generation to know hordes of adults who got divorced. If it wasn't your own parents who had midlife crises and split up, then it was your friends' parents or the neighbors next door. However, the divorces of the previous generation took place largely after the couple had children and even after the children had grown up and flown the coop. Our parents tended to marry and have children in their twenties, and divorce in their forties and fifties. In our generation, the timing of things is tracking quite differently.

Unlike our mothers, most of whom have only really been able to taste the possibilities of professional ambition later in life, our generation grew up believing we could have a lifelong career—in fact, we *should* have a serious career as part of being a modern woman. Women these days spend their twenties trying to figure out what color their parachute is and who the heck they are, whereas our mothers focused first and foremost on finding the right guy to marry and having kids. The career and identity outside of family came later. Young women today now ground their identity in several things—career, friends, hobbies, as well as romantic attachments—meaning that whether a woman is married or divorced is not the sum total of her worth and success in life.

Because we now have careers (if you're not a mother, not having a job is really the exception rather than the rule), we are far more financially independent than the women of our mothers' generation. Our earning potential gives us freedom to leave a marriage that makes us unhappy or to rebuild our lives after being left.

Another very important factor is that because we now focus

on building a career in our twenties, we often delay having children—indeed, according to Paul, the average age of first-time mothers in the United States has risen steadily since 1972, with many married couples waiting several years before having children. Childlessness in a young marriage is *huge*. Without children, getting a divorce is relatively (we emphasize *relatively*) easier on the heart and the conscience: you are hurting only yourselves (and most likely making yourselves happier in the long run) and don't have the incredible burden of worrying that you are ruining some little person's life.

In effect, by waiting to have children, a young married couple is granted an out before making the even bigger commitment of starting a family together. In the couple of years before breaking up, Kay and F. had been talking about having children, and it was Kay's inability to take this next step with F. (despite really wanting a child) that eventually gave her the clarity to leave the marriage. Having kids with him felt like another, deeper level of commitment that she couldn't make. Many divorcées in this book did not think they would have gotten divorced had they had children. They say they would have somehow made it work, kind of grinned and bore it, which implies that as divorce becomes less and less stigmatized, having children with someone is the *real* commitment.

Indeed, since the wacky antics of adults in the sixties and seventies, and the huge spike in divorces since then, divorce has lost much of its stigma. This is not to suggest that it suffers none; we discuss both internalized and externalized versions of the stigma still attached to divorce later in the book. But, overall, divorce has been democratized. Everyone knows numerous people (if not their own parents) in their own community from different social, economic, and ethnic backgrounds who have divorced, and reads about it every day in the papers. The statistic of about half of all marriages ending in divorce has been thoroughly tattooed on everyone's consciousness.

Finally, along with destigmatizing divorce, the sixties and seventies also heralded an age of personal fulfillment and self-empowerment, with more people than ever before engaging in some form of psychological counseling or self-help courses such as EST and Landmark's "The Forum." More and more, people feel they have a right to be happy and, in particular, a right to feel happy in their marriage. This is not to say that people of past generations did not wish for the same, but for one, they had more financial and societal constraints holding them back from getting a divorce if they were dissatisfied. And we may also feel this entitlement more strongly than past generations, since the rhetoric about "realizing your true self" and "getting the love you want" now permeates our culture—from Oprah to the overstuffed self-help shelves at bookstores to the irony-laced, Oscar-winning *American Beauty*.

We have very high expectations of marriage these days, expecting it to help us define ourselves and give meaning to our fractured contemporary lives, expecting it to anchor us and yet to stimulate us and help us grow. We don't just want compatible mates, we want soulmates who help us realize our best selves. Leonard Woolf once said to his wife, Virginia Woolf, "We ask a lot of life," to which she retorted, "But maybe we get a lot too." The same may be true of young people who marry—and divorce—today.

"JV Divorce"

Not only is it easier to *decide* to divorce, it's also logistically easier to divorce nowadays. As we discuss in the chapter on the legal process, more and more states have no-fault divorce, and more and more people do the paperwork themselves or hire a mediator. It's not quite the bureaucratic nightmare it used to be. If you divorce young, you also have fewer assets to divide than a couple who's been together for decades. You have fewer other entanglements as well: your two lives are most likely not totally fused, because along with being a couple, you were two young and fairly independent people with your own careers, friends, and interests.

And, probably most important, you have no children together. As we said earlier, without shared progeny, you have enormous freedom to walk away from the marriage and completely reinvent your life so that it's almost imperceptible to anyone that you were ever married. You can have as little or as much contact with your ex as you desire. This situation is in marked contrast to what it means to share custody of children, which behooves two responsible adults to have a lifelong relationship with each other even if they would prefer never to see each other again. While sitting in a divorce support group filled with older women with custody issues, our friend Maeve said she felt hers had been a "JV divorce."

All of this is not to say that getting divorced when you're young and childless is a piece of cake. Let's face it: it's still awful. It's incredibly disappointing, disillusioning, and destabilizing—and you're never quite the same again. However, misery is relative, and things could be worse. Along with having your heart and other important innards torn out, you could be dealing with major custody issues and the realities of single parenthood. You, on the other hand, still have two-thirds of your life to live, a whole wide world in front of you and a chance to focus on your own well-being and sanity (which, we'll grant, are pretty big projects to manage). As you'll read in this book, many previously marrieds say their divorce was the worst experience they've ever been grateful for.

60 Ways to Leave Your Lover

Every divorcée's story is uniquely poignant and complex. There are no easy explanations for why a profound commitment between two people disintegrates. And, often, precipitating events differ from underlying causes. Something like an affair or particularly disturbing behavior might initiate discussions of divorce, but the problems have often been there for a long time. While we can't possibly pin down all the different, specific circumstances of actual breakups, here are some of the more common root causes that can lead a marriage to fracture over time.

Getting Married Too Young and Outgrowing Each Other

When one night Kay asked her friend Trudie what had happened between Trudie and her ex-husband, Trudie paused for a few moments and said in her pithy way, "As I grew into my own skin, I think I outgrew the relationship." Behind this telegraphic headline, there is, of course, a long and winding tale of Trudie seeing herself married to H. (whom she thought was her soulmate) her whole life, of trying to make it work for years, and of hitting upon ever greater personality differences and depression on both their parts. However, when it came right down to it, she felt she had grown and changed a lot over the course of her marriage to him, and once she felt comfortable with herself, she no longer felt comfortable with him. H. actually initiated the divorce because he was as unhappy as she was, but the decision ended up feeling very mutual between them.

Like Trudie, many of our girlfriends who met and married young found that as they became truer to themselves, they had less and less in common with the man they married. Our friend Miranda realized she was much more adventurous and novelty-seeking than her ex, who preferred to putter about the house and lie low. Sydney similarly found that she was much more athletic and active than her ex, whom she experienced as being a serious couch potato on the weekends, when she wanted to be out running around and breaking a sweat. Rachel was originally drawn to her husband, W., because of his solidity and trustworthiness, which she yearned for right after college. Eventually, though, as her artistic temperament and bolder self came forth in her mid to late twenties, she found W. stifling and controlling.

Depending on how you look at it, our generation has the luxury or the burden to "figure ourselves out" in our twenties and thirties. Because the twenties are such a formative and transformative time, it makes sense that some people who meet and marry in their twenties might realize eventually that they married the wrong person. In some cases, women come into their own and realize the lack of fit with their husband based on who they are becoming, sometimes it is the man who has the precocious midlife crisis, and sometimes it is a mutual growing apart.

Sometimes it's not just personality differences but mood disorders that poison a marriage. Several women realized after years of being with a guy that they were in relationships with men with depressive personalities. Stephanie, a vivacious and outgoing woman, said about her ex, "He sucked the life out of me. I gave everything in my life to him, and he was a drain on my life—hungry, tired, agitated all the time." Stephanie realized that for years she'd been able to overlook his depressiveness, but as the years passed, she felt everything she liked about herself had died in their relationship and that she needed someone who brought out her vitality instead of killing it.

The Roommate Syndrome

Sometimes personality differences that arise over time manifest themselves as increasingly less compatible lifestyles. Megan, who met her ex when she was nineteen and separated from him at twenty-nine, reported, "L. and I were going in different directions . . . my career was really taking off, and he was doing the same old thing we'd been doing for years, hanging out with the same old friends, going to the same old bar. I was working a lot and coming home late, and we became just like roommates, like ships in the night, barely seeing each other or interacting much." She realized she wanted a really different kind of life than the one she'd been sharing with him.

Laura too had become something like roommates with her ex

before they split up. An actor and bartender, he worked at night and partied afterward with his coworkers, while she was a businesswoman who worked during the day and whose friends were mostly coworkers at her company. Although they lived in the same apartment, they barely ever saw each other and grew apart, acting and eventually becoming more like roommates than spouses.

Worldviews Apart

In some cases, part of the disconnect happens around beliefs and worldview. Delia and N. both had spiritual interests when they first met; in fact it was one of the things that drew them together. But, as they got older, N. became a dedicated Buddhist practitioner and began to criticize Delia's more secular approach. Among other issues in their relationship, the two had trouble reconciling their increasingly different viewpoints on spirituality and how to express it.

Along similar lines, Kay and F., who met soon after college as public school teachers in New York City, started off in their early twenties both being pretty fiercely liberal. As they got older, though, Kay began to question her liberal ideology and realized she was not at heart a very political person, while F. remained a pretty left-wing dude dedicated to fighting the power. At some point in one of their final arguments, Kay threatened to become a Republican (it didn't happen), probably just as a way of showing how different she had become and how little they still had in common in the politics department.

When the Seesaw Crashes

Sometimes, as one spouse grows stronger and more confident over the years, an old dynamic that worked before gets tilted off balance, and things don't work so well anymore. For instance, looking back, Dawn feels she was in an emotionally abusive relationship with her ex-husband for over a decade before becoming confident enough to realize how detrimental it was to her soul. She met P. in college, and they were married eight years. In hindsight, she thinks she married someone like her father, who was demanding and overbearing, and who constantly criticized her looks. Her husband, not unlike her father, would say things like, "I'd love you more if you weren't so fat." Or, pointing to an attractive woman, "Why aren't you as pretty as she is?" He also didn't approve of her doing well professionally and wanted her to be a domestically oriented wife, which didn't suit her ambitious personality (although for years she had tried to be "wifely" to please him). At some point, after years of emotional abuse, Dawn had an epiphany during one particularly egregious incident where P. flirted in a very obvious way with one of her girlfriends and publicly criticized Dawn for not being "beautiful enough." At that moment, something snapped inside her and she turned a corner. She knew then that it was over for her and that she wasn't going to take it anymore.

Getting Married Too Fast: From Swinging to Dangling from the Chandelier

Some young divorcées got engaged soon after meeting their exes, in the throes of early love, and later felt the marriage went awry partly because they made the commitment before they really knew the man they had agreed to marry. Andrea got engaged after two months of dating and being inseparable with her ex. "I was totally caught up in the whirlwind, I was totally romantic and dumbstruck. It was the first time I was really taken with someone. We got married in September, and right after our disastrous honeymoon, we landed in therapy!" Already on their honeymoon, major personality differences and incompatibilities arose—they spent their first night of marriage in a Super 8 Motel in a huge fight. The marriage continued to be incredibly challenging, and they separated four years later, having been in and out of couples counseling the whole time.

Erin's ex also asked her to marry him two months into their relationship. Erin recalls, "I was a little unsettled and met this guy who came from this great family, and we fell in love very quickly. It all went so quickly, it was just this tornado." They set a wedding date for a year and half later and then kept postponing it (they had three different wedding dates) because their relationship was so rocky. In retrospect, Erin says she knew something was wrong but felt she couldn't turn back. Their relationship was really only good for six months, but that initial euphoria still got them down the aisle and into a marriage that she soon wanted to exit.

Vickie similarly got engaged after only three weeks and then had a long engagement. But the marriage lasted only a year and features of his personality emerged during the breakup that she had never seen before, making her feel like she had married a stranger. Sometimes we realize that we have married the wrong person, not because we have outgrown him over time, but because we never really knew him in the first place.

Losing a Spouse to the Fog of Substance Abuse

Substance abuse, with all its attendant effects on personality and lifestyle, can also undermine marriages—and it's not necessarily something you can look out for early on. A substance addiction can steal away the person you married and, at some point, you may have to give up trying to help them and leave the situation in order to save yourself and build a healthier life.

When Cindy met M., he wasn't an addict, he was this wonderful guy who made her feel totally relaxed and great about who she was. They dated for three years and were engaged for one and a half of those years. When they got married, however, they bought a house together and happened to move right next to a house full of drug dealers. Over time, M. became addicted to crank. He would do things like go out to get some milk and not return all day. For a long time, Cindy got upset every time he let her down or didn't come home until late. One night, though, he came home at 3 A.M. and she recalls that she felt nothing—she just didn't care anymore. And then she saw years and years of this horrible life stretching out in front of her and realized she couldn't do it any longer.

Tanya's husband also wasn't an addict when she met him in Ecuador. But when they moved to the United States, he started smoking pot three to four times a day. Perhaps because he was insecure in a new country, in social situations he would always have to leave to go smoke pot. She was a teacher and one time a student stopped by and G. answered the door very high, which upset her. She wanted to become a principal down the road and realized that it would not be good to have a pot-smoking husband. G. was also apathetic and depressed. She felt like "pot was the equivalent to another woman in the relationship. It was this other personality he was attached to that took him away from me and from our relationship." G. argued that smoking pot was totally normal and a part of him, and he blamed her Christian upbringing for making her too stringent. After years of conflict around the issue, she gave him an ultimatum to stop smoking by a certain day and when he hadn't quit by that time, she kicked him out of the house.

I Do . . . Not Agree with Your Idea of Marriage

Occasionally, young couples marry and realize, once betrothed, that they have very different ideas of what it means to be married. One has a more traditional concept perhaps, and one a more progressive one. Dawn's husband, as we've seen, wanted her to be more domestic and encouraged her to act more like a traditional wife. Erin had an analogous experience. In describing her ex, she says, "He was old-fashioned Spanish, and he believed that I should be cooking dinner every night and doing all the grocery shopping, bill paying, all the cleaning." She, on the other hand, was raised to be a professional woman and have a relationship with a more equitable division of the domestic chores. Elizabeth had the opposite experience, whereby she "was trying to be a wife, picking up after him, doing his laundry, things I saw my mother do," and her ex responded very badly, seeing her actions as an invasion of his privacy.

Gina felt in a very different sense that her ex, E., and she had conflicting ideas about marriage. She wanted very much for her marriage to be a loving partnership, and he seemed to see it as an obligation. She says, "He wouldn't eat at the dining room table together, he wouldn't share chores, he was very selfish." She wanted them to share their lives together and feel like they were on the same team, and he wanted to live his life in a more autonomous and solitary way. During Gina and E.'s marriage, as well as with those of the other couples above, the two people were constantly at odds about what their relationship should look like, with both partners regularly frustrated and neither one of them satisfied.

Bad Communication: You Say
Avocado, I Say Guacamole

We're not sure whether bad communication is a symptom or a root cause, or both, but several of our girlfriends felt it lay close to the core of what split their marriages apart. In some cases, the issue was a lack of communication, an inability to build a bridge between each other when there were differences, and in others it was the nature of the communication: angry, scary, and not leading to resolution.

When Mehta's ex (a high-level executive) got laid off and couldn't find a job for months, he became depressed and angry but refused to talk about it with her. She felt they weren't a team anymore, at precisely the time when they really needed to be a team. Eventually, her feelings for him diminished, and she didn't know how to get her love or desire for him back. Nancy, who also felt she couldn't talk easily to her husband, said, "We had a lot of the same interests and were compatible in many ways, but not emotionally. This showed in the divorce. We weren't able to talk . . . we did not have the ability to communicate on an emotional level."

For two other women, Miranda and Caitlin, communication with the ex about their relationship could be scary and disturbing. Both of their exes had bad tempers, so that any kind of conflict or disagreement usually resulted in threatening outbursts of anger. Caitlin attributed much of the breakdown of her marriage to communication problems and her husband's "abusive way of talking." She felt their fights "never resolved anything." All couples have conflict, it's the way of the world. No two people are always going to agree about everything. But how you handle the conflict makes the difference in whether you walk away closer or more alienated from each other. If conflict either doesn't get addressed or is addressed in a negative, harmful, or frightening way, it can corrode a marriage and drive you further and further apart from one another.

The Heart's Hard Turning, the Heart's Slow Learning

It's incredibly important to understand What Went Wrong, and throughout the book we'll encourage you to actively engage in this sense-making. You need to dig deep in order to truly heal and move on from the divorce. But know that this process will take you some time, often several years, so don't feel you have to figure it all out at once. We and the women described above are at least a year away from our divorces and often much more. Have patience with yourself. Eventually, the chapters of your story will fall into line, you'll know all the major themes, the characters will be well drawn and three-dimensional, and you will be able to tell the story by heart—even though, once you've reached this point, you may find that you no longer need to.

CHAPTER TWO

Suddenly Single

*How queer everything is today! I wonder if
I've been changed in the night? But if I'm
not the same, the next question is, "Who
in the world am I?" Ah, that's the great
puzzle.*

—Lewis Carroll,
Alice's Adventures in Wonderland

Wherever your love went and however the split finally
happened, you're here now, in this strange new land of
Sudden Singleness (otherwise known as separation). We say "sudden" because, for one thing, the separation may have come as a
surprise if it was rather abruptly initiated by your husband. But,
even if you expected the separation and had thought about it,
dreamt about it, had nightmares about it, and played it out in your
wildest imagination, there is still a time when life starts over again
in a qualitatively different way, and it can be something of a shock.

No matter if it was your choice or your husband's or a mutual decision, you are most likely not quite ready to be out in the
world on your own. Extricating yourself (or being ousted) from a
bad situation is one thing; recovering from the divorce and re-

building your life is another. In Delia's words, "It was dreadful. I was heartbroken. It was sort of ironic because I'd been the one who left and made the positive choice for me, but I was still emotionally floored." The loss through divorce is massive—it's the death of a relationship, of a future together, of hopes and dreams, and of a good portion of your idealism about romantic love. As all the experts will tell you, it's important to realize that a divorce is second only to the death of a loved one in how profound the grief is and how enormous the stress is. This chapter is all about being kind and patient with yourself while going through one of the most difficult periods of your life. And, trust us, you will come out the other side eventually, so know that while the pain might be intense at times, it's only temporary.

The Shock of the New

Not long ago, you were safely ensconced in the bosom of coupledom. You belonged to someone, you fit in, you had the ground and planet beneath your feet. You had someone on your team, someone who was yours alone. You had a life that more or less made sense to you and your neighbors. You were married.

For years you had imagined the rest of your life with this person. You saw the children in your head and wondered whose eyes they would get, if they would look more like you or him, what beautiful and gifted creature the combination of your genes would produce. You had learned how to manage the in-laws and come to some kind of fragile acceptance of the fact that you would be spending the rest of your life interacting with this second set of parents. You were part of a twosome and everyone always used your names in conjunction with another, like Bonnie and Clyde, Bogey and Bacall, Ernie and Bert. You shared many of the same friends and had each other to mull over all their quirks and idiosyncrasies. You imagined getting older with him and played out how the two of you might look and putter about as octogenarians. You were part of something bigger than yourself. You were part of an institution, for God's sake. You were married.

Welcome to a brave new world. You may or may not have chosen this destination, but you're here now. And this new world is not necessarily inviting; there are no girls with hula skirts and leis welcoming you as you arrive at the gate. In fact, you deboard the plane and no one's there to greet you. It's late at night and the airport's empty, all lit up with fluorescent lights and pitch-black outside, everyone else asleep in their houses. All you know is you have never been here before, and it feels like no one else has either. You are bewildered and even the familiar looks strange. You want to go home but you don't know where it is. You are suddenly single when you never thought you would be again.

Speaking of home, you might ask yourself, what do I do when I go home? TV or rental movie? Trashy novel or magazines? You may discover new cable channels you never knew existed. Basically, you have no idea what to do with yourself because you're so used to doing everything with this other person. You may also have trouble deciding the smallest things. What do I wear to work? How do I get from point A to point B? What do I have for dinner? Kit Kat or Snickers? Chee-tos or pretzels? You're incredibly used to functioning one way (i.e., with a companion) and you haven't yet learned another, so every decision seems like a new one.

You might find yourself having an out-of-body experience and becoming a curious observer of your own life. Wow, I go to McDonald's when he's not around. I buy six pints of Ben & Jerry's when I just shop for myself. Hmmm, I take up the whole bed when he's not here to take up half of it. Interesting how light the laundry load is when it's just for one person! You notice who you are without him, and in some ways it's similar but in lots of ways it's different. You are your own separate person, you realize, even if you'd forgotten. You talk to yourself because you are so used to having someone else in the apartment to announce things to or bounce things off, and you wonder whether you're now psychotic (you're not).

However, you *are* in a state of shock. Your soul is undergoing an earthquake, and everything feels shaky and new. Know that this state won't last forever. Someday soon a degree of normalcy will return to your life and things will fall into place again—you'll develop new routines, new shopping lists, and alternative evening plans to prime-time television. You'll develop a life of your own, filled with things *you* enjoy.

32 Flavors and Then Some

Beyond shock and disorientation, you'll also likely experience the other classic stages and varieties of grief, sometimes all in a single day: denial, sadness, anger, acceptance, euphoria, disappointment, and ambivalence. Emotions are running willy-nilly through your veins and wreaking havoc on your sense of equilibrium. Try to just let them happen and don't overreact to any single emotion. Notice how you're feeling, perhaps share it with someone close to you or write it in a journal, and pretty soon that particular feeling may pass and an entirely new feeling may arise. Try as much as you can to just go with the wacky flow of it all for the time being—it's all part of the recovery process.

Swimming in Denial

Denial means living in something of a state of disbelief or oblivion, a conscious or unconscious suppression of reality that results in an inability to fully acknowledge what is happening in your life. Everyone else can see the writing on the wall, but it might as well be in Sanskrit as far as you're concerned. For example, you think the separation is only temporary while your ex feels it's permanent. Or perhaps both of you are holding on to the illusion that you have not broken up, but end up consistently making choices to conduct your lives more and more separately.

You may never go through a denial phase, or it may last a long time. All of us have a different psychological makeup that influences how we process something as huge as a divorce. Also, your particular circumstances may shape the extent to which you are in denial. If, for instance, the two of you were in couples counseling and spent a long time processing What Went Wrong, you may be closer to acceptance than if you were surprised by your husband's desire to separate. Kay, for instance, who had been in counseling on her own for several years regarding her doubts about her marriage, didn't experience much denial when she and F. broke up. She began grieving and experiencing all of her sundry, swirling emotions immediately. Delia, on the other hand, says that "it took a year for the fact to sink in," and she and her ex didn't start filing papers and making it official until after a year of separation had passed and they knew for sure they weren't getting back together.

Denial can be a useful and adaptive state. It allows you to go on with your life as opposed to dwelling in pain or the past. We human beings can't process an enormous loss all at once, so we tend to parcel it out, with denial being the reprieve between the bouts of painful reality. Another version of denial is numbness, where you have rationally accepted the demise of your marriage but it doesn't register in your emotional world at all. If you find yourself in such a state of not being able to feel anything, don't be shy about getting some professional help in bursting open the dam. Feelings can hide but they don't go away.

"Permanent PMS"

During the first year or two after the initial separation from your ex, grief—or the pain, sadness, and disappointment of loss—will likely be a frequent visitor. Grief can mean you are on the verge of tears much of the time and that you are vulnerable to the slightest insensitivities. Sometimes it may be hard to recognize yourself. When your shakiness makes you feel pathetic, reassure yourself that emoting is healthy and that letting yourself grieve will help you heal faster and more thoroughly in the long run.

Nancy recalls, "Initially, it's very overwhelming. I cried more in that first year than I have in my entire life. Even though I had a new relationship soon after, it didn't matter." Hope, who was left rather suddenly by her husband after he had a quarter-life crisis, echoed, "It was a terrible, terrible thing to go through. I remember sitting on my porch, sobbing to Carly Simon. I cried me a river for several years; it felt like I had permanent PMS. I remember once a colleague told me I had taken the last donut at the faculty meeting, and I was just so sensitive, I burst into tears. Every day was that sort of challenge." The whirlwind of feelings, many of which are unexpected and some of which are unwelcome, may leave you feeling like you're going mad. As Maeve expressed, "Even though I looked like I was really together, I felt like I was just out of my mind." Rest assured that you probably do appear a lot more sane than you feel and that this insanity will not last forever.

Miranda, who left her husband and never doubted the decision, was surprised to find herself still missing her ex, their home, their cats, and aspects of their life together. Sometimes she didn't know what to do with these feelings that seemed to contradict her conviction about the decision: "I went through a period of weeping and feeling desolate. It's a big loss. It's a disappointment of hopes, and it's a thing we built together, like a huge project, a constructed effort, and for it to fall apart is a massive disappointment."

Grieving can take a long time and can come in waves, sometimes when you least expect it. For instance, you may be flying high and having a ball and then you have a bad week, and all of a sudden you feel sad and alone. Another loss, such as the loss of a boyfriend or the death of a friend or relative, can also conjure up the loss of your ex. Ultimately, even if you know ending the marriage was the right choice, you still created a life together of which there were many things you enjoyed, and so it's natural for you to mourn their loss.

Rediscovering Your Inner Adolescent

Although you may or may not have been a self-absorbed teenager in high school, you may well meet her now. And she'll give you license to act immaturely in more ways than one. You may find yourself acting selfish and self-indulgent in ways you thought you left behind when you moved from lip gloss to lipstick.

Typical of teenagers, you will likely be at the whim of dramatic mood swings. One moment you're blissed out, filled with an unparalleled euphoria, thinking, "I feel so alive, I feel so young, I feel so new. Life f—— rocks. The world is my oyster farm!" Then, a nanosecond later, you're in state of abject misery. Not unlike the mercurial phase of adolescence, you are losing one identity and growing into a new one. But the process is not at all immediate, and along the way, you morph in all sorts of wild and woolly ways. The changes can be utterly unnerving, but they can also be intoxicating and exhilarating.

This time around, revel in the narcissicism that adolescence implies. Enjoy the temporary reckless disregard for anyone's wishes but your own. Basically, do anything your heart desires, anything that makes you feel good, since joy can be a relatively rare and fleeting sensation during this time. Don't call your mother back. Watch sitcoms. Rent bad movies.

You may never feel this young again. Don't worry, it

won't last forever; you'll soon recover your inner adult. Delight in the irresponsibility and carefree giddiness. It's one of the small gifts during an often difficult time.   🦢

The Hour of the Bewilderbeast

If your ex is the one who initiated the split, you might find your-self occasionally vexed by a deep and unsettling confusion about what happened and a profound sense of rejection. What the heck happened? What went so terribly wrong? Why is he giving up on us? What's wrong with me? What could I have done differently? How did I not notice what was happening? Sarah remembers feel-ing some of these things when her ex announced inconveniently while they were on a vacation in a remote town in France that he wanted a "trial separation."

You may spend a good deal of time in the post-separation phase sorting out his motivations and making sense of how his feelings changed. You will need to do this, but also make sure you attend to your own changing feelings about him and the marriage; you may discover that you were more unhappy and dissatisfied than you realized. If you're pining after him, you'll need to re-mind yourself daily (or have a friend remind you with a call or email) that if he doesn't want to be with you, you would never, ever be happy with him. And, we promise, he's not *that* great and certainly not great for you. You deserve someone who loves you to smithereens.

If you were the one who broke things off, you may occa-sionally question if you made the right choice, especially during the moments when things are not going so peachy in your own life. You may "only remember the good stuff," in Denise's words, and have to actively remind yourself why you left. If all the guys you meet are cads, you may think, "At least my ex was a nice guy . . ." Don't let these doubts fool you. There will be the wonderful things about your ex that you remember fondly. After all, you married him for a reason. But that doesn't mean that he was right for you as a whole package. Missing him is *not* the same as needing to get back together with him. If you were compelled to end the marriage—a very difficult thing to do, which means most people avoid it at all costs—there was something fundamentally wrong and it wasn't a mistake to separate. Some ambivalence is natural; let it teach you what you liked about your ex but don't let it erode your conviction or confidence about your decision.

Your Imperfect Storm

Another lovely emotion that might visit you on occasion is unbridled, intense, and almost blinding anger. This is one of those emotions that it's hard to figure out what to do with. Punch the pillows? Scream in your car in the woods? Become a punk rock singer? Throw things across the apartment? It can creep up on you and then once you're in the state, you find yourself able to relate to Bornean headhunters in a way you never thought possible. To make matters worse, the object of your anger is no longer in your midst, so you're angry at an abstraction. The upside of fury, however, is that you get in touch with a righteous indignation and a sense of the justice you deserve in life, which can be a motivating and empowering force in your post-separation life.

There are many reasons you may find fury welling up inside you. Perhaps you were wronged by your ex and he left you with little warning or for another woman. Or perhaps after you split up he began to act in unsavory ways, taking advantage of you financially or materially, or bad-mouthing you and trying to convince your family and friends to side with him. Caitlin, after finding out that her ex, who had been very abusive, wanted to sue *her* for "constructive abandonment," said, "I don't think I've ever been so angry in all my life . . . Emotionally, it was difficult, a very disillusioning experience." In Kay's case, she had initiated the split from F., but right when she was moving out, he began dating someone else. Although she no longer wanted to be with F., she still felt insulted that he would immediately start seeing someone else and found herself, surprisingly, incredibly angry (while also simultaneously feeling incredibly relieved of guilt).

Indeed, you may get in touch with a kind of rage you didn't know you were capable of—it's all part of the mix of grief and loss. We women can have a hard time feeling comfortable with anger and knowing how to express it. We encourage you to express it to close family and friends: call one of your confidantes and confess, "I'm totally pissed/angry/upset about something, can I vent to you for a while?" That way, they know that they just need to listen while you breathe fire for a spell. Other options include screaming into your diary or to a counselor. Most important, let yourself feel the anger and don't be ashamed of it or try to squelch it. The storm will come; it might be violent, but it *will* pass, and, as trite as it sounds, you'll feel better and calmer for having succumbed to its power.

However, you should avoid acting on your anger when it's running high, especially in matters regarding your ex, because you will likely do and say things you will later regret. It's best to wait until the storm passes before figuring out how you want to handle a given situation and avoid making any major decisions while you're in its grip. If you find yourself having a lot of anger and at a loss for what to do with it, consider a physical outlet such as kickboxing or karate. Jump-start those endorphins. It's amazing how satisfying it can be to objectify the source of your anger and go wild with all four limbs!

Who Ever Said No (Wo)Man Is an Island?

After having a companion for however many years, separation from your ex will likely leave you feeling lonely in a way you haven't for a long time (if ever). It can be strange to come home and hear echoes as your feet cross the floor because no one else is home. It can be strange not to have someone to take care of you when you're sick, help you bring the groceries in, or help you hang the new prints on the wall.

Kay nowadays really only feels the absence of her ex when she's trying to change the duvet cover (which for some reason is very difficult to do alone), while in the early days of her separation she thought about it a lot. It would hit her hardest whenever she had to fill out a form for work or at the doctor's office that required her to put something down for "In case of emergency, contact . . ." Once separated, she didn't want to put her husband's name there, but listing her parents felt like regression, and designating a good friend also felt inappropriate somehow. Dawn talks about how it was—and still is—hard to sleep by herself, so she sleeps with her one-hundred-pound dog. Elizabeth recounted that after she separated from her husband, she was fine when she was around other people, but it was when she was by herself that she would feel overwhelmed by loneliness. Her friends helped move her into her new place and then stayed for pizza and beer, but when they left, it all hit her and the place seemed excruciatingly empty.

However, if you felt very lonely in your marriage and increasingly alienated from your husband, you might welcome the kind of loneliness that comes from being truly alone. There's an honesty and purity to being alone with yourself after being lonely in a disintegrating marriage. This was true for both Elizabeth and Gina, who had slept apart from their husbands for quite some time before physically separating. Gina said, "I was lonely when I was married, so when I was single, I felt like at least I'm lonely for the right reasons. There was no one there as opposed to there's someone here but I totally can't connect to him." So, depending on your situation, the loneliness after separation may feel like progress.

The Glories of Self-Flagellation

Along with experiencing denial, grief, ambivalence, anger, and loneliness, you may also torture yourself with a three-pronged program of guilt, shame, and a profound sense of failure. No matter how much people may try to disabuse you of these feelings, we know it's not that easy to dismiss them. When you're getting a divorce, it's common to feel like the biggest loser on the face of the planet. You couldn't make something Very Important work, you failed on a lime-lit public stage, you're a dork, you're a good-for-nothing excuse for a warm-blooded mammal. Particularly if you're the one who initiated things, the guilt can feel pretty consuming.

Erin put it this way: "I felt a lot of guilt. I felt like I wasn't doing enough, that maybe I should have tried harder . . . I had never worked so hard in my life and not succeeded at something. I think you especially feel a lot of guilt if you have strong morals and values and believe in the institution of marriage. I always felt like I wouldn't get divorced unless my spouse was an alcoholic, drug addict, or something really bad." Kay also felt as though she needed some really concrete, understandable excuse for divorcing her ex, especially when one of her friend's mothers said, "Why did you leave? He didn't beat you, did he?" You will most likely be your own worst enemy in terms of judgment, but you may experience the occasional reinforcement from the external world.

Sydney relates: "My grandmother, who was a real role model for me, would have rolled in her grave if she knew that W. and I got divorced. I felt incredibly guilty that I couldn't make it work, especially when I thought of her. I gave myself a hard time." Leslie also engaged in serious self-flagellation. In fact, she thinks that's where the majority of her pain related to the divorce came from, as opposed to sadness or disappointment. "I had a lot of guilt about leaving, and the hardest part for me was living with my mistake. I went to a psychiatrist and she said she had never known anyone who had as much guilt, even people who had done really bad things—like murder people! A lot of my sense of self had come from the fact that I was a good person. I'd always been a good daughter, a good granddaughter, a good friend, and I'd never done anything wrong that anyone disapproved of . . . so I felt terrible about myself."

For the first few years after the initial separation, Leslie had dreams that her ex, C., had forgiven her. Then, at one point, she realized she wasn't having the dreams anymore: "I think I knew he was never going to forgive me, but I had forgiven myself. I've realized that the mistakes people make, including the ones I make, are not on purpose, so forgive yourself and others. It's a much better place to be than filled with guilt or anger."

So, for now, as tough as it may seem, try to quell the inner critic and reframe things in as humane and compassionate a light as possible. Tell yourself, as Dawn, who once felt enormous guilt and shame, still does: "You're not the devil, it's not your fault. Everything will be okay for everyone eventually."

Blissed Out Beyond Belief

Finally, along with all these more unsavory emotions, you will likely also have minutes, hours, days, even weeks of the most delicious euphoria and sense of freedom you've ever had. Especially if you've been miserable for quite some time in the marriage or after the breakup, you can find yourself so happy to just feel happy again. And your life is starting anew and is filled with change, adventure, and novelty. You can feel a most wonderful and intoxicating vitality.

Trudie described it this way: "I felt like a kid, it was like being a child again with this whole amazing world to explore." Gina voiced similar sentiments: "I had the feeling, the sky's the limit, I can do anything now. It was a like a vacation from my stultifying married life, it was fun. I was discovering all this food and music I liked but hadn't known I did . . . I began really celebrating life."

Isabel, whose breakup with her ex-husband was part of coming out as lesbian, also found the early period "thrilling, because I was finally being true to myself."

As with Isabel, some people may mostly experience the upside of divorce and little of the downside. Once Megan had made up her mind to leave her ex, it was finished for her, and she says she rarely—if ever—looked back. She found she really enjoyed living alone and cultivating exactly the life *she* wanted to lead.

The Big No-No: Dialing Your Ex

During those times when you feel *anything but* blissed out about your new singledom, you may miss your ex terribly; you may be dying to hear his voice console you. It will definitely depend on the nature of your post-separation relationship, but we recommend that you not call him in these times of dire distress. It's probably safe to assume he won't be able to console you the way he used to. He may have all sorts of defenses up now, he may need distance from you and, horror of horrors, he may have a new girlfriend. In general, you should make a concerted effort to turn to other people for help and start building a sturdy support system outside of him.

You'll probably be especially tempted to call him on holidays or dates that were significant in your relationship. Miranda, for instance, called her ex on Christmas and Vickie called her ex on Thanksgiving during their first years of separation. Kay felt incredibly strange at the end of September 11, 2001, not having talked to her ex, even though she knew he was fine since he lived in San Francisco, so she called him. Such reaching out during heightened emotional times is in many ways natural. However, if you'd rather not

---

act on such impulses because the conversations leave you feeling bad about yourself or are otherwise unsatisfactory, you'll want to prepare for particular holidays or dates by making sure you have a full schedule and are surrounded by people you love who can help you avoid doing something you don't want to do.

The Divorce Diet and Other Strange Behaviors

Grief does amazing things not only to your heart but also to your body, affecting many of your basic functions and your overall physical well-being. If you're like us and many of the women we spoke with, you'll find one of the first things it does is decimate your appetite. "Girl, you have *never* looked better!" all your girl-friends exclaim enviously. Suddenly, you find you have turned into the svelte young *thang* you were many moons ago. You haven't looked this good since high school. Our girlfriend Patti said, "I lost twenty pounds in one month. It was so hard to eat. I had no appetite. I'd eat a bagel in the morning and nothing for the rest of the day. Everyone at work kept asking me, why aren't you eating? I remember one lunch meeting, a colleague practially force-fed me a brownie. It was awful." Often you're hungry, but when you sit down to eat, you can't put more than a few table-spoonsful in your mouth. Our doctor girlfriend informed us that in medicine it's called "early satiety." Basically, your stomach goes into mourning as well as your heart.

If this phenomenon happens to you, know that while you may welcome this new twigginess, you'll need to beware that you don't become the incredible shrinking divorcée. And that you're still getting the necessary vitamins and nutrients to stay alive, or at least avoid developing a greenish pallor. A few months into her separation, Sarah fainted on a plane to San Francisco, not surprising considering one of her diary entries from that period reads "cornflakes and scotch for dinner." Try, try, try to eat something—and try to make it somewhat healthy!

On the flip side, food can become your ersatz companion. If you find yourself eating more than usual and gaining weight, you'll also want to try to eat healthy, even if you're going overboard. It may be discouraging to be gaining weight, but just as with losing weight, remember that this is a temporary stage. You will not have these eating habits forever. We promise. Once you and your body acclimate to the new circumstances, your appetite and eating will return to normal. In the meantime, keeping a journal of what you're eating may help you to stay aware of the problems in your diet and help you modify your habits. Also, you may want to enlist a friend to help you with your eating habits. She can check up on you on a weekly basis, or the two of you can plan to make healthy meals together.

The Midnight Demons

You may also have trouble sleeping, a common ailment for anyone going through a hard time. You may even be somewhat manic, whereby you are incredibly revved up much of the time and find it hard to put your head on the pillow, and when you do it's racing wildly and patently unable to count sheep. If you suffer insomnia or mania, learn the tricks of insomniacs: move out of your bed and to another spot if you can't sleep after an hour, and have a dull book handy to lull you into the land of Nod. Finally, we recommend Kay's mother's two surefire sedatives: warm milk with honey (the earliest remedy) and oatmeal (the adult version of Gerber's).

Alternatively, you may sleep too much, a symptom of depression, which is common during such a time. The problem with excessive sleep is that it feeds on itself; the more you avoid the outside world, the less you want to go out into it. We strongly urge you to fight this tendency if you have it. Ask your friends to plan things with you and force you out from under the sheets. But don't be too hard on yourself; it's also okay to retreat from the world on occasion during this period. You just don't want the seclusion to become an addiction. If you're spending truly inordinate amounts of time in bed and finding yourself unable to get to work, and you're not already seeing a counselor, find one as soon as you can. You may very well be a candidate for antidepressants. Nowadays there's very little stigma to better living through chemistry, and if there's any time people will understand your being serotonin-challenged, it's now.

Meet Jane Jetson

Spaciness is another common side effect of the kind of stress brought on by separation and divorce. If you find yourself becoming incredibly absentminded, it's wise to just admit to yourself and others that you are simply *not* firing on all cylinders. General spaciness—losing your keys, locking yourself out of your car, forgetting to call people back—is a well-documented by-product of undergoing major loss. Grief takes up an inordinate amount of energy, preoccupying your brain in such a way that many of the daily details escape you. Kay, who is ordinarily not very forgetful, continuously locked herself out of her house during the first two months on her own and became an expert at breaking into her apartment through the window using a neighbor's ladder and some Cirque du Soleil–style acrobatics.

Part of the spaciness may be an inability to concentrate and focus. Even if you're an avid reader, you may be unable to make it past page one or two of a novel for the first six to eight months after the Big Split. All you may be able to manage is a photo caption in *People* magazine. You may also have trouble undertaking and excelling at major personal or professional projects. Just try to coast and do the best you can.

Office 101: Work-Life Tips

In many ways, work can be a welcome refuge from the rockiness of your personal life. You may be really grateful for the structure, the tasks, and the feeling of being needed at the office. At a point where your self-esteem might not be at an all-time high, work can help affirm who you are and all you have to offer. Unlike so many of our mothers or our mothers' friends, women of our generation do have this going for us, and it's a palpable advantage. Some women told us that their careers actually really took off during their separation and divorce because they became absorbed by their work in a way they never anticipated. As Patti recalls, "I worked so much more that summer than I ever have. I just wanted to be surrounded by people. I just wanted to feel safe."

On the other hand, it's also entirely possible that work may be a huge chore and seem utterly pointless; you may find yourself having a hard time being motivated to take on projects, or even arrive on time in the morning. A certain amount of apathy is absolutely to be expected; if your apathy crosses the line into serious depression (more than a few weeks of trouble getting up and getting to work, for example), then be sure to seek some professional help. You may also want to consider a leave of absence from work for a period of time, two weeks or even a month, depending on your job and your boss. People often do this right around the time they are physically separating from their ex or if they find themselves in a deep funk and need quality time with family and friends or in counseling.

Generally, however, if you're basically functional, it's good to keep showing up every day and rely on work as a

source of stability in your life. Even when you feel like a
zombie, remember that you're probably doing much better
than you think you are, and your usual work ethic will return one day very soon.

Rock Out the New Routines

This early period is a time to discover (or rediscover) what makes
you tick. Explore the hobbies you love but haven't had time for
in years. Kay, for instance, spent hours every weekend refinishing
and painting furniture during the first six months of being on her
own, something she'd always fantasized about doing. Trudie de-
voted herself to growing a garden in back of her apartment building, wowing her friends with fresh basil, tomatoes, and more.
Such semiphysical labor can be very therapeutic during this time
because it allows you time to reflect while accomplishing something concrete. Now is also a great time to embrace your inner
Henry David Thoreau and organize and minimize your remaining material belongings. Sort through all your books and CDs and
figure out which ones to sell to used book and music stores in the
name of less clutter (and extra pocket money).

You can also think about taking classes in photography,
poetry, self-defense, interpretive dance—whatever grills your
cheese. Or contemplate volunteering; there can be a wonderful
consolation in getting out of your head and helping others. You
don't need to join the Peace Corps, but you can do something
you care about once a week or once a month. It may also prove
to be a great forum for meeting new people. In general, try to get
out and socialize with new folks. You'll find that you have an incredible openness during this period, and it's a perfect time to
make new connections.

And, most especially, do the things your ex loathed and relish doing them! For example, once Sarah had separated from her pedantic husband, she embraced her anti-intellectual side, enjoying sitcoms and *Cosmo* with abandon. Kay stopped paying an iota of attention to the news or any social issues in rebellion against her highly political journalist ex.

Finally, pamper yourself. It's completely justified to draw yourself a bubble bath every night after work, get a twice-weekly massage, clean out your favorite boutique, or do whatever feels like the most delicious guilty pleasure you can think of. Enjoy anything and everything you can during this most tumultuous and challenging time in your life and keep the faith that things *will* get better and saner with time.

"Sometimes You Just Gotta Trust Life"

Along with rocking out the new routines, the right attitude (and we know we sound like elementary school teachers, but it's true) can do wonders during this difficult time. Kay's ex's grandmother, Margaret Rose, is devoutly Catholic and always prays for "courage, patience, and persistence." We agree with Maggie Rose that a basically hopeful attitude and long-range view will benefit you tremendously as you stumble and fumble your way through the darkness of the early period. It's very easy to sink into the doldrums and even into an abyss during and after a divorce, and sometimes that's necessary for a spell. On those difficult days, you may need to consciously conjure up every ounce of inner optimism you can muster and *choose* to believe that the divorce was the right thing and that the experience will ultimately make you a stronger, more joyous person. This may require tapping into a reservoir of faith deep within you, a faith that, no matter how much things suck right now, there's a rhyme and reason to what has happened, and things will eventually work out for the best. As

Kay's friend, Anna, said to her once during a bleak time, "Sometimes you just gotta trust life." On days where it's very hard to conjure up that faith and trust yourself, it really helps to hang out with generally hopeful people like Anna and Maggie Rose, who can conjure it up for you.

The Power of Positive Spinning

Unfortunately, you may not always get public affirmation that the divorce is a positive thing in your life, so often you'll need to cultivate this feeling yourself. Laura's advice is the following: "Just embrace the divorce, don't be embarrassed. Do whatever you can to look at it as a positive thing. And, as much as possible, don't let other people get to you. Remember that you only live once, and you're the one who has to lead your life." In a similar vein, Tanya says, "You have to look at the divorce as an opportunity and not a failure. A lot of people only look at divorce as negative, but they look at many other difficult things in life as opportunities, and divorce shouldn't be any different. You need to keep telling yourself that and believing it deep down."

Along these lines, Gina felt funny when a female coworker was thrown a party to celebrate her upcoming wedding because it occurred to her that parties don't happen to celebrate upcoming divorces: "I thought, strange that I'm not getting a cake, I almost ruined my life by staying with my ex, and I'm now so much happier. Divorce shouldn't be condoned, but it should be seen as something that's necessary sometimes and a positive step forward in someone's life, like moving on to a new job. No matter what anyone thinks, I choose to see the divorce as a chapter in my life that makes me more interesting."

We urge you to proactively cultivate the kind of life-affirming, decidedly optimistic perspective on the divorce that Gina and others advocate. Consider throwing yourself a celebratory party, even if it's just a sleepover with the girls and lots of *vino* and chocolate. Or plan a trip with a close friend or group of friends in honor of the beginning of the rest of your glorious life. If you're close with your mother or sister, organize a spa weekend or week where you indulge yourselves and inaugurate the New You. During the early period, this positive spinning may be a struggle, but with time, you'll be able to embrace the divorce as an important chapter that makes you more interesting.

Strategies for Surviving Your Day During the Early Period

- Take pride in the small accomplishments: "I went to work, I answered the phone, I sent a fax." Remember Woody Allen's motto: "Showing up is 90 percent of life." Try not to dwell too much on The Future, but rather take it one day at a time and pat yourself on the back for staying alive and away from the railings of bridges.
- Start a journal (if you haven't already) so that you can record your chaos-inspired poetry, rants, speeches to your ex, new philosophies on life and love, etc. You may produce some of your best thinking to date. Really. Work the insanity in the name of creativity. You may even want to call it something like "Divorcée's Delight" or "Hear Me Roar!"—something that makes you smile when you pick it up.
- Make lists of everything you ever want to do in your life (however unrealistic and ridiculous), of things your ex loathed that you can now do freely, of things you don't miss (e.g., the CD he played obsessively, his slovenly habits), of things in life for which you are grateful. Sounds corny, but it does work during those bleaker moments.
- Indulge in little pleasures. Go for it, get a mani *and* a pedi. Get the whole milk in your mocha—get half and half in

your mocha for God's sake! Buy the twelve CDs. Whatever gives you a smidgen of happiness.

- It sounds trite, but go with the flow. Expect things to be crazy, and then your life may actually seem halfway normal.
- Be phenomenally accepting of yourself. You have never gone through this before; it's a huge deal, you're in entirely unchartered territory, and you're bound to act strange some of the time. Learn the critical importance of forgiving and having deep and abiding compassion for yourself.

CHAPTER THREE

"There's Something I Have to Tell You . . ."

Sharing Your News and

Getting the Support You Need

from Friends, Family, and Work

Some people go to priests, others to poetry;
I to my friends.

—Virginia Woolf,
The Waves

If you are anything like us, when your marriage unravels, you don't exactly relish the thought of having to go public with the news. It's never fun to hang your dirty laundry in the town square. As Greta put it, "Telling people was probably the worst part of it all." But, as hideous as it might feel initially, trust us. there are very real and immediate benefits to breaking the news to your family and closest friends. By pulling them into your reality, you get access to the support you need, and no matter what their reaction is, you will experience some relief that you no longer have to hide the goings-on of your heart and head from those closest to you. If, on the other hand, your family and friends have been aware of your unhappiness all along, telling them that you're ending your marriage may be invigorating for you and a relief for them. This was the case for our friend Erin, who recalls, "My friends and family 100 percent supported my decision, so it actually felt exhilarating to tell them. It felt almost like a celebration."

Working the Grapevine

Whatever your particulars, there's no need to compose a press release on your separation. Rather, if your life is closely tied in with the lives of your loved ones, it won't take much effort to get the word out through your network of family and friends. News of this kind spreads so quickly that you often don't have to make more than a few phone calls to inform your world. There are no formal guidelines here; in fact, you'll probably find that your modus operandi becomes telling people on a need-to-know basis. The point of this chapter is to help you get through those tough moments when you need to inform friends, family, coworkers, and miscellaneous others, with the most ease and the least pain possible. Once you've told people about your situation, it's all about building and maintaining a support system for yourself. Even if you're a self-reliant gal, you'll be grateful for some help through what can be a pretty dreadful period. This is an excellent time to reconnect with the people who matter to you most. And as awkward and painful as these moments might feel at the beginning, one day the words "I'm separated/getting divorced" will roll off your tongue fairly matter-of-factly.

Delegating to Deputies

You may want only your "A list" of family and friends to know in the beginning, and that's your prerogative. You may want to appoint a few deputies—a sister, for example, or a trusted friend—to communicate the news to your "B list" for you. It will probably be a relief to allow these representatives to inform important-but-not-top-priority people in your life, like your Aunt Pearl in Sioux City or your cousins in Kalamazoo. As our friend Valerie remembers, "Telling people was so painful. Even though my husband was awful, it would rip my heart out every time I had to tell the story. A childhood friend helped me relay the news so I didn't have to go through it all the time." Indeed, why bare your soul again and again, just to get the news out there?

On the other hand, you may feel moved to confess it to strangers on the street or anyone who will listen, and that's your prerogative, too. Something important to keep in mind, though, is that you're in a somewhat fragile state in the beginning and you don't know how most people are going to react. If they are anything less than utterly sympathetic, you could feel a whole spectrum of things, from disappointment to indignation. You need people around you who have your best interests in mind and can take good care of you, so it's best to try to practice discretion and seek out your closest loved ones.

Coordinating the PR Effort with Your Ex

Bear in mind that you and your ex may not inform others at the same rate, in the same order, or with the same details. If you're on speaking terms and want to avoid awkwardness, it's a good idea to confirm who's telling what to whom, and when. To demonstrate the importance of clear communication on this front, we offer a cautionary tale. One morning, several weeks into her separation, Sarah received a phone call from her estranged husband's parents. "Hello, dear!" they boomed, "Just calling to say we're about fifty miles away, closing in on the Big Apple for our Fourth of July visit!" Gasp. The in-laws were completely in the dark about the recent development in their son's marriage. Sarah's estranged had not "gotten around to it" so Sarah had to, rather uncomfortably, explain the situation and reroute them elsewhere. If you and your ex are on decent terms, consider making up a list of who needs to know the news, and which of you is going to tell which mutual friends, and when.

A Few Immediate Benefits to Sharing the News

There's no need to be in any great hurry to tell people you're separating, but the benefits of breaking the news do usually kick in right away. Here are just a few of the things you can expect:

- People will be kind to you; you'll enjoy cards, calls, and flowers, which can shine a ray of light on a difficult hour.
- You will start to minimize the amount of mail that arrives addressed to you and your husband.
- The separation will begin to feel real, and, if you or your estranged haven't fully accepted it already, you'll be further along in the process, just because you've told others.

Generally, as difficult as it can be, you'll probably find that verbalizing the situation has some therapeutic reward, too.

With a Little Help from Your Friends, Family, Pets, and Email Inbox

During this early period, you'll need a tremendous amount of practical and emotional support. Instinctively, you'll know who you feel most comfortable turning to, who you feel safest with, who you can talk to, and you'll seek these people out. Actively reach out to the people you trust most and let them take care of you. Chances are, they'll be honored that they can be there for you at such an important juncture in your life. There may also be some people you thought you were close to who somehow don't react in a way that's consoling. Or you may find that your friends who are struggling with their own miseries may relate to your blues but drag you down further. In general, you'll need to really look out for numero uno during this period and focus on the people whose company really helps you, reassures you, and cheers you up. Even if you're already in a new romantic relationship, you'll realize that the nonromantic ties of family and friends are absolutely critical when you're separating.

Reach Out and Touch Someone

If you're like Kay and Sarah, you might have trouble asking people for help, so allow yourself to be more demanding during this time. If people don't know quite how to be there for you, give them ideas. You can suggest having dinner once a week, or invite them over to watch your favorite TV show, or implore them to invite you to absolutely *anything*. Or ask them to call you once a day to check in and see how you're doing. Or ask you if you've eaten anything. Or make you dinner. Or come over for takeout and a movie.

Valerie, for instance, couldn't stand being alone after her separation, so she invited one of her best friends to come over every night. The friend basically moved in with Valerie for a while; she'd appear at the doorway after work with a bottle of wine and a video. Valerie says, "My friend filled the gap and gave me something to look forward to after work." In another rescue mission, Hope's best friend flew out from California to the East Coast to be there for her soon after the separation. He took her out for a burger and beer and said, "I love you, I'll always love you, and about the divorce, that's why they put erasers on pencils." She never forgot that. People who love you will often do extraordinary things if you just give them the opportunity.

They Knew You When You Were Normal

Many divorcées turn to their family and/or oldest friends at this time. There's something deeply comforting and anchoring about people who have known you an incredibly long time and can see that you're going through an especially hard, wacky period in your life. They understand who you are beyond this isolated stumbling block and they can help you reconnect with who you are as well.

If they are living, your parents especially may suddenly find themselves supporting you in ways you might not have experienced much in adulthood. You've been independent, and, particularly if your parents are older, they may even have started to become dependent on you. Get comfortable with the idea of reversing this trend for a bit and make use of your parents. As Robert Frost tells us, "Home is the place where, when you go there, they have to take you in." Remember, we're the first generation to have divorced parents who can actually relate to what we're going through. Megan told only her mother at first, who had also been divorced and had very sage advice. Delia moved back in with her mother (who had also gotten divorced from her father) and sister. Miranda told only her mother in the very beginning, and it helped to have her on board right away: "The next day I got a FedEx package with ten self-help books, and the day after that I got twenty-five more."

Sometimes it can be a surprise to find out how supportive your parents are, especially if you never thought they would be. Cindy remarked about her traditional Japanese mother, "I moved back home when I moved out, and I was shocked that my mother was so accepting, even though she never knew all that had gone on because I didn't tell her along the way . . . I think she just saw how much pain I was in." Elizabeth had the same reaction about her very traditional, Catholic family: "They were amazingly supportive. They said, you guys didn't look happy. They just wanted me to be happy . . . Suddenly, I had a network of people there for me." Similarly, Caitlin was amazed by how helpful her mother's friends in particular were when they heard: "These sixty-something women were so affirming! The irony was that my own generation of thirty-something women, who were supposed to be post-feminist, were not so supportive. My mother's friends realized how important it was to be true to yourself, whereas women my age were concerned about what my choice reflected about their own marriages."

Right after she separated from F., Kay found herself reconnecting with her oldest high school friends, none of whom lived nearby (much of the contact was by email). She found they knew her so well and so long that they could easily put her wild mood swings in context.

A word of caution: mutual friends shared during the marriage, even if some of them were originally your friends, may not be the greatest confidantes during this time (for more on coping with mutual friends, see chapter 7).

New Blood for Your Rusty Veins

On the flip side, sometimes your parents and oldest friends, either because of their values or because you've fallen out of touch with them and they are far away, cannot serve as baseball mitts for the curveball that is you (we'll discuss exactly why this might be later on in this chapter). Some women make up for this by reestablishing friendships that had faded somewhat during their marriage or by developing new friends to fit their dynamic, ever-evolving selves. Megan started going to local business council meetings and met a whole new group of people who only knew her as the single, independent woman she was becoming and not as her past self. Tanya became good friends with a woman who also became her roommate and introduced her to a whole new, exciting group of friends. Trudie, who had had very few female friendships while married, reached out and forged relationships with single girl-friends and women going through similar situations. During the first six months after her separation, she would call two of them on her cell phone every morning for moral support as she walked to work.

It's not uncommon to become incredibly tight and dependent on one or two serious confidantes during this time, as Trudie did with her two morning advisors. In a similar vein, Maeve had a morning walking partner who was her "one deep confidante," because it's important to have one true person that you can just let it all out with. For Rachel, this person was an old guy friend who became her roommate, and for Cindy, it was an old friend of her brother's who she'd go running with. These confidantes can serve almost as surrogate romantic partners—without the romance. They are the people you can call at any hour and with whom you can have those all-important intimate conversations, but without the risks and baggage of a love relationship. (For advice on the ins and outs of romantic attachments post-marriage, see chapter 8 on dating.)

Sometimes It's Best to Leave It to the Professionals

We promise we aren't getting any kickbacks from the American Psychological Association when we recommend at different points throughout the book, including now, that you consider seeking professional counseling if you haven't already. We're certainly not saying you should lie on the couch for the rest of your life. We're just saying, you are undergoing a hugely stressful life event, and it can really help to have someone neutral with whom to sort through all the madness, someone who is exclusively interested in you and your recovery.

Many of the divorcées we interviewed felt strongly about this point. They usually entered therapy only for a year or two and then stopped when they felt a lot better. Gina says, "For a long time, I couldn't say 'divorce' without crying. I went to a counselor until I couldn't cry anymore, until I had to make up things to talk about, and then I knew I was done." A few important benefits to seeing a counselor or therapist: (a) all those shrinks do have a point about "the talking cure"—it really does work to talk and cry yourself to cathartic oblivion; (b) you are assured complete confidentiality; (c) they're objective, and their feelings about your ex won't cloud the picture (unlike, perhaps, even your closest friends and family); and (d) you are distributing where you get support and aren't overburdening those closest to you.

Woman's Best Friend

Finally, if you don't already own a pet, you may want to consider getting one as a source of comfort and companionship. Studies show that people are more successful coping with stress in the company of a pet; heart rate and blood pressure actually go down when you're getting (and giving) affection from a feline or canine friend. Vickie, for instance, was helped immensely by adopting two cats. She did this partly so that the apartment wouldn't feel so empty and partly to spite her ex, who had been allergic.

Sarah's friend Polly went to the pound and fell in love with a handsome stray mutt, who became her constant companion. It can be incredibly nice to come home to a furry someone, who expects nothing of you except some food, water, and basic affection. Another friend, Stella, who had never dreamed of owning a pet, got inspired by someone she knew to buy an English bulldog, which she now adores and can't live without. She also finds walking her dog a great way to meet people, especially of the opposite sex. And because owning a pet forces you to take care of a little creature, your schedule has to be somewhat regular, too, which can provide balance and routine when you're feeling at sea.

Navigating the Reactions of Your Inner Circle

The ubiquity of divorce hasn't made the causes or emotions of it much easier to digest for many people. This means that, at the same time that you're seeking the support you need, you might not always be greeted with open arms. Sheesh. It's enough effort to take care of *your* needs, and now, on top of everything you're coping with, you have to contend with the reactions of others, which can range from shock to grief to "good riddance." These reactions may or may not match your own present state of mind, so processing the emotions of your inner circle can get complicated. While this is not a time to be overly concerned with what other people are feeling or thinking, it can be helpful to acknowledge that even some of your dearest friends and family members, particularly your parents, might have a hard time coping with the news.

Any number of reasons can be behind their uneasiness, but let's look at the big one: *they love you.* Of course! No one wants to learn that a beloved daughter, friend, or sister has had a difficult marriage, much less reached this difficult decision to separate and probably divorce. If they didn't know about your situation until now, they may feel bad that they haven't helped earlier in the process. As Miranda put it, "Some people find it deeply unsettling that someone in their life could have something go wrong without their knowing."

Sometimes, the parental reaction is more complex and you don't feel particularly coddled and swaddled. As an only child of divorced parents, Vickie, for example, dreaded telling her mother and father. "I'm not emotionally close to them. I didn't want to show failure to them." Vickie's parents, it turned out, did not look down on her for her divorce, but not everyone is so fortunate. For example, our friend Laura has very traditional Catholic parents who questioned her decision and blamed her for not upholding her vows. Their harsh reaction taught her a lot about them and how deeply held their worldview really was. For Laura, what helped mitigate their disapproval was that she realized that she didn't have to be imprisoned by their provincialism and trapped in a joyless marriage like theirs. In the process of examining her family's reaction, she better understood her own motivations and needs.

For Mehta, raised in a very traditional Thai family, telling her mother about her separation was harder than telling her husband she wanted a divorce. Although Mehta never spoke with her father about the divorce, she did reach an understanding with her mother, and in fact their relationship deepened, as her mother revealed her unhappiness in her own marriage and expressed an understanding of why Mehta would leave.

In an even more positive way, our friend Leslie's divorce provided the catalyst for changes within her larger family dynamic. Her parents were initially shocked by the news of her separation, but it then caused them to reexamine their own marriage and, in general, helped foster a more forgiving spirit within the family as a whole. "There's less pressure to be perfect all the time and to fit into this perfect mold, more understanding for people's faults and shortcomings," says Leslie of her family today.

Too Much 411 . . . Too Little 911

The fact that our generation is the first to have experienced such widespread divorce within our parents' circles means that in some respects, a parent may be more understanding of what you're going through. Sometimes, though, the familiarity of divorce in their lives only complicates things further, especially if one or both of your parents attempts to identify with you. As Hope relates, "My mother, who had a starter marriage, kept telling me, 'I know what you're going through.' But my marriage was very different from hers, and I just wanted to say, 'You have no idea how I feel.' " The identification impulse is well intentioned, but it can be confusing: it refocuses attention on the other person's problems rather than yours. (And if it's your mother talking about divorce from your father, you might prefer she didn't go there, at least right now.) So do your best to communicate what you need from your family members, realizing that even though they love you, they're just processing the news too.

Sad, Mad, Glad . . . Egads!
The Rainbow of Reactions

It was our experience, confirmed by that of our interviewees, that as you start to tell people in your orbit, their initial emotional reactions fall into one of four basic categories: sad, mad, glad, or "egads!" You're likely to encounter all of these at one point or another as, generally, people are pretty averse to change. As we said before, these responses might not always be in sync with your own emotional state, but in the process of telling others, you'll discover your own reservoirs of strength and self-knowledge.

It's important to realize that people will inevitably bring their own baggage to bear on your situation. Just try not to internalize their issues so much that you confuse them with your own or second-guess your feelings and your decisions. Now is the time to focus on yourself and seek out the people who can best support you.

We've already established that one of the main reasons people will be upset is because they love you. Let's look at some of the ancillary reasons why people might react the way they do.

1. *"Egads!" They're shocked.* They just "can't believe it," they "had no idea," or "you seemed so perfect together." Since it's often considered taboo to talk about marital tension with anyone beyond your husband or your therapist (if you have one), some friends and family may be shocked to hear the announcement of your separation and/or divorce. As Miranda put it, "From my family, my cousins in particular, I got the 'but you seemed so happy' and 'he's such a great guy.' People say this to you as if they deserve an elaborate answer." Sometimes, people close to your

husband will feel like they need some kind of explanation, but re-alize that whatever reasons you can give them right now may not seem adequate, as they've established their own relationship with your husband. It's possible that at first they may not be capable of understanding how someone they love (you) could stop loving someone else (your husband) they love. To some extent, reactions of surprise might be strangely comforting to you, especially if you are coping with your own disbelief; if that's the case, don't be afraid to say so: "I know, I can't believe it either."

2. *They're sad.* As all the experts say, when couples divorce, there're often more than two people left grieving; your loved ones will grieve the end of the two of you as a couple and will be sad on account of your sadness. When a marriage comes undone, many people feel their own version of disappointment and dreams dashed. Gina remembers how some people broke down and cried when she told them her news. Though she too was crying a lot at night, her response to the tears of her friends was, "Look, be happy that I'm going to be happier." It can be helpful to step outside of yourself and realize that people are feeling their own loss, and they need time to process this experience and adjust to your new reality.

Complicating this is the fact that friends and family members might have become attached to your husband as an individual. Even if they didn't adore him in the beginning, they may have learned to, partly out of love for you. He may have been a fabu-lous brother-in-law, friend, or uncle. And if people close to you really loved your husband, when you separate, they will be sad about losing him and anxious about what kind of relationship (if any) they'll continue to have with him. They know things aren't going to be the same and are grieving this change.

3. *They're mad—at him, at both of you, or just you, especially if you initiated the process.* Anger can come from various sources. Maybe a friend or family member feels hurt that they didn't know

what was going on. If there was an infidelity on either side, they may be experiencing some bewilderment, and anger is a natural response to this as well as to loss in general. They are probably also responding to what might feel like a sudden change in the status quo, a change over which they had no control or influence. And as *you* know all too well, change of this kind feels awfully destabilizing. It's helpful to realize that your marriage has been part of their reality, and that many people will simply need some time to adjust to you as a single person. They might also need some time to hear more details of your story, if you are able to share. In all likelihood, whatever anger your family members and friends might harbor against you will dissipate with time, as they begin to see beyond their anger and become more sympathetic to your situation. Even if they don't sympathize with you, chances are that one day they'll be able to appreciate that the marriage had to end. If they're not able to do this eventually, then as excruciating as it might feel (and as trite as it sounds) you'll know you've separated the wheat from the chaff.

4. *They're glad.* The overly glad reaction, as in *"Good riddance!"* can sometimes be as hard to hear as anything else. People may suddenly feel free to tell you anything they've ever thought about your spouse—how much better off you are without him, what was wrong with him, and so forth. You may hear unsavory stories or negative perspectives for the first time. As Patti said, "People can say really awful things to you. They'll insult your ex, thinking it'll help to hear 'you're too good for him.' " Depending on how you feel, these harsh words may be hard to hear, or alternatively, you may welcome some of the anti-ex talk. While it's okay to indulge in some of this trash-talking with your inner circle, most of the time you'll feel better rising above the bulk of the well-intentioned insults. Overly denigrating your ex (and/or encouraging others to do so) can make you feel a bit cheap and like your marriage was a weird chimera.

Communicating at Work and Beyond: Whispers at the Watercooler

For practical reasons, you'll want to be sure to inform your human resources department at work once you are separated or divorced, since you'll need to remove your husband as a beneficiary on your insurance, and maybe the emergency contact as well. Although you don't *need* to, you also might want to tell your boss, and perhaps other members of the immediate team with whom you work. Vickie felt compelled to tell people at work right away because, as she puts it, "I wanted to resume use of my maiden name and because I was such an emotional wreck I felt there had to be some explanation." Our friend Elizabeth, on the other hand, had changed jobs while she was getting separated, in part to have a new environment where people didn't know her and her husband. She decided to take her time and not to tell anyone at her new job for three months, which helped her to get her bearings and avoid having to worry about whether her boss was scrutinizing her performance. Only you know how open you can and want to be with your boss and colleagues at work. Telling people at work definitely falls within the optional/extra credit category, so do it only if and when you feel like it.

If you do decide to tell your boss and others, briefer is usually better. If you are likely to cry—and hey, that's only natural—bring a water bottle and some Kleenex. A simple "I thought I should tell you that I'm going through a divorce right now" should suffice. We don't recommend email, since the recipient can forward your message anywhere, and then you lose all control over the information. As you share with others the basic facts of the change in your life, you'll want to stem the tide of watercooler gossip by asking them to be discreet and keep your news in confidence.

Let's be honest, you might not be a peak performer right

now, but you should also realize that absolutely everyone goes through a personal crisis at one point or another. Life is full of hard knocks; if your boss and coworkers haven't experienced a divorce firsthand, then chances are they have coped with a death, an illness, a health challenge, or what have you. Unless they are completely heartless, they will be sympathetic to your situation. When Sarah told her boss, a fifty-something man, he told her that he'd had an early first marriage and that the reason he stayed an extra year in Vietnam during the war was that he didn't want to come home to face the pain of his divorce. As he put it, "Combat was easier." Sometimes you even forge new connections with people you'd never have thought you would just because you've shared your news.

However, even if you have the most understanding boss in the world, you'll want to do your best to follow up the news by showing her or him that your work will not be affected. Along these lines, it's a good idea to try to minimize the amount of divorce paperwork you have to handle from the office or at least on office time. The ole "doctor's appointment" or "migraine headache" may allow you to come in late on a day when you need to complete paperwork or make telephone calls. And don't be afraid to ask for time off. Most bosses would prefer that you simply stay away from the office, if necessary, rather than stay there, firing on less than all cylinders or leaking like a faucet.

The Name Game

First of all, let's just forget the term "maiden name." It might have made sense for our mother's generation, but we've always thought it sounded pretty bogus for our generation. (How many of us were maidens when we got married anyway?) Instead, we'll refer to your surname from birth as your "family" name—isn't that better? If you changed your name when you were married, and plan to resume your family name when your divorce is finalized, there's no need to wait to be known professionally and socially as your former self. It might feel really exhilarating to do this right away, and get new business cards printed up, for example, or change your email address at home and at work.

On the other hand, if you'd rather not broadcast the reason for your name change, particularly at work, you might prefer to do this in stages. For example, you could insert your original name into your signature on correspondence and into your outgoing message on voicemail, so that people get used to seeing it and hearing it, especially if you've never been known under this name in your office. When your name change is official (see page 134), you can simply drop your married last name altogether in correspondence and introductions.

Eventually, you may have to circulate an email to let colleagues know about the name change. Some people will innocently react with a "Congratulations!" assuming you've just gotten married, which can feel a tad unnerving, but accept the congrats. You deserve them. When Gina announced her name change, and received this reaction, she found herself saying, "Actually, it's the opposite, but congratulations are still in order."

Telling Miscellaneous Others: Your Dentist, Doctor, and Dry Cleaner

Sometimes, the act of telling the miscellaneous other people in your life will hit you in a way you weren't prepared for. Perhaps you still share the same dentist, doctor, or dry cleaner as your ex?

They innocently inquire about your husband, and you make a split-second decision as to whether you want to go into it. The questions and condolences may make you queasy. Or maybe you're just tired of telling the story. So don't. Do it when you want to. And switch vendors if it makes you feel better.

Sarah decided to change dry cleaners when she realized she felt a weird self-consciousness creep up on her when she brought only her clothes (without her husband's shirts) to the dry cleaner: "No shirts? What happened to husband?" When told the news, the kind Chinese proprietor, delighting in her use of American idiom, offered, "You hang in there, Mrs.——— !" Sometimes, however, you don't want the well-intentioned sympathy, you just want anonymity.

Kay, for example, took two years to reveal the Big Split to Tyler, the receptionist at her dentist's office. For some reason, in this place with scary metal instruments, she still wanted to have the comfort of married status. Also, she felt she would somehow be letting Tyler and the whole public world down if she admitted she and F. weren't a unit anymore. Eventually, after receiving one too many bills for F.'s dental work, she got over her silly self and broke the news to Tyler, who didn't even bat an eye while he fixed their accounts in the computer.

Losing the In-Laws

When two people decide to divorce, they don't just leave each other. They also break up their mutual families. Sometimes, this is a relief; maybe there was a good deal of tension with the in-laws. Maybe you really loathed your sister-in-law. Many times, however, the impending loss of the extended family you came to know through your ex provides yet another layer of sadness. For example, for Gina, the thought of losing her in-laws proved to be the hardest part of her divorce. She'd become very close to her husband's sister, brother, and mother, and, in general, his family traditions had really become hers. Likewise, her husband had become close to her brothers. When they broke up, they decided to make a conscious effort to maintain these family ties, and so far, it seems to be working.

Only you can figure out whether you should maintain contact with your in-laws. When you have no kids, you really are free to determine the kind of relationship, if any, you want to maintain with your husband's parents or siblings. Although your relationship will never be the same, and one day there might well be another daughter-in-law, you may still feel a good deal of fondness for your ex's family. If your goal is to stay in touch, by all means, do what feels right while acknowledging a certain degree of awkwardness due to the situation. Common sense and decency will help guide you. For example, if one of your ex-in-laws is sick with a serious illness, you may be inspired to send an expression of your good wishes. Realize that you do not, however, have any obligation to them, so don't put yourself through unnecessary stress about how to maintain ties with in-laws if you don't want to.

Particularly if ending the relationship was not your choice, it's a good idea to examine *why* you want to stay in touch with your ex's family. Is it possible you really want a way to keep tabs on him? Or perhaps it's that you just want to find a way to stay in his life. Sometimes people will make a big effort to stay in touch with their ex-in-laws because they are brokenhearted and the ex-family represents the old connection. These impulses are perfectly natural, but try your best to avoid indulging them because you don't want anything to interfere with your healing process.

What do you do if *your* family members want to remain in contact with your ex? Just as you might miss your in-laws, your relatives may miss your ex. But let's be clear: they should not keep up contact if it will upset you. When Sarah's ex proudly told her that her sister had sent him a Christmas present, and that her brother-in-law had sent him a card with family pictures, she was filled with a strange displeasure that was hard to articulate. From then on, Sarah made it known to her family that because things were, at the time, bitter and sad, she wanted to have veto power on all correspondence. On the other hand, if you feel fine about a certain degree of interaction, you can make that known to all involved and they can proceed accordingly. The bottom line is that it is your call, and it is your responsibility to let your loved ones know what you feel comfortable with.

Shifting from "We" to "I"

Since this is the communications chapter, it seems appropriate to bring up something that no one seems to prepare you for: that shift from "we" to "I" in your everyday speech. You know how it goes: you've got that big bank of mutual shared stories, and every time you recall an event, a trip, an anecdote that was shared with your ex-spouse, you begin by exercising that couples pronoun, "we." It may take a while to change this reflexive way of speaking; as Elizabeth put it, "Sometimes 'we' will slip out. It's hard because I had this whole life that happened for six years that I can't erase." But shifting from "we" to "I" can prove empowering. Whether it was hiking in the Grand Canyon, missing that plane flight, or taking that Burmese cooking class, *you* were there! Using "I" instead of "we" in your daily storytelling is also a polite gesture to others. For example, the new guy in your life probably isn't going to love being reminded that you were a "we" before he was a "we" with you. Finally, getting to "I" is an important part of breaking the news to yourself, and accepting your new single status in the presence of others.

CHAPTER FOUR

Losing a Bed, a Bank Account, and a Roommate

Physical and Financial Separation

Thank goodness for sofas and jointly owned automobiles. As soon as the argument can degenerate into a battle over property, the personal emotional ground can begin to be abandoned.

—Ellen Gilchrist,
"Meditations on Divorce"

As writer Ellen Gilchrist suggests with some wry humor, beginning the physical separation and the negotiation over concrete things in your shared life can feel like a strange relief after all of the emotional battles you've probably waged with yourself and your ex. But the reality is, the heartache will linger for a while, and your emotions will probably find a new way of expressing themselves in the division of assets. Moving and physically separating yourself from your ex is one of life's more challenging processes, and it's made all the more delightful by having to adjust to life on a single income. When your feelings are still raw and rough, it's incredibly hard to think sensibly and practically, but no matter where you are in the process (considering a separation or already in one), at some point you'll need to sharpen your pencil and start to plan your new solo life in all of its practical glory.

In this chapter, whether you're the one staying or going, we'll offer ways to go about it all that can help make the logistics and all the attendant emotions as bearable and future-focused as possible. We'll also cover some basic steps you'll want to take in separating your finances, your material possessions, and other kinds of assets that need to be sorted out in order to make your separation and divorce a reality. Even if you can't see the light at the end of the tunnel right now, we promise you, things *will* get better. And if you're like us and the scores of women we interviewed, you'll find that the physical separation, once under way, gives you a new sense of the relationship and a new sense of your own strength, wisdom, and capacity for happiness.

Economics Get Emotional

Even if you're on excellent terms with your husband, be mindful of the fact that for many couples, the moving process and the division of money and shared belongings is an area where much of the pain, or the reason your marriage is ending, comes into play. This is because, in many ways, it's easier to argue about these seemingly objective, concrete, and tangible things than it is about the subjective, hazy, and hard issues of the heart. This means that it's important to keep your wits about you as you negotiate the new terrain and, in all areas, try to be true to yourself. While we're not suggesting that you treat your husband like an outright foe—and in fact, we were both fortunate to have husbands who generally acted graciously during this process—we do know that there are many instances among our interviewees of husbands who became absolute gladiators in this arena (and we don't mean in a cute Russell Crowe kinda way). The bottom line is, we want you to keep your interests front and center, and we believe you can do this while being a decent and honorable person to your soon-to-be ex.

Should I Stay or Should I Go? Staying Put or Moving Out

While many books and other authorities might suggest that you should stay put for better bargaining power—especially if you're a homeowner, or if there are significant assets in the shared space—this decision is highly personal and highly specific to your individual situation. Nevertheless, in our experience and research, the person who initiated the divorce is *usually* the one who has to move out, and the person who didn't (at least initially) want the divorce *usually* gets the option of staying.

There are exceptions, of course, and sometimes finances or ownership will dictate what happens. Our friend Megan, for example, who had initiated her divorce, stayed in their house because she was the one who could afford the mortgage payments. Similarly, our friends Greta and Caitlin, who both decided to end their marriages, stayed in their places because they owned them prior to marriage. Other times, your emotions just tell you what to do, as was the case with Vickie who, though she didn't want their divorce, moved out for some fresh scenery. In either case, whether you stay or go, this is the time when you are undertaking the separation in earnest, so you should be mindful of the fact that you're about to experience a fairly crazy time, complete with some soaring new highs and some less-than-lovely new lows. This is often the time when the reality strikes you (and your soon-to-be ex) most acutely. Realize that this is part of the process. Give yourself over to those cathartic opportunities that arise as you move, purge, clean, renovate, and redecorate. Soon you'll be well on your way to starting life anew and letting the healing begin.

Interim Arrangements: Gimme Shelter!

It's possible that even though you've figured out who's staying and who's going, you don't have the resources to move immediately into something permanent. If this is the case, don't be shy about asking friends and family to put you up for a few weeks, even a few months. If you're not near your friends or family, get recommendations from them for friends in the area who could give you shelter for some period of time. Or, if these ideas just aren't possible, consider moving into a hotel for a few days or a week until you get your bearings. Credit cards are for crises like these. There's no harm in putting some mileage on your plastic for the peace of mind that you'll get by living on your own, even in a hotel.

When Temporary Cohabitation with Your Husband Is Your Only Option

We probably don't have to tell you that this is a highly undesirable situation, to be avoided if at all possible. If it's cost-savings you're after, think hard about the psychological and emotional costs such an arrangement will probably bring. As our friend Erin, who endured six months of living with her husband after they'd technically separated, put it, "I wouldn't wish it on my worst enemy!" She and her husband were fortunate in that they had a two-bedroom, split-level condo, so her domain was upstairs, his downstairs. Nevertheless, it was extremely stressful. He became obsessed with the idea that she was cheating on him (she wasn't; she was diligent about not even dating anyone even though they were legally separated), and every communication was a confrontation. She got through this time by keeping very busy, working around the clock, and returning home just to go to sleep.

Your case may not be as dramatic as Erin's was. You may find that you have to stay in your old place while you're searching for your new one, especially if the real estate market is tight. This is what happened to Elizabeth; she remained in the house with her husband for three months, both of them sleeping in the same bed because the futon was uncomfortable. Such an arrangement is bound to feel bizarre, and Elizabeth admits that she found herself, out of habit and concern, doing wifely things for him—buying his favorite ice cream flavor at the grocery store even though they weren't eating meals together, for example. If you find yourself in a similar situation, don't beat yourself up. It's incredibly hard to release a person and all of their preferences from your brain and heart. Do move on as soon as you can when you've found a room of your own—limbo is no fun.

If You're Considering Moving in with the New Flame

If you have one, moving in with a new flame may seem like a tempting idea because (a) you're wildly in love with him, (b) this new relationship might have been the catalyst for ending your marriage, therefore you feel it would somehow justify things, (c) let's face it, you could use some companionship, and finally, (d) you fear the financial ramifications of living alone. Despite all these seemingly good reasons, we caution against this, on two major fronts:

- Legal/practical: if the divorce becomes contentious, and some do when you least expect it, you really don't want to give up your leverage, and you will be doing so by moving in with your new man.
- Psychological/emotional: even if you end up spending most of the time at your new man's place, there will probably be times when having your own address and the potential for privacy will mean something to you— a safety net in case things don't work out with the new

relationship. After all, you're going through a really difficult time right now, and the fact of your separation/divorce is bound to occasionally complicate the new romantic connection you're making.

If money is tight and you know you won't be spending oodles of time at your place, consider getting a roommate so you have your own address but pay less than what you'd pay on your own. This might feel like "back to college" but it can be a good compromise between moving in full-time with your new beau and living on your own. And you might meet some new people as a result, never a bad thing when you're rebuilding your life.

If You've Decided to Move

As you search for a new place to call home, your budget may be feeling some strain these days on account of your newly single income, but we want to emphasize how important it is to figure out something that will please you about your new place, new 'hood, new city. Take some time to think about what you might want to do differently now that you have a chance to indulge your own preferences entirely. Maybe the place you shared with your husband didn't get much natural light, so you realize it would be great to move to a sunnier pad, as Kay did in San Francisco. Or maybe you were living among the so-called smug-marrieds and want to experiment with a more jazzy, restaurant-filled section of town. If you were living in suburbia, as our friends Valerie and Patti were at the time they separated from their husbands, consider moving to a more happening area—if not into a city, then perhaps a hipper, funkier neighborhood within your town. As longtime urban dwellers, we confess we might be biased, but even if you are a total solitude-lovin' introvert, we urge you to place yourself in an area where you can at least have the *option* of finding friends, food, and interesting diversions just down the block or a stone's throw from your doorstep.

Handling Move Day

Once you've found your new nest, you need to start preparing for the Big Move. Basically, moving sucks under *any* circumstance. In fact, according to a recent feature article in *Home* magazine, on the stress index, moving ranks right after death and divorce! And this particular move can feel uniquely unpleasant because, however excited you are about your new life, you're bound to also feel some twinges of sadness, nostalgia, and anxiety. Keep focused on your new opportunities, staying on task as much as possible. Here are three key suggestions to make the process as stress-free as possible:

- Even if you don't hire professionals, you can be professional about your move. This means, set your date and don't waver. Devote the whole day to it, resolving to get it done in the course of eight hours. The concentrated sweep, the surgical strike, will most likely be better for everyone—most of all, *you*. It's kind of like pulling off a Band-Aid, the faster and more decisively you do it, the less it hurts.

- Insist that your husband absent himself completely from the process. You really don't want him lurking in the hall, awkwardly attempting to help, or getting maudlin. This may take some advance planning, so try to settle on your date quickly and give your ex some lead time.

- Call your friends. Even if you hire professionals (and if you can, financially, by all means do), you can really use the moral support of a pal or two. It can get very lonely out there with the moving guys. Plus, your friends can keep the coffee flowing, the doors open, and help with general troubleshooting like watching the open van. Of course, at the end of the day, you

should reward yourself and them with copious food
and drink.

Announcing Your New Coordinates

*W*hen your move is set, and if your place is reasonably permanent, it's a good idea to think about sending cheery
change-of-address cards with your new coordinates. People
who have been thinking about you but are not in frequent
contact with you will be very glad to get this information,
and you can append personal postscripts if you are so in-
clined ("Hope to see you at book group" or "Let's get together soon").

All Moved In . . . Now What?

Be sure to give yourself enough time to unpack, call the cable guy,
get your phone installed, get oriented to the neighborhood, and
generally set up your new home—exactly the way *you* want it.
Moving in to a new place and new area can be discombobulating
so you'll want to be sure to take enough time off from work to
get reasonably settled in your new abode. Consider having a
friend or two over to help you with one category of your belongings, say, the kitchen or the bookshelves. There's also something to be said for creating a party for yourself and setting up
shop completely on your own. In any case, smile and dial some
delivery food, break out a bottle if you like, and dream about dec-
orating. Now you have a chance to cultivate your personal style,
be it Spartan, chic, or country charm. And even if you don't
"need" new bedding, consider getting a new quilt, comforter,
sheets, or pillows. It can feel awfully good to have new nesting
materials, and the puffier the better. One of our girlfriends or-
dered up a giant pillow, monogrammed with her premarriage ini-

tials, celebrating her return to her family name. Sometimes, those small gestures in self-care work wonders for the soul.

When You're Staying Put: Making Your Old Place Feel New

If your husband is the one moving out, plan to be away from your place and thoroughly occupied, preferably with good friends, while he's taking his stuff. Advise him that you really need him to move out efficiently in the course of his appointed day. You may want to go hiking, go to a spa, or go shopping with girlfriends. Get out of town if you have the opportunity. But whatever you do, do not stick around. The last thing you want is to find yourself getting weepy over possessions, or worse yet, break your own back helping him move something!

When your husband leaves the premises, it can be tough to cope with the holes in the floor plan, and continue living in the space the two of you shared. That's why this is a great time to consider some subtle makeover techniques to make your old place new. For starters, you could . . .

- Hire a cleaning service to clean your place top to bottom. You could also do this yourself, as our friend Caitlin did. She said there was something oddly therapeutic in smelling the strong ammonia fumes wafting through the floorboards.
- Repaint. Maybe not the entire place, but something like your bedroom might be doable. Go for a fabulous color—fuchsia or lime green.
- Invite a friend over to help you conceive new arrangements and move things around. It's amazing what turning your bed to a new angle can do.
- Buy a book on feng shui and make some floor plan changes to get the positive energy vibes flowing freely.
- Take down pictures of you two if they're still up. For

some people, these are the first items to go, others the last. Whatever seems right, but there will come a time when you really don't need these reminders of him and you. Replace them with happy enlargements of your family and friends.

- Figure out what you need to make it feel homey and then go shopping with some friends—flea markets, IKEA, antique stores, anywhere that fits your fabulous new style.

The Clean Slate Approach

It's entirely possible that you might say, as our friend Trudie did, "I wanted to start from ground zero and create a space all my own." Trudie's husband moved out and took all of the furniture, and she stayed in their empty place and lived an ascetic life at the beginning, even sleeping on a bench (which her friends called the "nun's bed"). She felt that somehow, furnishing the new place would make the ending final, and even though she wanted the separation, she just wasn't ready to go there for a few months. Nevertheless, she boldly hosted a dinner party and everyone happily sat cross-legged on the bare floor! After about five or six months, she did buy a bed—a double bed—and conquered her negative associations of "double bed equals marriage equals death." In today's acquisitive culture, and when you just don't want to be reminded of your ex, you might find it really liberating to let go of all of your things and become a minimalist. Of course, you don't have to go to Trudie's extreme; you can also take some joy in going shopping for new pieces of furniture and new possessions to celebrate the new you.

Two Roads Diverged and You Took... Deciding Who Gets What

Next on your agenda: figuring out what lawyers refer to as the Division of Marital Assets—in other words, how you and your ex divide your domicile and specifically, those items and assets that were acquired during your marriage. No matter what your situation, if you've been together a long time or a short time, this process can feel darn prickly. It's our goal to give you an overview of how some couples have gone about this so that you can figure out what works best for you. In this section, we ask you to ask yourself what you really need and want of your shared possessions. As we've said before, you'll survive these negotiations in better shape if you approach them in as cooperative a spirit as possible. Even though this is a totally irrational time, and even though there may be times when you really don't want to be rational with him, if you can conjure up some common sense and be willing to compromise, you'll emerge from the scene feeling better rather than worse (although you may never feel great about the experience).

But Don't Negotiate with a Terrorist

If you feel you are in danger with your ex, you really don't want to get caught up in discussions over who gets the blender, so preserve or take only the things that really, really matter to you (be it family pictures, jewelry, your yearbook, or your diary), get the heck out of Dodge, and put yourself in the hands of loved ones and a lawyer as fast as you can. Our friend Maeve, for example, remembers the day she left her husband: "I was out of my mind with fear, anxiety, fear of what he would do . . . I crammed my car full of my stuff, found a place for the cat, left my beloved books, and took off." If you're in an abusive or potentially abusive relationship, consider putting a restraining order on your husband so that he can't plunder your possessions. If you really need to stay in the house, change the locks and ask a friend or a relative to stay with you. When Valerie was stalked by her husband after they'd separated, she said, "I felt like a candidate for a witness protection program, doing everything I could to start a new life." Play it safe and listen to your most cautious self if your husband is prone to a violent temper, is threatening you outright, or is otherwise harassing you.

What's Mine, Yours, or Ours?

If you have pretty uncomplicated finances and are on decent terms, like Kay and her husband were, and you don't have lawyers, you may be able to settle all of the division of assets on your own—in which case, feel free to skip this section of the chapter. If you've got a contentious situation, however, it's a good idea to get a basic orientation as to how the law works on property division. As you'll learn in chapter 5, states vary in their laws for property division upon divorce. So depending on where you live in the country your assets and liabilities (debt) are subject to the classification of either "personal property" (anything you acquired *before* the marriage, which includes gifts from the man who would become your husband) or "marital property" (anything acquired *during* the marriage). Then there's a third category, "exempt property," which in many states refers to personal property acquired during the marriage but not subject to division at divorce (for example, an inheritance or a personal injury award from an insurance company). Finally, there are a few states that treat marital property as "community property," which means that anything gained during the marriage is shared by husband and wife and must be divided equally between you, fifty-fifty. At this writing, community property states include California, Colorado, Idaho, Louisiana, Washington, and Texas. And then there's "equitable distribution," which some other states observe, according to which all shared property should be divided equitably (which does not necessarily mean *equally*, but "fairly") no matter when it was acquired (before or after your marriage). It's absolutely enough to make your eyes cross, isn't it?

Bear with the distinctions, because there can be benefits to knowing your particular state's rules, particularly if there are areas of conflict between you and your husband that may be moot depending on how the law comes down. For example, Greta's husband was trying to go after an inheritance she received from the death of her father before she was married. It turned out that, not only did he look really money-grubbing, but by law in their state, he had absolutely no claim to this money as Greta had kept it in a separate money market account for the duration of their marriage. It was exempt property. If, however, Greta had taken the inheritance and put it into a joint account, then it would have been considered comingled, and therefore possibly subject to division. Finally, according to the law in many states, like New York, if you own assets that you acquired prior to the marriage and that are still titled in your name at the time you are splitting up, say, a house, mutual fund, a certificate of deposit (basically anything that appreciates in value), *the interest or profit* of the investment that was accrued during the time of your marriage is considered marital property and is subject to division. In other words, in such states you or your husband could lay claim to half of the interest or the profits from your house sale. It's as if the tenure of your marriage was the umbrella under which these investments grew.

Obviously, the question of what constitutes "equitable" or even "equal" distribution can get hazy, and you can't assign a real price tag to absolutely everything, though lawyers in these states will try. Sarah's friend Ella almost had to sacrifice thousands of dollars when she fought for custody of her beloved dog. Happily, she doesn't regret it one iota; her divorce was finalized four years ago and her beagle is still her affectionate companion. (For more on pet issues, see "Who gets Rex?" page 91.)

Note that, in general, if you have a complex real estate or asset/liability situation, you should probably consider a lawyer to handle your case. The money you pay in legal fees will be well spent in the long run. At the same time, however, the more you can reasonably accomplish on your own in terms of dividing stuff, the better. There is one general rule, however, as far as possessions go, and that is this: it is best to try to sort these matters out before one of you moves. If you don't go through lawyers, it'll be up to you to reclaim anything you leave behind, and as dreadful as it may seem to be Stormin' Norma right now, we promise you, it's preferable to having to be Repo Woman later. In so many cases, possession really is ninth-tenths of the law, and if you want it and you're the one moving, you better take it.

This applies even if—or maybe especially if—you are undertaking what you think is a trial separation. Our friend Nancy learned this the hard way: she moved out with the understanding that they were taking a break to think things through and so she didn't take anything that they had acquired during their ten years together. "I only took things that I needed at that point . . . some clothes, some kitchen stuff. I didn't take much at all, which turned out to be a mistake. My big regret in retrospect is that I moved out so quickly and that I gave him my set of keys when he asked me for them . . . He told me, 'I didn't want to tell you beforehand because who knows what you would have taken!' " Again, if you're the initiator, beware of your own guilt and the fact that your husband could trade on it to his advantage. Again, we don't mean to suggest that your husband is out to get you, but divorce is an altered state and people you'd never expect to "act out" (like Nancy's husband) do sometimes act out.

Here are some general points to consider if you're able to do some of this yourselves, sans lawyers.

Divvying Up Possessions

- Even if you live in a community-property state, anything that was yours before you were married can probably stay yours, unless, of course, he's really fond of that hideous oil painting and you're eager to unload it. Likewise, don't try to abscond with a family heirloom of his or the *James Brown's Greatest Hits* that he brought into the marriage.

- When you have two of anything, try to avoid fighting over who gets the better one, be it a futon, a TV, a book-case. It's really not worth it. Be thankful you don't have to replace something.
- Generally speaking, you each should keep things that were in your family, especially anything with sentimental value.
- If you know where one of you is moving, try to let partic-ulars of a location dictate certain decisions, for example, if you know you'll have central air, don't haggle over the right to keep the air conditioner, just be glad you don't have to pay to store it or haul it down the stairs to dispose of it.
- If there's something neither one of you wants to keep, someone's got to give it away or sell it. In Trudie's case, this took the form of an enormous desk that she'd always disliked. In the end, she and her husband fought so much over getting it removed (it was supposed to be his re-sponsibility) that she took charge and arranged for the Salvation Army to pick it up. Moral of the story: conserve your psychic energy and get the job done if you have to.
- If and when you get down to dividing things like china, glasses, silverware, if you have less than six of anything, it might be easiest to preserve the set rather than end up with piecemeal division. Replace what you didn't get and move on.
- Keep a running record of what goes where, in case it needs to be included as part of your separation agreement or final settlement.
- Don't sweat the small stuff—and so much of it *is* small. Above all, pick your battles. Sometimes you'll find that surrendering in certain situations can give you a special Zen-like power. Go with it.

Optimal Conditions:
Finding What Works for You

In an ideal world, if you can bear a few hours or half a day together in your home, you could consider a My Turn–Your Turn approach: wander around and choose a couple of things at a time in each room and closet. Or, if you'd rather not be in his presence (or he in yours) consider drafting a list of the mutual things and either mark the list with your suggested divisions, or send it to him and review it over the phone. The more you can settle between the two of you, particularly on things like furnishings, the less you have to rack up in legal fees (if you go that route).

If you're already pretty estranged from each other, sometimes even figuring out how you're going to begin to communicate about the stuff can be trying. As Miranda told us, "We negotiated the major things by fax. K. was opposed to email because he felt it was a public means of communication, as if people would care about my armoire! Or that oriental rug I wanted, as if that's going to appear in the papers!" Of course, you might actually prefer email. Sarah's friend Ella was so upset by everything that she appointed her best friend to be her ventriloquist, to answer all incoming emails about practical matters from her husband. It annoyed the heck out of him, but it did help keep the emotions in check and the mission was accomplished in a businesslike way, with the friend acting as her agent.

Who Gets Rex?

As DINKs (double-income-no-kids), we are lucky not to have to worry about child custody battles. However, if you're attached to a shared dog or cat, dealing with pet custody can be extremely painful. Technically, pets are considered possessions, but of course, our bonds to them can be so much more than that. In many cases, it's helpful to decide to prioritize the pet's best interests as one would a child's best interests. Our friend Trudie, for example, kept her apartment when she and her husband split up, and the cat stayed with her because they felt that the cat would be too traumatized by a move. When she moved out and her husband then moved back into the rent-controlled apartment, the cat stayed there with him. "The pet stays with the place" was their approach. Other possibilities include joint custody arrangements, but these tend to be tricky unless you're on really terrific terms with your ex. However, some people do successfully work out arrangements that are analogous to child custody arrangements, with primary residence for the pet and visitation hours even spelled out in their separation or divorce papers.

Sometimes, however, despite the best attempts at clarity and honor, painful mishaps will happen. For example, Sarah's friend Ella had worked hard for sole custody of their beagle, but the beagle nevertheless remained a bone of contention between Ella and her ex. Ella left the dog with a spry seventy-year-old neighbor when she went on vacation, only to have her husband surreptitiously dog-nap her while the neighbor was on the phone. "Poor Hazel," says Ella, "The kind dog-sitting neighbor was completely defenseless as my ex-husband stole the dog for three weeks." Eventually, the beagle was returned, but only upon a lawyer's injunction! If you do lose your pet to your husband, consider getting a new dog or cat. As we discussed earlier, the benefits of pet therapy are well documented, so head over to the pound and take a look. Or, if you can't handle the responsibility, consider volunteering at a pet shelter, many of them offer volunteer programs for people who want to walk a dog every week or so.

The Ring Thing

The ring issue can be a tough, very personal, and emotional one for many women who had traditional engagement rings or wedding bands. And you can't easily look for guidance in etiquette books or advice manuals (they just don't go there), so there really is no right answer except the one that feels best to you.

Technically, the ring is yours to keep because it was a gift before marriage, but you can be as creative, thoughtful, or practical as you want to be in your approach to the problem.

- Cindy really felt that Return to Sender was the best option: "The night I left, I gave him back the two-carat diamond ring he had given me. I knew I wasn't going to do anything with it, and I felt better giving it back. My mom and others have chided me for that, saying I could have gotten money with it, but I felt better returning it to him."
- Valerie: "I kept my ring, but gave it to my parents. I didn't want to see it. My mom sold it. I figured my parents had paid for the wedding, I really wanted them to keep whatever cash they'd get from selling it. My mom said, 'I'll use it for you someday,' and indeed, a few years later when I remarried, my mom paid to fly all of my siblings and their spouses to the West Coast for my wedding."
- Hope: "It was a family ring on his side, so I really felt better giving it back to him."
- Vickie: "I took it to the jewelry district and sold it for a fraction of what it was worth, but I just needed the money."
- Caroline: "It was a gorgeous diamond! I kept it in my sock drawer for years after my first marriage ended. Then I fell in love and got engaged, and we sold the ring to an estate jeweler who applied the proceeds toward a totally new emerald and diamond ring. Enough time had elapsed that it felt good to repurpose the first-husband gift in this positive way."

Of course, there's nothing urgent about the ring question, unless of course he asks explicitly for it back, or unless you are really dying for cash in your pocket. Many divorcées do nothing. Even when their divorce is years over, the ring still sits in the bottom of their jewelry box. Hey, it doesn't take up space, and after a while, you'll forget it's even there. One day, you might decide to do something with it, but in the meantime, let it be a dormant vestige of a chapter of your life if that's what feels most appropriate.

Bare-Naked Finger Syndrome

Sarah remembers the day she took off her wedding ring and how excruciatingly naked her fourth left finger felt. Some nights she couldn't sleep it felt so odd. To make matters worse, summer was the season of her separation, and she had a tan line where her ring used to be. Following the advice of her sister, she decided to get a new ring for herself, something that would have some heft and sparkle to it but that wouldn't look traditionally marital. Tiffany's, of all places, had just what she was looking for. It was a sterling silver ring designed by Elsa Peretti and called, appropriately, The Elongated Teardrop. Among her friends and family, "elongated teardrop" became an excellent shorthand for the painful time, but the retail therapy and the elegant hunk of silver did improve Sarah's outlook immensely. If you wore a wedding ring and fear the bare-naked finger syndrome, we heartily recommend finding a new something to slip over your digits and remind you of your resilience.

Other Mementos of Marriage: Your Dress, Your Wedding Pictures

Unlike the ring, which you can stow away easily, your wedding dress and photo album/proof book might be taking up closet or shelf space. If your dress is in a giant hermetically sealed bag and you are confident that neither you nor any relative would want to borrow it, then you could consider giving it to charity for a tax deduction. If the dress is designer, some women's colleges even have fashion museums or fashion archives attached to them, and they might be especially eager to have it. If the dress has been passed down from your mother or grandmother, ask a family member to store it for you (you can do the same, even if it wasn't a family dress).

As for your photo album, it's possible that you and your husband might both want to keep it, for a nostalgic moment, for posterity, or because it probably contains nice family pictures of people who might not always be around (grandparents, aunts, dear friends). If you had a formal photographer, chances are you have more wedding photos than you need, so maybe one of you can take the formal album assembled by the photographer and the other can take the album or box assembled by one of your friends. Of course, right now, part of you might want to put all the wedding photos down the incinerator, but in all likelihood, you'd probably live to regret it. So again, take a deep breath and find a place to store it where you won't have to come across it until you're ready.

Cents and Sensibility

If you're like most women, you probably feel some degree of anxiety about the prospect of managing on a single income after a dual-income marriage. Both of us recall being hit hard by this reality, but like so many difficult things about divorce, we believe that this is a challenge that comes with a terrific opportunity to take control of your financial fate and become empowered by the process.

What to Do About Bank Accounts

Once you've decided to separate, if you have a joint bank account, you should withdraw half of what's in your savings and possibly the checking, too, depending on the state of your outstanding bills (obviously, this is no time to have the electric bill bounce, so be careful with the checking account). If you are on good terms with your husband, it's fine to tell him you're planning on doing this, but if he's at all volatile, note that you don't *need* to tell him. It is standard practice to withdraw half of what you have in the joint savings account. If you don't have an account in your own name, set one up immediately—we repeat, *immediately*—and put this portion of the funds into that account. Try to keep it there relatively undisturbed until you sort out the division of assets, in case something comes up. One other important detail: if you have direct deposit of your paycheck going into your joint account, don't forget to get this rerouted to your own new account right away.

If you have a joint checking account and are on reasonably good terms with your husband, you two might want to consider keeping this account open until things are finalized in order to pay off the mutual expenses that remain, including, of course, your divorce expenses. If you go through a lawyer or mediator, you'll have those fees to pay but other related expenses that could be shared include car maintenance, pet care, tax payments if it's around tax time, or an appraisal of your apartment or house if you plan to sell it. However, if you're not on good terms with your husband, you'll want to minimize the stress that these financial dealings can bring, and should consider closing out the checking account and splitting it in half right away.

Financial separation from your husband is crucial and generally speaking, the sooner you do this, the better. Our friend Miranda wishes she'd acted in a more timely way on this front, as things rapidly escalated with her husband and, as she puts it, "It took me about a month to realize that I couldn't keep a joint account with someone who was so hostile to me." Even if things are amicable between you, you'll be ahead of the game by making this and other relatively simple moves to begin divvying up the assets.

Joint Credit and Debit Cards

If you have joint charge cards, cancel them as soon as you have decided to separate, but do inform your husband so that he's not caught flat-footed at a business lunch (as delicious as that idea might seem, it'll only embarrass you later). One of the bright spots is how incredibly easy it is to cancel credit cards. Visa and American Express just aren't going to care about your marital woes, and they won't ask any questions, so don't delay on this important step in financial extrication.

If canceling the charge cards seems extreme to you, or if neither one of you has alternative independent credit, then as a short-term step you can also explore reducing the spending limit, so that he won't go out and rack up a big bill. And, of course, this can be helpful for *you* as well. We won't deny the immediate gratification of retail therapy, but you'll want to watch yourself so that you don't go overboard. When you get your joint credit card statements, you can begin to separate your expenses from his and split or divvy up the mutual expenses.

Important: If you don't have credit cards in your own name, take one out as soon as possible, and do so *before* you cancel any joint accounts so that it's supereasy. You'd be amazed by how many smart, professional women make the mistake of not getting their own credit established (or reestablished) before their divorces. Our friend Leslie, for example, a high-tech strategy executive, realized too late that she didn't have credit cards in her name anymore. So, do be sure that you not only get your own credit as soon as you can, but also that your credit isn't tarnished through your husband's failure to pay the bills. Recognize that, even if you're on cordial terms with your husband, it's such an unusual time for both of you that you can't fully rely on each other anymore to follow up on these kinds of details.

If you and your husband have hefty credit card balances on your joint accounts, negotiate as best you can who makes the minimum payments in the interim period before you are officially separated or before you've seen a lawyer or mediator and drafted the settlement agreement. For example, Kay and F. simply split the debt: she took American Express, and he took a credit union loan. If the debt is not easy to figure out or negotiate, you may want to have these obligations clearly spelled out in any separation or divorce agreement. This is important because a credit card company that issued you a joint account can, generally speaking, collect from either one of you, even after you've separated, and even if the debt was incurred during the time you were married. And further, any charges your husband puts on the credit cards might be his responsibility according to your settlement agreement, but not according to the creditors.

If you have merged everything, as many couples do, there's a certain thrill to establishing a new account(s) in your name. When Sarah married T., they had been advised to combine everything right away. The person who married them had counseled (a little too exuberantly, Sarah realizes in retrospect) that total financial fusion between husband and wife is an important step toward complete intimacy, and indeed, for many couples, it does function this way. But once you decide to separate, or even contemplate separating, lifelong intimacy is no longer a goal or a reality, and so you've got to start prioritizing your privacy. Especially if he's the one still getting the bills to your joint accounts, be prepared for him to peer into your spending habits and question why you bought those plane tickets for your much-needed trip to the Bahamas.

Most lawyers will advise you to curtail your major expenses at this time or be discreet about them in case your husband's lawyer is trying to prove that you are not as needy as his client is. For example, when Sarah's friend Ella purchased a new Saab to celebrate her near independence, she was advised to arrive at the final appointment with the lawyer by public transportation or to borrow a car from a friend.

Inventory Time

In many ways, getting divorced is like disbanding a business, and in most cases, it really helps to have the most complete knowledge of your marital finances and assets as possible. Therefore, ideally before you embark on the legal process, it is a good idea to copy as many, if not all, financial documents as you can and put them into a portfolio that you keep in a safe place (maybe a locked drawer at work if you're still living together). Include the following key items from the time that you have been married:

- Your and his tax returns
- A recent pay stub of his if possible
- Recent bank statements
- Statements on your investments (mutual funds, stocks, both of your 401ks)
- Insurance policies
- Mortgage information or property deeds
- Car loan(s)
- Wills or other trusts

This type of inventory-taking may feel weird, but if you have lawyers or a remotely complex divorce, forearmed is the best way to be. As you are technically still your husband's wife, you are entitled to these documents, so don't worry about doing this detective work. It's completely legal, even if it feels odd and on the sly. If you've never been the one to handle the finances, then consider this process the beginning of your education and empowerment. You *should* know the state of your individual and mutual financial picture.

If you really can't put your hands on all of these items, don't worry. It's entirely possible that you and your husband will be able to work things out to your satisfaction without having lawyers scrutinize your W-2s. But if that's not the case, and you do end up hiring a lawyer, he or she will get at your husband's financials through a last-resort process called "discovery" whereby your lawyer goes on a scavenger hunt to collect all kinds of information from your husband's lawyer (and vice versa). However, we strongly suggest that you amass what you can so that you know as much as possible about your situation, which will put you in good stead with respect to the upcoming process and will get you in the habit of being more aware of your accounting.

On the flip side, be sure to safeguard your own personal papers, especially things like like your diary and journal, as this may contain confidential information that you'd hate to have fall into the wrong hands, especially if things become heated and contentious. You don't want to worry about your husband or his family happening upon your private ramblings.

A Word About Leaver's Guilt

If you are the one leaving, it's very important to be vigilant about not letting your guilt make you either apathetic about the finances and assets or overly generous in giving your share away. This tendency toward either apathy or overgenerosity is an all-too common affliction of women who leave men (and for that matter, men who leave women). Or you may be so desperate to get out of the marriage that you essentially say, "I don't care. I don't want anything." Our friend Erin fit this category. At the time, she really felt like she didn't have a choice: "I gave him everything . . . Some people say it was crazy because I gave him so much, but I would have given him the shirt off my back. I was so unhappy he made out like a bandit." Sometimes fear will impact your actions, as it did with Maeve, who relates, "I let him have everything in our bank account, which wasn't much, but I made more than he did, and was afraid he might sue me." Our friend Dawn confessed, "I barely took anything. I had decorated the whole house and hired an interior decorator, but I felt so guilty, I didn't want to take anything."

No matter what the circumstances of your marriage, you are entitled to your half and you should rightfully claim it. Try to look beyond just escaping your present situation. Just because you've decided to leave the marriage doesn't mean he deserves a fabulous severance package! Remember that in any unhappy marriage "it takes two." So fight the "I feel so awful for him that I'll just leave him everything" impulse and start to consider that someday—sooner than you think—you'll stop feeling so guilty and you'll be glad that you took some time to get yourself on the best possible financial footing.

Similarly, if your husband's the one who left the marriage and is feeling guilty, don't go crazy taking advantage of him either, although it may be tempting. One day, when both of you are happier than you ever were together, he'll feel less guilty and may turn around and ask for things back, which could spark a whole new blaze of legal drama. Even if it never occurs to him to do this, it's a good idea to try to take the high road and split things as equitably as possible whenever possible. Again, if nothing else, you'll enjoy the good karma that comes your way.

Taming of the Shrew

If the divorce wasn't your idea, and your breakup was nasty, you probably feel some bitterness right now. At one point or another, you're bound to be tempted to exact revenge in the time-honored tradition of "You'll pay, you slimy no-good louse (or replace with your favorite epithet)!" We understand. Really, we do. This is completely natural. You probably feel like you had that IKEA rug pulled right from under you and are suffering in the most unexpected ways. By all means, go ahead, get in touch with the fury, but try, *try* to channel it in the direction of your therapist or your new karate class and leave it out of your negotiations with your ex about money and material things. Remember that revenge is like greasy fast food for the heart; it's delicious at first but soon leaves you feeling queasy and is certainly not a healthy diet for the long haul. As money guru Suze Orman puts it in her book *The Courage to Be Rich*, "Whether you are the one who is being left or the one who is leaving, the way in which you behave during this period will live on with you, long after the pain of the divorce has faded."

Managing and Thriving on
Your Income Alone

Just as it's helpful to take stock of what you and your husband have together, it's critical that you take stock of what you can do on your own. The best place to start is with a budget sheet. We know, you might not feel like this drudgery right now, but working up a budget is important in the divorce process in several respects. It's good for your own edification and personal awareness; it will fortify you in your negotiations with your husband; and, finally, if you decide to use a lawyer, she or he will want you to prepare this information at some point fairly early in the process. We suggest that you fill this out realistically, but that you also figure out ways to give yourself those pleasures that will make a difference in your solo life. For example, once you or your husband moves, it's amazing how the mail drops off, so you might want to give yourself a few magazine subscriptions to keep your mailbox filled with glossy mags to read while luxuriating in the bath. Gradually, you'll find the areas where you're able to economize. Maybe you prefer to have Jiffy Pop and edamame for dinner two or three nights a week so that you can have your bimonthly pedicure. You have to treat yourself right during this life change.

Don't worry if you can't sock away the savings the way that you did when you were a part of a couple; eventually, you'll get back on track. You need to nourish your body and soul right now, and for some women, that means figuring out new ways of living and getting comfortable with spending money on yourself. Gina, for example, received some money from her divorce settlement and while she would usually have saved it, she spent some of it on traveling and other material items because she felt that this was a time to enjoy herself and indulge her desires, having catered to a less-than-generous man for many years.

The Savvy Divorcée's Budget: Accounting 101

Becoming more savvy about what you spend and how you can economize can be a great boon to your self-esteem. Grab a pencil, take a good thirty minutes, and take a stab at the worksheet below.

	MONTHLY	ONE-TIME
Housing		
Moving		
New Furniture		
Rent		
Mortgage		
Condo or Co-op fee		
Storage		
Cleaning Help		
Telephone		
Electricity		
Cable		
DSL		
Cell Phone		
Insurance		
Miscellaneous		
Legal		
Lawyer		
Mediator		
Transportation		
Car Payments		
Fuel		

	MONTHLY	ONE-TIME
Upkeep		
Garage		
Insurance		
Public Transport		
Taxis		
Tolls		

Food/Drink

Groceries		
Entertaining		
Eating Out		
Takeout		
Liquor Store		
Bars		
Coffee/Snacks		
Lunch at Work		

Entertainment & General Diversions

Movies		
Theater		
Magazines and Newspapers		
Books		
Vacation/Travel		

Beauty & Health

Hair: Cut/Color		
Makeup		
Massage/Spa		
Grooming (manicure, pedicure, etc.)		
Gym		

	MONTHLY	ONE-TIME
Classes		
Doctor's Visits		
Health & Dental Insurance		
Prescriptions		
Eyewear		
Therapy		

Miscellaneous

Charitable Contributions		
Other (loans?)		
Other (savings?)		
Other		
TOTAL		

Okay, now ask yourself,

- How's my income-to-expense ratio looking? Is this manageable?
- Can I still sock away some savings, or am I just going to cope with paying my expenses for right now and start saving when I become a bit more solvent?
- Are there any areas that I can scale back on?
- Of the divorce-related one-time expenses, could I get some relief by asking others to help? For example, do I need a full cadre of professional movers or could a group of friends help with some of this work?
- In the household category, if I had full cable as a married woman, do I really need it on my own?

Consider asking others to take a look at the numbers with you. You might be pleasantly surprised by how helpful an accountant can be, for example, or even a trusted family member or friend. Obviously, you'll want to pick your financial advisors closely.

When the Numbers Don't Look
Good—A Few Things to Consider

Maybe you're falling short, period. The balance sheet is not working. Expenses exceed income. Let's face it, you're making a shift from a double income under one roof to a single income under the same or new roof, and it's no surprise that things might look grim. Housing is probably your biggest monthly expense, and maybe you assumed you could stay in your current place. But with the new situation, you may want to look at a less expensive neighborhood and more affordable rent, or consider living with a friend for a time. Sometimes live-in company can be a good thing post-separation. If these options don't work for you, you may want to consider making some career moves or professional changes in order to increase your earning power. As Nancy recalls, "Right away, I was terribly affected because I was in graduate school. He cut me off . . . then I decided to go back and practice law." Sarah's friend Helen stayed in the same industry but switched from publicity into sales, which meant a significant salary increase, enabling her to keep up her standard of living. Kay also made a career move around the time she split from her husband, partly because she knew she needed to make more money now that she'd be on her own.

Another option, depending on your family's financial situation, is to turn to loved ones for some temporary support. It can feel embarrassing to ask for help like this after being financially independent for several years. But remember that this is an unusually difficult and unstable time for you, and close family and friends who have the means would much rather help out than see you struggle. If you're uncomfortable asking for outright sponsorship, you might start by asking a parent, a sibling, or even a dear solvent friend for a no-interest or low-fee loan. A temporary reliance on credit cards is also perfectly fine, if you stay on top of the payments.

Gazing at the proverbial bright side, if you've never been great at managing your money, now is the time to start anew and take control of your financial present and future. Take a look at the book list at the back of our book for some reliable places to start.

Turning Straw into Gold

As you go forward, always remember that becoming financially independent again and learning to live alone after a substantial period of coupledom are amazing accomplishments—and don't let anyone tell you otherwise. It will seem as though you've been through a kind of fiscal and material boot camp, only you're the leader as well as the trainee. Even if it feels like a struggle, you are developing tremendous self-reliance skills. Don't stop summoning your friends and family when you need them, but realize that it *is* in you to survive and thrive on your own too.

CHAPTER FIVE

Untying the Knot

The Legal Process

*The world breaks everyone and afterward
many are strong at the broken places.*

—Ernest Hemingway,
A Farewell to Arms

One of the most daunting realities of getting divorced is initiating the legal process; whether you want the split or not, you're probably not savoring the prospect of the paperwork and the finality it brings to your relationship. Although some people feel very ready to proceed as soon as the word "separation" is mentioned, many others need more time to process the reality and finality of it all. Whatever your situation, you'll want to take your time and make sure that the decision feels like it's yours. Just because your friends and family are urging you to call a lawyer doesn't necessarily mean you should—this very moment, at least. Consider that, while everyone's situation is unique, most people never feel completely excited about beginning this process. Everyone has a different timetable, and although you may hear "What are you waiting for?" or "Why the hurry?" from some people, only *you* can really know how quickly or how carefully you should proceed.

Once you realize you are as ready as you'll ever be, it's time to put your research skills to work and, as we advise you throughout the book, take advantage of your friends' and colleagues' offers to help. Like so much in life, once you dig in and dissipate the dread of it all, you'll probably start to experience some relief that things are happening and that you're moving forward in some way.

Readiness Is All

Sarah's friend Petra spent nine months living apart from her husband, dating others for distraction but unable to contemplate really ending her marriage until she went on a two-week trip to Africa with her mother and sister: "The dramatic distance and the beautiful scenery really helped the healing process. It was like a cloud just sort of disappeared and when I got back, I was ready to pick up the phone and start the proceedings." On the other hand, Kay and her husband started their paperwork fairly soon after splitting up, partly because they had been breaking up for some time and partly because he was involved with someone else and it made him uncomfortable to still be legally married.

In Sarah's case, T. moved out very suddenly in June one year and they spent that summer and fall separated, just cooling off from the heat of what felt, at the time, like his decision. After an initial few weeks of shock, Sarah gradually adjusted to the idea of being unmarried again. Although divorce was, in hindsight, inevitable, neither one of them felt immediately ready to consult lawyers and draft the paperwork. For Sarah, what helped accelerate the decision to make it final was falling into something wonderful with someone else. Suddenly, she could visualize life post-husband, and it actually looked pretty appealing.

In some cases, of course, women do not have the luxury of

waiting for the right time and the right state of mind to proceed on the legal front. If, for example, your husband has already retained a lawyer or if he's harassing you, proceed directly to "The Legal Process—Finding What Works for You" on page 111, where we describe how to find a lawyer.

Dealing with a Reluctant Husband

Maybe *you're* perfectly ready but your husband isn't. He's dragging his feet, doesn't want to get divorced, and generally doesn't want to accept the reality that the marriage is over. Or maybe he is surprised and shocked, with no grasp of the issues, like our friend Leslie's husband. If this is the case, it might be the time to get into (or resume) counseling. You may need the help of a safe environment with a neutral third party to give the relationship a proper burial. If your husband is unwilling to go to counseling and unwilling to move forward, you may need to spend some time strategizing with your lawyer and/or a trusted confidante, like a best friend, sister, or parent.

Our friend Miranda knew she would face huge resistance from her husband K. and she also knew that in her state, the only way to obtain a no-fault divorce is to first obtain a separation agreement, which must be in effect for a year before you can file for divorce. Because she knew K. would be alarmed if she blurted everything out at once, she communicated her desire for "some time apart" in careful stages, buying herself some time to consult a lawyer and craft the right things to say to K. Desperately unhappy and determined to get K. to sign the agreement, Miranda left property out of the paperwork so that they wouldn't have to negotiate anything at the early stage. She also confessed to us that it was key that she keep up the pretense that, if they only took some official space apart, things might work out, so she maintained contact with K., meeting with him regularly until she got the agreement. When K. realized that a separation agreement was grounds for divorce in their state, he was as livid as Miranda knew he would be. But she stuck to her guns, telling him, "There's no chance of us getting back together if you don't sign the agreement because it's what I need and it's what I want." Mission accomplished, and as Miranda put it, "To get the thing started was a huge relief."

As Miranda's example shows, how you frame your decision to leave is very important when you think your husband isn't going to cooperate immediately. When Megan realized her marriage was over, her husband was taken aback by her resolve, but she felt it helped make things final. She put it to her husband: "I have made an irreversible decision about my life and I have to tell you about it. You can ask me anything you like, but you can't change my mind."

If you're the initiator, you may be feeling guilty about your decision to leave. This is utterly natural. Just try not to let the guilt get in the way of what you need to do for yourself. Worse comes to worse, be assured that in almost every state, you *can* serve your husband with divorce papers without his consenting to a divorce, but let's hope that, like the majority of women who initiate divorce, you're able to get the legal work going without too much holy acrimony.

The Legal Process: Finding What Works for You

There are several ways to go about untying the knot legally. In this section, we want to give you an overview of the process so that you can find out what best suits your needs, budget, emotions, and time constraints. You have many more options than your mother's, or certainly your grandmother's, generation did, which is a good thing. Divorce legislation has evolved pretty substantially over the last forty years, making it easier and increasingly more equitable for women ending their marriages. In particular, no-fault legislation, which we'll explain in detail in this section, has simplified the legal process to a great extent.

Despite these advances, divorce laws can feel complicated and sometimes highly antiquated. We will give you some information on how you can be your own guide through it all, and whether mediation is your best option. But first, let's review the most traditional course: getting a lawyer.

Deciding Whether or Not You Need a Lawyer

If you meet any one of the following criteria, you are a good candidate for considering hiring a lawyer:

- You and your husband own property of any kind.
- There's little you *don't* fight about right now.
- He's harassing you, either physically, mentally, or verbally by phone, email, faxes, or letters.
- The fault lines run deep (maybe there is someone else, maybe one of you has a drug habit, etc.).
- He is a lawyer, or his father/brother/best friend is one (especially a matrimonial lawyer).
- You know he's already consulted with and/or retained a lawyer.
- You are in business together.
- One or both of you have significant debt.
- One or both of you have significant assets other than real estate.
- One of you is having an affair.
- You are in physical danger.
- You are suffering a clinical depression or other illness.
- You are not all that concerned about saving money at this point. You just want a really good advocate for you and are too exhausted to do the research yourself.

If any of the above describes your situation, we strongly suggest that you consider getting a referral for a "matrimonial lawyer" (as divorce lawyers are ironically known). Where do you start getting referrals? One obvious place to start is by asking lawyers you know for referrals to matrimonial lawyers, lawyers who specialize in family law, or solid general lawyers who have handled divorce cases. Therapists, ministers, doctors, and, of course, other divorcées, are also all good sources to ask for referrals. You never know where you might discover your advocate: when our friend Kate separated, she went out on a blind date with a guy who had been recently divorced, and he recommended his lawyer to her. Though he (the date) wasn't a keeper, Kate did happily retain his lawyer!

If you are dreading even making these calls to gather the referrals, deputize a sibling or friend to send out the queries. It shouldn't be hard to get a referral, but if you run into a dead end or just really crave anonymity, we recommend you resist the temptation to blindly flip through the yellow pages. As with all services, quality matters greatly to your experience. If you're at a loss, you could start with the website for the American Bar Association at www.abanet.org. Once there, consult their family law section. You could also consult the American Academy of Matrimonial Lawyers (www.aami.org), which has stringent membership standards. The first concern most of us will have about retaining a lawyer is the cost—you picture Arnie Becker in the old eighties TV show *L.A. Law* running up a huge tab for you. While we can't say that divorce with legal representation is inexpensive, there are ways to be savvy about the process that can save you some money. And, just as you would with so many items in life, you *can* get an estimate for how much your divorce will cost you. Most lawyers will be able to give you this information after they learn some details about your case. You can (and some would say, should) interview a few lawyers until you feel the best fit. In her essay "In the Country of Divorce" writer Daphne Merkin said she went through two divorce lawyers before settling on "a smart, scrappy woman in business for herself."

Preparing for Your First Meeting
with Your Lawyer

You'll want to secure some time to meet with your lawyer in person if at all possible, because a law office can tell you a lot about the experience you'll have if you decide to retain this lawyer. Does it feel sleek and corporate (read: possibly beyond your budget) or shabby (read: you'll probably feel shabby)? Are you kept waiting forever? (Never a good sign; you need your lawyer to be reasonably available for you.) Is the location one you feel comfortable frequenting? (Not hard to get to, safe section of town, etc.)

In setting up the appointment, it is perfectly fine to ask if you will be charged for the initial consultation. Most lawyers do not charge for the initial consultation, but it's much better to get this squared away ahead of time in case it influences your selection process. During the appointment, remember that you are interviewing the lawyer as much as he or she's interviewing you. Sometimes a lawyer will begin asking you so many specifics that you'll be left with your questions unanswered. (Should this happen too much, the lawyer probably isn't the right advocate for you.) Finally, you might want to consider bringing a family member or trusted friend to your appointment, for a second opinion and to make sure that all of your concerns and questions get addressed.

Key Questions to Ask Your Prospective Lawyer:

- Tell me about the laws in my state (this will be helpful to you even if you don't retain the lawyer).
- Explain your fee structure—do you need a retainer up front, and how much is it?

- What is your hourly fee?
- Could I get the fee structure set out in writing? (If the answer is no, you'll want to look elsewhere.)
- Do you accept credit cards? (Some lawyers actually do now, and this might be a big plus for you.)
- In addition to the retainer, please explain additional fees (you can expect to be billed for postage, messenger fees, copying costs, etc.).
- Do you know my husband or my husband's lawyer? (The latter is not necessarily a bad thing, many would say, because the case might be handled more expeditiously.)
- How many divorce cases have you handled? (This is especially important if the lawyer is young and doesn't specialize in matrimonial law.)
- Will you personally handle my case, or will you be working with an associate? If you'll be working with an associate, may I meet him or her? How does the associate's work impact the fees and hourly rate?
- Do you have a minimum unit of time you bill for? (For example, if a call only takes a couple of minutes, they might bill you for fifteen minutes.)
- What problems do you anticipate in the filing of my case?

It's also a good idea to go into your appointment with some information on your situation. You may be given a questionnaire to fill out at home, along with a worksheet to help you figure out your net worth, listing your assets (which you may have already done if you followed our advice in chapter 4!). The kinds of questions the lawyer might ask you are how long you were married, what you do, how much you earn, how long you've been living apart (if you have been living apart), and how you consider the marriage beyond repair (this is to make sure you're serious about proceeding).

Be prepared to divulge some very personal stuff, maybe not in the first meeting, but certainly in subsequent meetings. It can be rough. Our friend Valerie had her father's friend prepare her papers, and she said that "for the most part, it felt like a business transaction, but the hardest part was telling the attorney all of the details . . . he was a family friend, and I had to reveal all of these embarrassing things." Of course, it's important to realize that lawyers don't ask you these personal questions out of some voyeuristic pleasure. They really want to get to know your situation so that they can best represent you.

What to Expect When You're Hiring a Lawyer

If you've found the right fit, your lawyer will, in all likelihood, ask for a "retainer." A retainer is like an advance or a deposit. If your case is relatively simple, the retainer will probably represent about three hours of their work, and in most cases, this means you are looking at paying several hundred dollars up front. After you pay the retainer, the lawyer subtracts his fees from the amount you've paid until he's exhausted the retainer, at which point you'll start to get bills. (Even before the retainer has been used, you'll want to get a statement so that you have a sense of how things are progressing.) Alternatively, your lawyer could ask you for a second retainer.

Before you pull out your checkbook, make sure that you have a draft of the "retainer agreement." (Retainer agreements are totally standard, so if your lawyer doesn't want to draft one, this could be a flag that something's fishy.) The agreement should specify not only the hourly rate at which you'll be billed, but also that you will be refunded whatever portion of the retainer is not used. Additionally, it should explain what happens after the retainer is used up: will you need to pay another retainer, or will you just be billed weekly or monthly? Although you might feel an urgency to sign on the dotted line, you should take some time to review the retainer agreement, and maybe run it by a lawyer friend, colleague, or parent. The retainer agreement isn't just a financial document. It serves as a blueprint for your relationship with the lawyer and his or her firm. You'll want to check that the retainer specifies the following:

- The hourly rate and payment schedule.
- How out-of-pocket expenses (photocopying, overnight mail, secretarial services) are billed. Specifically, do these charges get subtracted from your retainer, or are you charged separately? (Either way is fine, you just want to know where the money is going.)
- Provision for your cancellation of the contract (how do you get out of it if you hate the lawyer, reconcile with your husband, or shift gears and see a mediator).
- Commitment to copy you on all correspondence and generally keep you apprised of progress on the case.
- Provision for not being billed for any time spent discussing your bill.
- Commitment that if the attorney you are retaining needs to bring another lawyer on to the case, you will be notified and apprised as to that attorney's rate.

What you'll encounter in the way of hourly fees varies a great deal of course, but it's pretty standard to see $250–350 per hour in major metropolitan areas. Perfectly skillful lawyers exist elsewhere for $150–175 per hour, so you may want to do some comparison-shopping.

Tips for Controlling Costs with Your Lawyer

- If you live in a major city, consider a lawyer in the suburbs, where rates are usually less expensive and where you might get more attentive help.
- Be efficient with the telephone, and try to be all business. No matter how close you feel to your lawyer, she/he isn't your therapist! You don't want to waste precious minutes bad-mouthing your husband or calling your lawyer with miscellaneous little questions. Store up the little questions for when you have to have a more extensive call, since your attorney may treat a two-minute call like a fifteen-minute call.
- Ask for a monthly report, even if your retainer isn't used up.
- Just as you would monitor a project budget at work or a renovation or construction project on your house, ask that you be contacted in advance of major expenditures on your case. Maybe it's going to cost you a whole lot of your lawyer's time in fighting to keep a particular item or series of items. You want to be given the chance to rethink things based on cost.
- Try to keep track of your time on the phone with the attorney so that when you do get the bill, you can compare costs for telephone work.
- Ask what you will be billed for photocopying and whether there is anything you could handle yourself. (At an average rate of 25 cents a page, this can add up; you might prefer to take documents to Kinko's.)

Who Foots the Bill?

Who pays for legal fees will vary depending on the issues in your case. Common sense would suggest that whoever is initiating the process or whoever has the more robust resources might pay for the fees, or might pay a larger portion of them. As Nancy put it, "My feeling was, he wanted the divorce, he can pay for it." Sometimes guilt is a contributing factor. When Mehta decided she wanted to divorce her husband, she knew he had just been laid off and didn't have any money, so she handled everything, in part because, in her words, "I didn't want to hurt him any more than he'd already been hurt. I felt sorry for him." Sarah remembers splitting the cost of the fees even though her husband was the one who wanted the divorce. He had moved out suddenly, but left her every major asset from their marriage, so she didn't feel right asking him to pay more than half of the fees.

Sometimes, the potential maintenance of goodwill is more important than the actual dollars. It's hard to remember this at a time when you might feel a tad vengeful, but in the long run, it will save you agony. Particularly if lawyers are involved, the more you haggle with each other, the more you'll end up paying in legal fees, so it pays to walk away occasionally. In general, you really are better served by being amicable or at least civil with your soon-to-be-ex-husband than you are being hostile or acrimonious with him. Easier said than done, we know, but if you still have emotional issues to resolve, try not to do it through the legal process. Of course, if being civil doesn't feel genuine yet (and we can reassure you, that's totally normal) put on a good show: as Sarah's friend Petra likes to chant, "Fake it 'til you make it!"

When Cheap Is Expensive

In some ways, Sarah wishes she had hired a lawyer. She and T. got recommendations for lawyers from their couples therapist and Sarah did have a consultation with the one who had been recommended for her. She remembers how kind he was, a gray-haired, elegant lawyer who right away put her at ease by showing a picture of his daughter who was also going through a divorce. After the initial consultation, however, Sarah found out about mediation, which is often a more economical way of untying the knot. When Sarah and T. went for their appointment, it was in the home-cum-office of a sad-sack guy who was probably a failed social worker turned divorce mediator. Eventually, the job was done, but since the mediator was not a lawyer, he had to refer them to a freelance attorney who drew up the paperwork. The attorney had the twisted habit of sending every bit of correspondence with a LOVE stamp (the cupid variety that Sarah had avoided for her wedding invitations three years before). It ended up costing both Sarah and her ex about $700 each, which was roughly what had been estimated for lawyer fees.

At least the mediator route was a step up from the divorce clinic Sarah's husband suggested they try before committing to the mediator. Hopeful of saving some money, Sarah and T. mounted the dingy stairs to a place she would later learn T. had found in the yellow pages, the "1-800-DIVORCE—When Diamonds Aren't Forever" variety. Suddenly, the sad-sack mediator and lawyer team looked better and better. And, in a strange way, there was an upside to the episode: it galvanized Sarah out of the sadness into some good old-fashioned righteous indignation. The moral of the story is this: cheap isn't always cheap, and cheap can also *feel* cheap. Economy is a good thing, but quality, dignity, and peace of mind are also crucial given how hard the whole process can be.

Mediators

Essentially, mediators are to divorce what midwives are to childbirth—an alternative path. Mediators came into vogue in the seventies, as a way to avoid the adversarial system of lawyer versus lawyer, which can be vicious and expensive, especially for divorcing parents. Some go so far as to associate mediators with the New Age movement and a "free to be you and me" mentality.

In mediation, you and your husband visit a mediator together, and the mediator is the one who tries to help facilitate the negotiating so that you can reach a settlement, divide the assets, and get the filing under way. With mediation, there are no adversarial lawyers. Instead, the idea is that you have an impartial third party helping you part ways with as little acrimony and expense as possible. Sounds sort of appealing, doesn't it? And it could be the best option for you, but you have to take some care in selecting your mediator because they vary greatly in experience, qualification, and knowledge. Unlike the lawyers you interview, all of whom should have passed their state bar, there is no national approval process for mediators. There is, however, the Academy of Family Mediators. You'll want to visit the website of the Academy to make sure that anyone you are contemplating calling is on their approved list: www.mediators.org. Specifically, you want to confirm that your mediator has achieved a practitioner-level status at the Academy.

Although some mediators are trained as counselors (with degrees in clinical psychology or social work), their goal is not to act as your therapist and certainly not to get you back together; it's to resolve conflict that might impede the progress of your divorce. (And, although some mediators have law degrees, they are not representing you.) Most mediators will assume that your marriage is over in all but the paper, and they are generally not interested in your story, except insofar as it might impact how you decide to approach the division of assets. As Carol Butler and Dolores Walker, practiced mediators and authors, put it in their book, *Divorce Mediation Answer Book*, "In our practices, we sometimes complete a mediation and have no idea why the marriage has ended; it has never been mentioned."

One of the first issues in mediation is which one of you prospects for and places the call to the mediator? Even this simple process can stir up controversy. Our friend Nancy said that because she got the referral to the mediator, her husband assumed that the mediator was "on her side." Before they had even had their initial consultation, her once mild-mannered professor-husband called up the mediator, started yelling at him on the phone, and accused the mediator of being biased toward her. Needless to say, they didn't get very far with mediation. Another friend said that just because their mediator was a woman, her husband assumed the mediator was "on her side." Sometimes, one of you will really like the mediator and the other doesn't like him or her. If this is the case, move on. It's pretty important that you both feel that you can work with this person. A lack of comfort for either one of you could be detrimental to the negotiation process. If you decide to pursue mediation, and want to avoid such pitfalls, we suggest you try to make this a joint venture as much as possible. Get your referral(s) from someone you both know and trust and make sure you and your husband have both "bought in" to the concept from the beginning.

Some Pros and Cons to Mediation

The problem or opportunity, depending on how you see things, is that if you and your husband are still sorting out the emotions, a mediation session can feel like a therapy session. There you are, sitting together in someone's office (it may feel like déjà vu if you tried marriage counseling) and that person is asking you about your thoughts on how you will divide your assets, and, before you know it, you're reaching for the box of Kleenex. One of our girlfriends, Gina, who went through a mediator, said that she kept her composure about everything during mediation but started to sob when it came time to discuss the division of stuff. This process just killed her, and there she was with these two men, the mediator and her husband, and it felt really awful.

With mediation, you have to be willing and open to compromise. Of course, you have to do this to some extent whether you've hired a lawyer or whether you're doing it yourself. But one of the key differences in mediation is that you have to share and be reasonable, spending a good deal of time (at least a couple of hours) with your soon-to-be-ex-husband and a complete stranger trying to find a happy or at least acceptable compromise.

The openness of the process distinguishes mediation from adversarial representation. A former divorce litigator Sarah knows decided to become a mediator because she was so appalled at the climate in New York City law firms. She explains, "You can be sad or angry in the context of mediation, but it doesn't get exploited by one lawyer or another." For many couples, this freedom of expression is one big benefit of mediation. And, if you have limited cash resources but major assets to divide, mediation can be less expensive than each of you hiring lawyers.

How to Figure Out If Mediation Makes Sense for You

You are a good candidate for mediation if you meet any of the following criteria:

- The decision to divorce was a relatively mutual one or became mutual.
- Your relationship has never had a strong power imbalance (i.e., neither one of you has been dominant).
- You've been living apart from your husband for a while, and the emotions have cooled a bit.
- You've settled some or many of the issues already (you have established separate bank accounts, for example).
- Both of you really believe in the idea of mediation and are generally getting along and communicating pretty well.
- You have one or two large issues that really bear discussion and need resolution (e.g., custody of a pet, selling of a house), and you are willing to discover and propose possible trade-offs together, but you'd prefer that the discussion be moderated by a neutral third party.

- You don't want to undertake the process by yourself, but you are concerned that hiring a lawyer is going to be beyond your budget.

Questions to Ask During Your First Mediation Appointment

Many of the questions you'd ask a lawyer you also want to ask a mediator. Review the list on page 114 and add these questions to it:

- Are you an attorney, or do you work closely with one? (You don't want to have to begin a whole separate search for someone to draw up the papers.)
- What are your (other) professional credentials? (As mentioned earlier, make sure that the person is associated with the American Academy of Family Mediators.)
- How many cases have you mediated? (It's all fine and well to get a hungry young thing, but you really don't want to be their guinea pig.)
- Do you like to caucus? (This means, meet with each of you individually before the first joint meeting. Some mediators will do this to determine if the couple is even capable of mediating.)

Even if you hire a mediator who is an attorney, don't be surprised if the mediator encourages you and your husband to have your own lawyers review the documents. This is fairly standard, since the mediator is not representing either one of you. Again, you'll want to weigh this in your cost-benefit analysis to see if you might be better off with lawyers all the way around.

DIY (Do It Yourself) Divorce

According to a recent article in *USA Today*, some sources estimate that as many as half of all divorcing couples today decide to file without the help of lawyers or mediators. When you represent yourself in your divorce, it is called filing *pro se* (Latin for "for yourself"). If you have the time and energy, preparing the papers can be a great thing to do, as Kay and her ex-husband did in California. The most obvious benefit is the cost savings, but the other benefit is taking control of the legal process yourself. Kay and her ex were on good terms and had already divided what little shared property they had, so they decided a do-it-yourself divorce was the cheapest and most hassle-free approach. Kay's ex, who had worked in a law firm and felt very comfortable with all the paperwork, researched the laws and printed the forms off the Web. He drove the proceedings and they met occasionally to fill out the forms and make the necessary decisions. Overall, Kay found it to be a fairly painless process.

If you meet the following criteria, you are a good candidate for *pro se*:

- You are on good or decent terms with your ex-husband. (You may need to interact a few times in order to get signatures and move the process forward.)
- You are capable of getting a good grasp on your state laws and are unafraid of the legal jargon.
- You own no property and don't have many assets to divide in general.
- You've been married for a short period of time (less than three years).
- You and your husband are both working and self-supporting.

When should you not consider doing it yourself? If any of following applies to you, think twice about *pro se*:

- Your husband has already retained a lawyer!
- You anticipate a contentious divorce.
- You have limited time and patience for paperwork.

- You have significant assets or debt, or complicated tax issues.

If you do opt for *pro se*, make sure that you have all of your bases covered. According to *The Unofficial Guide to Divorce*, do-it-yourselfers commonly neglect to consider these areas in the settlement arena: tax return preparations, pensions, insurance provisions, military benefits, and debt repayment. So, be careful—you don't want to overlook a major issue and then have to go to court to get it resolved postdivorce. Also, if you changed your name after you were married and plan to resume use of your family name, you'll want to make sure that there's a provision giving you this right built into the final judgment of divorce. This will make changing your name on credit cards, bank accounts, and elsewhere much easier.

Resources for Pro Se

In Print

There are a number of books that explain divorce law on a state-specific level. If you're willing to do the research, you should be able to find such books at your local library, bookstore, or online bookstore. The best known of these is a series published by Nolo Press: *How to Do Your Own Divorce in*——(name your state) which contain forms and step-by-step guidance on handling your divorce in a particular state.

Dot-Com Divorce

There are also some solid software programs and online options today, many of which offer all of the forms. The best known of these is a website started by a Seattle attorney: www.complete case.com. As of this writing, the site is available for uncontested divorces in Washington, California, Florida, and New York (an uncontested divorce means that you and your husband have reached a settlement and will not be hashing things out in court—

so, "uncontested" does not mean "no-fault") and the total fee for preparing the papers is $249. The site has received a lot of favorable publicity in recent years, with *USA Today*, the *LA Times*, and the *San Francisco Chronicle* all devoting articles to it. It differs from the average self-help website in that it prompts couples with all kinds of questions and then uses their answers to help populate the forums. You still have to submit the papers to a court; at least for now, there's no electronic filing for divorce papers like there is for taxes. There are also software kits available at Office Depot, Staples, and over the Web. Be sure that you pick one that offers state-specific support. If it doesn't, it won't do you any good because getting divorced is a state affair.

Avoid Becoming
an Unwitting Bigamist

Even if you do the papers yourself, with or without the help of a kit, it's a good idea to have a lawyer or lawyer friend examine them before filing, just in case you've missed something. You do want to make sure that all the i's are dotted and the t's crossed, lest you one day want to get remarried and discover that you were never officially divorced.

Legal Centers

The last twenty years have seen the rapid growth of low-cost legal centers offering document preparation services. Not surprisingly, these centers have stirred up a good deal of controversy in the legal community, so much so that they are outlawed in some states. However, some of our interviewees had a perfectly fine experience using them. For example, our friend Elizabeth used a divorce center in California, and she really liked the paralegal who helped her and her ex: "He was this New Age crystals dude who was nonjudgmental and made it as easy as possible."

One of the biggest and seemingly most credible chains is known as We the People (www.wethepeopleusa.com). Established in 1985 in Florida, then franchised in 1992, We the People is a legal document storefront service staffed largely by paralegals. Disclaimers abound on their websites: "We are not attorneys and we do not provide legal advice." Rather, they bill themselves as *pro se* document assistants, a kind of H&R Block for processing uncontested legal actions, the logic being that "at least half of a typical attorney's practice is the processing of legal documents, often performed by non-attorney employees." At the time of writing, the average cost for using their services is about $350.

In Arizona and Utah, you can even file your divorce at an automated kiosk at the courthouse, just like an ATM or drive-though McDonald's. Such "drive-through divorce" options are usually available only if, in addition to having no kids, you have no property and you have no questions—because you won't find anyone there to ask advice of.

Is There Such a Thing as a "Quickie Divorce"?

Not really. Quickie divorces do not exist in the United States, unless you consider Nevada's six-week residency requirement a painless option. We suppose it could be if you have the resources to hang out at a spa in Nevada for a month and a half. Another option would be the "Dominican divorce," which has been obtained by the likes of Jane Fonda, Elizabeth Taylor, Diana Ross, and Lisa Marie Presley. Because the Dominican Republic only has a one-day residency requirement, there is a mini-industry of divorce processing out of Santo Domingo. Indeed, there's a firm, coincidentally out of Nevada, that specializes in catering to the adventurous divorcée willing to go to foreign shores to get the hassle over with: www.nevadadivorce.net. This site is surprisingly helpful and professional-looking, if you aren't turned off by the fact that links to government sites exist alongside links to Travelocity and inviting pictures of what seems to be their sponsor resort in the Dominican Republic. And, lest you think you have to bring your husband for a mock-honeymoon-divorce weekend, according to the site, only one of you has to be present to obtain a divorce in the Dominican Republic. However, the site's statement that "our divorces are generally valid internationally" might give you pause. Be sure this is really what you want to do, and consult legal counsel before, during, and maybe even after your trip to make sure all of the necessary bases are covered.

Fault Lines: Divorce Law and Affairs of State

One of the first things to realize is that divorce is basically an affair of state. This can come as quite a surprise. You might think, as our friend Nancy put it, "Why is the state getting so involved in how *my* marriage ends?" But it's because, whether you were married in a church, synagogue, or beach cove, your union was sealed in a civil contract. Laws for undoing that civil contract will vary quite a bit depending on what state you live in (it doesn't matter where you were married, it only matters where you're living now).

In most states, however, you are beginning a legal process in which one of you has to be the plaintiff (or, in some states, "petitioner") and one of you the defendant. In other words, one of you has to sue the other for divorce. The first step in the process is filing what is known variously as a "petition for divorce," "petition for the dissolution of marriage," or "complaint for divorce." This document will include basic factual information, including your names, addresses, social security numbers, the date and place of your marriage, a description of any property you hold together, and, if you changed your name when you were married, specifications to resume use of your family name. The petition also states the grounds for divorce. When the divorce is officially filed, you can expect to pay a filing fee ranging from $50 to $250 or more, depending on what state you live in. The defendant in your case then files an answer or response to the petition. (This process is what people refer to when they say "she served him with divorce papers.") In no-fault divorces, the petitioner/defendant communication is minimal.

What Does "No-Fault" Mean?

Here's an odd fact about how the term "no-fault" came into common divorce parlance: it was originally a shorthand expression journalists invented to describe changes in automobile insurance legislation in the seventies. It was used so widely in the press that it was then appropriated by the courts to describe the growing number of divorces where no specific blame was asserted. A hundred bad (but maybe apt) metaphors come to mind: your marriage was an accident waiting to happen, you and your husband got involved in a head-on collision, and so on. Indeed, the terms "fault" and "no-fault" are mercifully ordinary compared to some of the legalese you'll encounter in getting divorced.

All states now have some version of no-fault divorce. According to the American Bar Association "a no-fault divorce is one in which neither the husband nor wife officially blames the other for the breakdown of the marriage." Some sixteen states, including California and Florida, are exclusively no-fault, meaning that blame cannot be asserted on either you or your husband. Even in a no-fault state, however, you need to specify a basis or cause of action for divorce. Common bases for a no-fault divorce include irreconcilable differences, incompatibility, irrevocable breakdown, and separation. Note, however, that not all of these bases are available in all no-fault states. Common bases for a fault divorce include adultery, cruelty, drug or alcohol addiction, and incurable insanity. For the very latest information, we suggest you check the family law section of the American Bar Association's website: www.abanet.org.

Mandatory Separation as a
Condition of No-Fault

Many states require a period of separation in order to file under no-fault grounds (the period of separation required varies from three months to three years). At the time of this book's printing, the following states require spouses to live apart for a period of time before a no-fault divorce can be granted: Arkansas, Louisiana, Maryland, Missouri, Montana, New Jersey, New York, North Carolina, Ohio, Pennsylvania, South Carolina, Tennessee, Vermont, Virginia, and West Virginia. If you live in one of these states and are planning to file for a no-fault divorce, you'll want to find out whether your state requires you to file a separation agreement before filing to obtain a divorce. Some states do, some states don't. Finally, it's also important to note whether the clock starts ticking from the date you sign those separation papers or if it begins with the actual date you or he moved out. Illinois, for example, does not require that you file a separation agreement, but it does require a period of time living apart and honors the move-out date as the start of a separation.

Some states seem to have very antiquated laws. In New York, for example, the only way to obtain a no-fault divorce is to file for a separation agreement. It's only after a year of separation with a court-filed document that you may file for divorce. For Sarah, this meant discovering her "inner ironist." The yearlong separation felt like a macabre reversal of the engagement process, a year of getting disengaged: taking off her wedding rings, separating the possessions, and enduring a full year of referring to her estranged husband as, well, just that: her "estranged." He wasn't technically "the ex" yet, and he certainly didn't feel like a husband. In short, he was the opposite of a fiancé: he was her "ex-husband-to-be."

Filing "Fault" versus "No-Fault"

Some people decide to file for a fault-based divorce because no-fault is not readily available in their state, or because the waiting period/mandatory separation period is so long. Others file for fault because they have fault lines that they want registered publicly, either for their protection (say, in the case of domestic violence) or for their sense of justice, or for some combination of the two. The list of possible fault grounds is fairly extensive and, again, what's available varies according to state. However, the following allegations or cause for action are available no matter what state you live in: adultery, bigamy, cruelty, desertion, deviant sexual misconduct, drug addiction, endangerment of your life, felony conviction, gross neglect, habitual drunkenness, and physical abuse. For these charges, most states also waive residency requirements and waiting periods. In filing for many of these fault grounds, no proof is needed in order to approve your cause of action. However, if you are filing under charges of adultery, the court will need proof of your allegations because your charges involve a third party.

The statistics say that most people now file for no-fault divorce, but for several women we know, this was not the case. One practical point to consider about filing under fault charges: you will probably have to appear in court. This shouldn't overly influence your choice. For some women, the court day can serve as an effective ritual for closing the marriage, something that our society hasn't yet found a way to formally observe. And in some states, like New Jersey, no matter how you're filing (fault or no-fault) you have to appear in court.

Grounds for Fault

Sometimes identifying the grounds is just pain on top of pain, stirring up all kinds of complex feelings. Our friend Nancy's husband N. sued on grounds of adultery because he could (she was having an affair) and because he wanted it over quickly. But because N. felt so humiliated, he originally wanted to file under the allegation of "cruel and abusive treatment" because he kept insisting that "it wasn't just the affair" that caused the breakdown of their marriage. His lawyer called Nancy to push for this action instead of adultery, suggesting that "everyone knows cruel and abusive just means irreconcilable differences." Nancy stayed true to herself and replied, "I don't care what people think it means. It's a public record. He's got to face up to it. He kept saying it wasn't the adultery. If it's the adultery, let him sue me on adultery. I'm not letting him sue me for cruel and abusive treatment—he can't prove that." (Adultery, by the way, is the only cause that has a set of possible defenses, including forgiveness and adultery on the part of the plaintiff.)

We advise you to follow Nancy's lead and stay true to yourself. Our friend Patti had the misfortune to marry a divorce lawyer, so when her marriage unraveled, she felt that she was at a serious disadvantage but didn't think to get her own lawyer. Instead, she thought she'd be serving him right if she made him do all the paperwork. It turned out, however, that even though he was the one at fault (having an affair with his secretary; Patti said, "I felt like a cliché") *he* sued *her* for "mental cruelty" in order to expedite the paperwork. He claimed that their state, Illinois, had a superlong waiting period for no-fault, but she went on the Web and found out it was only six months starting from the time of physical separation. So Patti put her foot down and insisted on no-fault. She confessed that "in court, we actually both decided to lie about the original separation date so that we'd be closer to waiting out the required period of time."

Generally speaking, for our demographic, the fact that you are filing for a fault divorce will not impact your settlement. Rather it's the symbolism suggested by the charges that is sometimes hard to swallow. Try, try, *try* not to get overwhelmed by who's "at fault," whether you're suing or being sued, and connect instead with your most pragmatic self and realize that no one else is going to care how you filed. Your safety, freedom, and general well-being are what really matters.

When Are You Officially Divorced?

You are officially divorced only when you receive what is variously known as your "decree of divorce," "decree of dissolution" (California), or "judgment of divorce." This is a document drafted by your lawyer or by you, if you did the papers yourself, and it is always signed by a judge. You will receive a copy of the decree from your lawyer or maybe directly from the court. In either case, make sure that you have a copy that has been stamped by the court; you will need to pull out this document a fair amount if you are changing your name.

Emotions: All's Fair in Love, War, and Divorce

Many people receive their decree by mail, which is often a very odd feeling. Some women report that it feels anticlimactic getting that piece of paper, because so much time has elapsed and all the drama is over. And then sometimes there can be this disjuncture between how you think you should feel and how you actually do feel. Sarah recalls coming home one day and there it was (the envelope from the state offices looked so banal she thought it was a parking ticket or tax reminder), sandwiched between the cable bill and *Glamour* magazine. She put it in her sock drawer and promptly called her mother, expecting to cry. But, by the time she got the decree, it had been a full year and a half since she and her husband had separated, and so much happiness had filled her life during that time that getting the actual document felt good.

Similarly, our friend Laura recalls, "The day I got my divorce papers, I called some friends and tried to play the wounded divorcée, but I realized I was being so fake, trying to feel and act like I was supposed to, but in reality, I was doing handsprings." Maeve was so desperate to be free of her husband that she felt jubilant on getting her decree: "I did a little tap dance in the street, jumped in my car, and spent $1,600 on new clothes. I just felt new. I just felt like I had to dress this new person completely differently—more sexy. It was pretty much a celebration."

At the other end of the spectrum, it's also perfectly natural to feel a new wave of sadness with the finality of it all. No matter who initiated the divorce, the gravity of the language can feel like cold steel between the eyes. Trudie, who did all her paperwork herself, thought she had accepted the dissolution of her marriage, but the finality of the paperwork just really wiped her out. Miranda had a similar experience. Although she had left her husband and was happily involved in a new relationship, she was thrown off by receiving the final decree in a way she hadn't anticipated: "You'd think after all that time, all those fights, and all this money, that you shouldn't feel a trauma, but the moment can take you by surprise." So, although you'll probably feel some relief, don't be surprised if the process brings you to a new level of grieving, too.

Society has no rituals to mark what is usually a serious life passage, the moment when you are officially divorced. Every woman has a different way of reacting to the moment when it is finally made official. Mourn if you need to. Be alone with your memories if that's what feels right. Call up your girlfriends and tell them to bring a few bottles of wine over. Whatever you do, be proud of yourself for untying the knot. Whatever your situation, take strength in the fact that you've conquered an enormous and trying task, and that you're now that much further along on the road to freedom.

CHAPTER SIX

In the Company of a Vivid Ghost

Encounters with Your Ex

*I call him my husband half of the time and
my ex-husband the other half . . . Like it
or not, he has an important place in my
personal history. He has a title.*

—Ann Patchett,
"The Sacrament of Divorce"

Whether you desire it or not, you will need to have some contact with your ex in order to complete the legal proceedings and generally extricate yourselves from each other's lives. There are better and worse ways to handle this contact so that you leave with more rather than less of your dignity intact, and feeling more rather than less empowered.

We chose the title for this chapter after several divorcées we talked to described encounters with their ex as akin to "seeing a ghost." Indeed, Sarah described a post-separation meeting with her ex, T., as "being in the company of a vivid ghost." When she said this, Kay knew it would be the title for this chapter because it so aptly describes the surreal experience of being in the presence of someone you once knew intimately but now no longer know so well, who has ceased to exist as the person he was to you but still somehow exists in the world, who remains a phantom floating around your imagination but who somehow can also sit in front of you in a restaurant like any normal person. In this chapter, we explore both the emotional and logistical challenges of this new way of relating, offering tips for how to handle both.

In the Beginning: Extricating from Your Ex

From the paperwork of the divorce to sending each other the DSL and dentist's bills, in the first year or so there's often lots of necessary contact. It can be amazing to discover how many little tendrils tied you two together, and how many you have to disentangle. In a modern, bureaucratic society, getting divorced means endless administrivia. For instance, you need to inform a hefty number of institutions of your new status, including banks, credit card companies, the Internal Revenue Service, the Department of Motor Vehicles, your doctor, your Bikram yoga studio—the list goes on. In the course of separating your two identities in the eyes of all these organizations, you often have to interface with your ex.

Although the two of you will be communicating about mundane matters, the interactions can feel loaded because you both have lots of emotions still swirling about. As a result, people's worst sides can emerge during these early encounters (including your own). And, because you are no longer invested in seeing him in as kindly a light as possible, all your ex's worst traits reveal themselves in the most glaring of ways. The things that while you were married bugged you only mildly will feel like nails on a chalkboard now. Indeed, being in touch with your ex after the love has died is a true lesson in the power of perspective (not to mention the power of love to blind).

Listening to the Angel Instead of the Devil

There are a number of tried-and-true practices you can follow to keep things peaceable during the emotionally volatile early period. The first reason to keep your cool is that the cultivation of a decent, amicable relationship with your ex can eliminate some of the stress and even give you a sense of pride. Granted, such a relationship is not possible if your ex is not a decent or amicable person or if the fault lines run very deep, so don't waste your time if either (or both) of these is the case. But, even if you don't want anything resembling a friendly relationship with him down the line, the more calmly and respectfully you approach contact with him, the more dignity and self-respect you'll have afterward and the more you'll be working to achieve closure in the relationship. We therefore recommend you access your Inner Angel—not because we're saintly or even because we promote saintliness, but because we're looking out for your best interests. The Dalai Lama, Jesus Christ, and all those spiritual high-achievers are onto something when they say it *feels* better to act decently and honorably. It may not be what makes you feel better in the moment, but it makes you feel better the next day and the next. So, as you navigate the early days, try the following.

Rack Up Moral Capital in the Bank of Life

We recommend that, sometime soon after you separate from your ex, you consciously decide to take the high road in all your interactions with him going forward. We're not saying you have to be Mother Teresa, but we encourage you to be as courteous and respectful as possible in your negotiations with him. Not only will you feel better about yourself, but frequently politeness and decency will breed the same in him. Be the grown-up and initiate the right spirit of relations between the two of you (assuming he hasn't already). Offer to take care of X, Y, and Z and hopefully he'll offer to do A, B, and C (or you can subtly suggest this). If he isn't acting equitably, that's annoying, but instead of wasting precious energy over when he will finally call the electric company, take charge and inform him of changes graciously. It may feel counterintuitive to be courteous and respectful sometimes, but it's a thousand times more pleasant than feeling resentful and bitter.

Prepare Thyself!

With every possible encounter, ask yourself what your objective is. Sometimes, you'll find that what you really want deep down, for example, affirmation or affection, you can better get elsewhere (e.g., from your good friends). Other times, of course, you have an honest agenda of items for his eyes and ears alone. Before encountering him to discuss something in particular, try to get very clear on what you want out of the encounter, how you want to feel afterward, and what things truly matter to you (if you're going to be negotiating about anything). Cindy, for instance, knew she had to steel herself before she met her ex in order to avoid getting back together with him. She was still very much in love with him even though she couldn't be with him anymore (he had major substance abuse issues), so she made herself reread her journals filled with accounts of his neglectful and disrespectful behavior to remind herself of why she had left before facing him in person. Try to be thoughtful and methodical about your interactions, and avoid anything impulsive. Do whatever you need to do—call your mother, get a Swedish massage, eat a big brownie—in order to encounter your ex with as much confidence and strength as you can muster.

Don't Sweat the Small Stuff

Some quibbling and bickering over minor issues is bound to happen, but try to keep it to a minimum. Follow the old truism to pick and choose your battles. If you really want that print from Bali back, make clear that this item is very important to you and since you chose it and bought it, you'd really like to get it back. Or if he wants to hang out with your best friend and that's really not okay with you, send him a clear message about your preferences. However, if he took a tablecloth you like but don't care about that much, let it go. Don't use it as an excuse to vent other frustrations. You'll find another tablecloth you like. Or, if he hangs out with an acquaintance you don't care that much about, it's probably best not to make a big deal about that either. Recognize that you may be seizing upon this issue as a channel for your anger and frustration at the larger situation. Minor issues can easily become arenas in which to play out the deeper issues that split you apart in a highly ineffective and unsatisfactory way, so try to avoid engaging in conflict about things you don't care about *that* much.

Keep Your Supreme Excellence to Yourself

Refrain from rubbing in your ex's face just how great you're doing when you email, talk, or see each other. It's a natural feeling to want to show him how much better off you are without him, but the instinct also means you still feel you have something to prove to him. If you're thinking along these lines, you need to focus on proving your amazingness to *yourself*. You're the only one who truly matters. Everyone else's opinion of you, including his, will follow your lead.

In general, if you have a lot of hurt, resentment, blame, or anger toward him, it probably makes sense to see a counselor to sort through the muck and purge yourself of these feelings. Until you reach a good measure of resolution about what happened between the two of you, it will be hard to have anything but charged relations and, more important, move onward to the rest of your excellent life.

Email Ex-changes

As denizens of the digital age, we now have the ever-efficient and handy medium of email with which to communicate with our exes, and it has many benefits. It allows you to get a message across quickly without having to face the complexity of actually interacting in real time with your ex: responding to what he says, hearing his voice, or seeing him in person. Especially for more minor issues, email can be ideal. Also, if you're frightened to speak or be with your ex in person for any reason, email is a particularly good communication channel.

However, email can also have its pitfalls, and you should use it judiciously. Its strength, lack of immediate interaction and non-verbal communication, can be its weakness. In the absence of face-to-face contact, some people can become more vitriolic, coarse, and uncensored; because you can't come back at them right away, they can sound off at you. Similarly, you may reply (or feel pressure to) before you are composed. Indeed, sometimes email becomes a way to let off serious steam. If you find that you or your ex is using email in this way, you may want to try talking on the phone or meeting in person instead.

Along these same lines, email communications can be easily misunderstood and can sometimes breed a false sense of camaraderie or agreement. Especially when it comes to more serious topics, like how to handle the legal proceedings or what the heck happened in your relationship, email is probably not the best choice because you're getting a fraction of the information you would be getting in person. If you have something big to tell your ex (e.g., about a new beau, engagement, or child) and you're on decent terms, it's probably best done by phone, in person, or old-fashioned snail mail. Case in point: Kay's ex informed her of his engagement in a reply email to an email she had sent him asking whether he had seen her skis recently, creating something of a huge shock for her on a very stressful day at work.

Sometimes someone uses email precisely because it allows them to stay at arm's length. They can reach out to you without really getting in touch with you—kind of a tease. It's a perfect communication channel for profoundly confused individuals. Beware of your ex trying to keep you hooked by sending the occasional provocative email because he feels you moving on with your life. When it comes to the real stuff of relationships, email is for cowards. If your ex really wants you back or has something important to tell you, he will muster up the moxie to call you or arrange to meet.

One last word of warning: remember that email leaves a permanent record. As with professional emails, you'll always want to pause before pressing the Send button to think, do I really want these thoughts/feeling/rants/raves documented for eternity? How would I feel if my ex forwarded this treatise to his nearest and dearest (*always* a possibility you have to consider)? And, more practically, can my ex use these against me in some way in our legal proceedings or in any other manner? The written word is a powerful thing—don't let your pointed prose get used against you.

In the Twilight Zone

Many divorcées report that their exes engaged in some patently bizarre behavior in the first year or so after the breakup. Again, feelings are flying around pell-mell, and especially when a guy is not great at processing his emotions, they find their way into his behavior even if they're not coming out in his words. You can expect to have your share of strange encounters and surreal scenarios before the dust settles. Here's how to cope with some of the more familiar situations, even when they rattle you or stir up feelings of your own.

Inexplicable Oddness

Part of the trouble in extricating yourself from your ex is that you both possess special knowledge that comes from having been a couple and shared life together for any number of years. You've been accustomed to being each other's walking memory, telephone book, and best friend. It can be tempting, then, to reach out and call each other out of habit and simple ease and convenience. However, beneath this impulse may also be an unconscious desire to stay in touch, a willing obliviousness to the new separateness of your lives, and an avoidance of feelings of loss. For instance, two weeks after Sarah's ex moved out of their apartment and got his own place, he emailed Sarah asking if she could remember where they had bought their mattress (of all things!) the year before, because he needed to get himself one. Sarah enjoyed the irony of the moment further when she answered him in the affirmative with, "Of course I remember: 'Kleinsleep—have more fun in bed." Obviously, mattress stores in Manhattan, where they lived, were easy to come by. Something—perhaps plain old convenience, perhaps feelings he wasn't even aware of, perhaps some combination of the two—prompted T. to communicate with Sarah about this silly yet rather intimate matter.

Megan's ex stopped by her flower shop once a week every time he went to the bank next door for the first year or so after they split. He never bought any flowers or had any real purpose for being there; he just showed up and chatted. He seemed to need to be in her presence without having anything particular to say. She eventually tried to send the message that although it was okay that he was there, he was not exactly welcome, and the visits became somewhat more infrequent.

Don't be surprised if your ex displays somewhat out-there behavior, especially in the immediate aftermath of the breakup. As in the case of Megan giving her ex hints about dropping by her shop, you may need to draw boundaries for your ex, either subtly or more directly. He may not even be conscious of how bizarre his behavior is, so if the interaction is bothering you, you'll need to be the adult and set the standards for what's acceptable and what's not.

Still Sorting It All Out

In other cases, your ex may express emotions he knows he has and wants you to know he has; he's still figuring out what happened and feels the need to share his confusion, anger, or sadness (or all of the above) with you. Maeve's ex actually sent her a letter a day for a while after they broke up. She chose not to read a single one. Trudie received semi-regular emails from her ex in which he would muse about why they had broken up, writing things like "What was it that killed us? Was it that I liked to play pool and you liked to go out and listen to live music and I didn't?" Another time he wrote her about a dream he had where the two of them got back together, which gave her a major case of the heebie-jeebies since she was very far from wanting that to happen.

If your ex is just contacting you to sort out his feelings, you'll have to determine how much you want to engage with him. His neediness may be overwhelming, and you may need to protect your space. You can choose to do as Maeve did and simply ignore his attempts to communicate with you (especially if, as in her case, he is going off the deep end, or if the communications are simply totally unproductive). If you think it will help *you* to process things, you can enter into a dialogue with him. However, if his (or your) emotions are running high, it may not be the best time to be talking through things with him. You'll have to gauge what makes sense for you, but be sure to base your choices on what's going to help you to resolve things and move on, otherwise, you may find yourself engaging in a largely futile and unsatisfying relationship autopsy.

When Your Ex Turns Creepy

Sometimes the communication is not as innocuous as Maeve's ex's obsessive letter-writing or Trudie's ex's painful e-ponderings. During the first few months after they split, Vickie's ex would call her from pay phones, "screaming obscenities, telling me I was a f——ing bitch. He told me he felt freed from my shackles. I was begging him to see a therapist, he was acting so crazy." Andrea's ex came over to the house they had shared while she was away one weekend and found condoms in the dresser next to the bed. The condoms were actually ones that Andrea and her ex had gotten at a party while they were still together, but he accused her in a very loud and dramatic fashion of already sleeping with somebody else (which she wasn't doing) and ruining the chance for them to get back together.

Sometimes exes can go further than just expressing anger and hurt and can act violent and dangerous. Patti's husband cheated on her with his secretary and then asked for a divorce. Once she agreed, he lost his bearings: "I had to get a lock on the bedroom door. He would call me every five minutes at work, harassing me. He got so desperate to talk to me that once he came over and pulled the fuses in the basement and then pounded on the bedroom door. I called his father and told him I'd call the police if he didn't stop. My ex heard me call his dad and so he gave up."

If, as in Patti's case, your ex is violent and unpredictable, you should seek legal counsel and consider a restraining order. In such a situation, you should definitely avoid ever meeting with your ex alone—take a relative or friend with you *always*. You may have trusted him once, but he cannot be trusted now; he's in an altered state and you need to take serious precautions. In general, you'll want to minimize contact with him, consolidating lots of things to tell him and hand off at once. You may want to have your lawyer, and even your relatives and friends, deal directly with him so that you don't have to at all. Loss and rejection can bring out dangerous impulses in people that they wouldn't normally display, so you're dealing with a different and more dangerous person than you knew before, and you need to act accordingly.

The Red-Hot Intensity of Revenge

Some exes who feel very hurt by the decision to divorce do not become violent but still have the desire to get back at you and make you feel some of the pain they are feeling. Sometimes revenge can take the form of refusing to interact with you at all and cutting you out of his life completely, which was what happened to Leslie, who felt terribly guilty for leaving her husband and ended up feeling extra horrible because he would have nothing to do with her and was utterly unforgiving for many years.

Often revenge is not an act of omission but an act of commission. For instance, when Janine was away one weekend from the house she had shared with her ex, he came back and took all the furniture they had gotten together. She arrived home to a virtually empty house. Recall Caitlin's husband who charged a large sum of money to their joint credit card after they separated, knowing that she would have to pay for it. He also called her sister and met with her girlfriends, trying to convince them that Caitlin was crazy and to be on his side. When someone's ego and pride are profoundly wounded, they can lash out through strange and vindictive financial and material maneuvers. (There are steps you can take to protect yourself financially. See chapter 4.)

If you initiated the split and your husband has a history of bad-temperedness, you should probably stay vigilant to potential acts of revenge. And, if your ex does engage in such acts, it's best to cool off and wait some time before figuring out how you want to respond. Often, if the act isn't ultimately that terrible, no response can be the best policy because you don't want to incite his anger further. However, sometimes he needs to be put in his place. You'll have to figure out the best way to do this given your particular situation, but you'll want to make sure you don't fan the flames of his fury or put yourself in jeopardy. In order to figure out the best way to proceed, you should discuss the situation with family and friends (also so they're aware of what has happened) but possibly also with the police, a counselor, or your local domestic violence organization.

Backhanded Revenge: See How Great I'm Doing Now!

A corollary to your ex wanting to cause you pain is the desire to rub in your face just how great he's doing. Sometimes an ex wants you to know you didn't hurt him or wants to emphasize that the divorce was the best thing for everyone. But the mere fact that he wants you to know these things is proof that he *was* actually injured by the whole thing. Valerie recalls, "Every blue moon for the first couple years after we'd separated, I'd get a phone message. It was always when he was drunk, and he was always boasting about how he'd closed a big deal at work." Sydney had similar experiences with her ex: "W. called me and all he could talk about was money, how he was making millions and his wife was making millions, going on and on about how great he was in superficial ways—the money, the house, etcetera. It was kinda gross."

Only you can decide how to deal with such gratuitous boasting, but we recommend just listening and being receptive without faking congratulations or joy for him. You may be tempted to counter his tales of success with some of your own, but you probably won't feel any better if you do. Just let him say what he needs to say and don't engage in the game of one-upmanship. He'll probably feel pretty silly after a while, which will allow you to get off the phone and back to your life. If you secretly do feel bad about how well he is doing, recognize that he's painting a rosy picture for you because, again, he's trying to get back at you or to prove something. Remind yourself of what was problematic about him and your relationship, and focus on your life and what you're excited about in your present and future. In short, don't let him be successful in rubbing his success in your face in order to make you feel bad!

Rest assured that, with time, these random and often volatile encounters will happen less and less, and your life will stop being punctuated by this inexplicable oddness. The demise of a marriage is like a huge earthquake in people's lives, and there are often aftershocks for some time afterward.

If You're on Good Terms:
Grieving Together

Particularly if you're on good terms with your ex, you might find yourself in the odd position of grieving the loss of the relationship with him. Especially if you met young and "grew up together," you might have enough of a friendship beneath all the drama to give the relationship something of a proper burial. Some couples get together explicitly to try to make sense of things and others get together simply to catch up, then find themselves grieving together. Grieving together can include mourning the loss of your shared lives and the loss of your future life together, recounting fond memories and honoring what you shared, and getting angry at each other for the ways in which you hurt or didn't understand one another.

Tanya, who broke up with her husband, G., at the same time as her mother was dying, found herself often sleeping in the same bed with G.—after he had moved out and without having sex— and grieving with him about the end of their marriage and her mother's impending death. Kay and her ex, F., had monthly talks to process the end of their relationship, and they invariably ended up with the two of them crying, hugging, and affirming how much they cherished what they had shared for over eight years. Kay, who had taken the majority of the CDs when she moved out because she had chosen and bought them, gave F. about half the collection back during one of these monthly talks—the half he would appreciate and listen to more than her.

Delia and her ex, N., had many conversations where they sobbed together over their mutual brokenheartedness. They also got very angry about the ways in which they felt wronged by each other. In general, they spent a good deal of time grieving and processing the demise of their marriage, including giving each other parting gifts. Megan's husband, whom she'd been with for over ten years, insisted that they meet several times in the year after they split up to try to understand what happened and build a friendship. Although she was reluctant at first, she's now grateful that he forced the two of them to make the effort. Sydney and her ex, W., also met regularly for lunch after they separated: "We actually got closer and became better friends after we officially split up. I'd tell him what I was learning in therapy and he was really interested. They were really nice lunches, but they sometimes did get emotional and go to some dark places, with both of us crying."

Sometimes an ironic thing can happen once you're no longer officially together. You find that you actually communicate better and see each other more clearly and kindly. Because you no longer have the pressure "to make it work" and all bets are off, something opens up and you become just two human beings trying to make sense of things. There can be a confusing poignancy to these conversations, with one or both of you wondering, if we'd been able to understand each other like this when we were together, could we have made it work? It's important to remember that you are only able to have such authentic dialogue now that you are safely apart from each other, which doesn't mean you could have had it on a daily basis in a relationship.

Grieving together is only possible if neither person feels too terribly betrayed by the other and if there's still a friendship beneath the stormy histrionics of the breakup. It sounds contrived, but you may even consider making some ground rules before talking so that you can call each other on things if one of you becomes hurtful or starts laying blame. Or you can simply agree at the start that the spirit of the discussion is about understanding and resolution not fault-finding, and catch each other if either veers from this agreement. Debriefing your relationship can be a very painful process, but if the two of you focus on understanding and avoid vindictiveness, it can be an amazingly cathartic and life-affirming experience as well.

You Never Know Who You Might Meet . . .

Chance encounters with the ex, depending on when and how they happen, can be any number of things: traumatizing, confusing, humorous, uneventful, and great. Time and place have something to do with how such an encounter unfolds, as does how settled your respective feelings are.

Caitlin describes her first encounter with her ex on the street during the first year after they split up as "deeply awkward and emotionally confusing. I had the impulse to hug him, but I didn't. I felt lost. We had literally bumped into each other. We talked for three or four minutes, very friendly . . . It was a relief to see him acting pleasant, but it was also very sad. It was like I'd seen a ghost." Indeed, chance encounters can feel especially surreal and otherworldy. After all, you're face-to-face with someone you once slept next to night after night and now you're running into them on a street corner. The dissonance in levels of intimacy, past and present, can send you reeling and dredge up feelings you hadn't particularly planned on having that day.

Timing and distance from the actual separation naturally make a huge difference in how these spontaneous meetings unfold. In the first six months after they parted ways, Trudie bumped into her ex unexpectedly at an event. Seeing him threw her into a tailspin and made her panicky and grief-stricken. Now, a year and a half later, seeing him barely phases her.

Similarly, in the first six months after breaking up, Leslie ran into her ex at a café on a Sunday morning. She was with a new boyfriend and had an excruciatingly awkward exchange with her ex. They didn't talk again until seven years later, when they ran into each other at a conference. She remembers seeing him from afar and thinking, "This guy who is such a character in my imagination is just a guy walking through the halls of a conference."

They actually met for drinks and had a remarkably heartfelt conversation about what had happened between them and how they were doing now—a testament to their emotions being far more resolved than at the time of the encounter in the café.

As with Leslie's second chance encounter with her ex, sometimes such serendipitous meetings can lead to a newfound sense of resolution. Elizabeth asked her ex, who's an accountant, to do her taxes the year they officially separated since he knew all her finances and didn't mind doing them. When he came over to get all her papers, they ended up having the first caring and "real" conversation they'd had in years, and it left Elizabeth feeling more at peace about the relationship than she had up to that point.

Don't be surprised if a random meeting with your ex (or one of his relatives or friends) renders you somewhat off-kilter for a few days. The emotions will die down with a little time, and eventually the encounter will be a tiny blip on the colorful radar screen of your life. It's possible, too, that a chance meeting at the right time could yield an unexpectedly fruitful conversation. Sometimes fate seems to bring you together for just such a purpose.

As for running into your ex with his new flame, this kind of encounter can definitely be something of a shock, especially if you didn't know about his new liaison. But even if you'd heard that he was with someone else, actually witnessing it in 3-D can be quite unsettling. How you feel about this sighting will have a lot to do with how you are feeling about him, the divorce, and your own life at that particular time. For more on your emotional reaction to the encounter, read the section later in this chapter called "When Your Ex Finds Someone Else." In terms of how to handle the situation in the moment, it's best not to ignore your ex and his girlfriend (which is very seventh grade) but to be cordial and casual, perhaps even approaching them first in order to alleviate your own stress and get the encounter over with. If you're with your own date, definitely bring him along for the introductions. Make it short and sweet: be brave, be brief, and be gone. Save the histrionics for your girlfriends; you can scream, sob, and laugh hysterically with them, but try to have as much of a poker face as you can when in your ex's presence. If you feel yourself on the verge of losing it, feel no shame about leaving the situation quickly and going home to your bed to eat a big bar of chocolate and call all your nearest and dearest.

From Here on Forward: Leading Separate Lives

There comes a time when you have basically extricated yourselves from each other's lives and are now leading two separate ones. How do you relate to each other? This question will depend largely on the nature of your interactions during the breakup and during the disentanglement phase. Because you two are childless, the options are wide open and truly a matter of preference. Some divorcées never see their exes, some have very occasional contact, and some see their exes fairly frequently. Don't worry about what other divorcées you know are doing or what you think you *should* do. Do what makes sense for you and your relationship (or non-relationship).

The Choice of No Contact

Some divorcées cease having contact with their ex after the initial period of logistical disentanglement. In some cases, interaction with the ex is toxic or painful for one or both of you and so is best avoided altogether. If you two make each other looney and communication never leads to anything but more misery and agitation, why torture yourselves? In Andrea's words, "Contact just petered out. It didn't make sense. Our relationship was too hot and cold and crazy. There's just some people it doesn't make sense to stay in touch with, if you're just not good for each other. Why? There's no purpose."

If your ego has been very bruised from the breakup, you may

make the very healthy and legitimate choice to regroup without any interference from the ex. Vickie says, "I've never asked for his new phone number, and I never gave him mine. I didn't want to know about him, and he had lost the right to know anything about me. I guess I just realized that to hear *anything* from him would hurt me." If, like Vickie, you need to recover your self-confidence, it makes a lot of sense to stay away from your ex and focus on healing yourself and being around people who remind you of how amazing and lovable you are.

On the flip side, if your ex was very hurt by the divorce and has communicated a wish for no contact, it's important that you respect this. After 9/11, Isabel felt compelled to find out if her ex, who was very bitter about their breakup and could have been working in the World Trade Center, was alive and okay. She did some research but could find nothing conclusive about his status. But, she reports, "I never called or wrote, though, because I decided that popping back into his life or his family's life would have been a selfish thing to do." If either one of you still has deep wounds about the divorce, you need to respect that. As strange as it may be sometimes, distance and time will be the best salves.

In some cases, your ex may desire contact with you but have a new girlfriend or wife who's not comfortable with him being in touch with you. While this situation may be very difficult for you and you may find yourself judgmental of a new partner who cannot accept you in his life, you need to be respectful if he cuts off contact for this reason. Our girlfriend Sydney encountered this scenario: "As soon as W. was married, he wouldn't go to lunch with me anymore. He told me that his new wife doesn't like it, so to be fair to her, I can't do it." The situation made her sad because she enjoyed being in touch with W. and relied on his counsel for many professional matters, but she realized she had no choice but to honor his decision.

Perhaps you don't feel strongly about contact or no contact, and instead feel mostly apathy and disconnection from that part of your life. This is okay, too. Janine remarks, "I have no desire to contact him, but I really truly do hope he has a nice life. He's a really good person and deserves it." In these cases, it's not that the contact would be toxic, it's just that there's no motivation or desire for it.

Falling out of touch with your ex, then, makes sense in a variety of different situations. However, even though it makes sense doesn't mean it doesn't also feel slightly odd at moments. As Nancy put it, "It's very strange, to have someone who was part of your life for so long, and then—nothing."

The Occasional Acknowledgment of What Was

*M*any divorcées and their exes do not want to stay in close touch but feel a desire to occasionally acknowledge that they were important people in each other's lives and that they still value things about the other and the relationship. We spoke with numerous divorcées who wrote and received cards or e-greetings on birthdays and other important dates. These gestures are not about building a friendship but about extending an olive branch to each other and making a small tribute to what you shared. Sending and receiving these missives can stir up old emotions that are not always invited, but overall, these intermittent communications tend to contribute to greater closure and general good karma.

The Post-Marital Friendship (PMF)

In some cases, it may be possible and desirable to build something resembling a friendship with your ex. Because you have no bambinos, such a friendship is totally voluntary, and you have the freedom to make it whatever you want it to be. Generally, in these situations, no one was inordinately hurt by the breakup, and the relationship had already evolved into more of a friendship than a romance.

However, we use the word "friendship" broadly here because a PMF with your ex is unlikely to be a typical friendship. You may be able to call each other up freely and hang out regularly to catch up on each other's lives, but only when you don't care one iota if he's with someone else (and vice versa), will you truly be able to be friends. Until this day comes, though, which may be never, you can be on very good terms with each other and be there for each other in certain ways but not others.

Kay, for instance, has stayed in fairly close contact with her ex since their split. They have regularly gotten together to stay abreast of each other's lives. Right after the separation, they'd see each other every two weeks, but now, several years later, they see each other more like every three or four months. However, Kay has yet to meet F.'s new wife and didn't attend their wedding. So, while they remain important in each other's lives, they do not share everything with each other and there are certain areas which remain off-limits.

Megan, who asked for the divorce from her ex, has also developed a PMF with him, largely because he initially made a real effort to understand what happened between them and build a friendship. She says, "We grew up together. We did really crazy, stupid things you do when you're young. And because of that, I think we'll always be friends." She has met his new girlfriend (and in fact seems to run into her all over town) and says she feels no jealousy whatsoever. However, she's also not interested in hanging out with the two of them.

PMFs, then, are somewhat unique beasts in the land of friendship. You still cherish the person and feel close to them, you still feel comfortable calling them up and talking to them about many things, but there are likely realms that you cannot share with each other the way you would with another good friend. And being in each other's presence can also feel somewhat strange.

You can still be very intimate about many matters and you're reminded of the intimacy you once shared, yet there are places neither of you can tread now. You know this person and yet you don't fully know this person anymore. You are intimate strangers.

When Your Ex Finds Someone Else

According to the experts, when your ex finds a significant other, even if you are not at all interested in getting back together and even if you have your own romantic interest, you may revisit the experience of losing that person all over again and go through a period of heightened grief. Our girlfriend Delia initiated the breakup with her ex and moved to another city, but when her ex hooked up with one of their mutual acquaintances and the woman got pregnant, she relates, "It was a big dash of cold water for me." Even though she knew her ex truly wasn't right for her, the speed with which he had moved on was jolting and augmented feelings of loss.

While many divorcées may experience a massive *ouch!* when their ex finds another main squeeze, some actually experience a sigh of relief. Our girlfriend Leslie, for instance, felt a massive amount of guilt about leaving her ex, so when he reconnected with his old girlfriend and began dating her, she says she felt nothing but pure and unadulterated relief and absolution.

Depending on what feelings you have about the divorce, you will react accordingly to the news of your ex with a new flame. Don't be surprised if you have complex feelings: some happiness for him, some feelings of abandonment, some resentment, some relief, and some sadness. Be careful during the time immediately following this news because you may find yourself feeling especially vulnerable and susceptible to making some bad decisions. For instance, beware the impulse to start sleeping with random guys just to get some male attention or to sink your teeth into a less-than-ideal relationship just to keep pace. In other words, resist the temptation to start measuring your success in building a

new life against his. Instead of doing something that will ultimately make you feel worse, we encourage you to honor your
myriad feelings about his new situation and process them with
friends and family. They will occupy you for a while, but as time
passes, the wacky emotions will wane and fade away. We also advise you to work hard at staying focused on living your life at the
particular pace at which it unfolds, without regard to what is happening in his.

Ghostly Visitations

No matter how much or how little contact you have with your
ex, he will remain a figure in your consciousness, flitting about
now and then, here and there—in dreams, reveries, rants, and re-
flections. Such is the nature of human connection. People from
our past stay with us in the recesses of our minds even if we see
them very little in real life. Like a ghost, your ex is no longer with
you the way he was, but he is not exactly gone for good either.
He comes back into your imagination on occasion to say hello,
check up on you, and sometimes torment you.

Laura, who hasn't seen her ex since the day she moved out
her stuff, says she encounters him mentally every time she travels
because she has to show the divorce papers with her passport (because she changed her name back and the passport hasn't come up
for renewal). It makes her think momentarily about the marriage
and what he might be like now. She says, "Even if you're not
emotionally invested at all anymore, you can never escape it or
forget it entirely."

The passport example is just one of many triggers that can
spur you to think back on your ex and the relationship. Maybe
you hear about him through the grapevine. Maybe you pass the
restaurant where the two of you always used to go or the place
where you met or the apartment where you lived together, or

you see someone who looks like him . . . the list goes on. Don't be surprised and don't beat yourself up if you find yourself thinking about him and what happened even years after the divorce has been finalized. We human beings may be able to tear ourselves physically apart but extricating each other from the interstices of each other's minds and hearts is another matter entirely.

Room in Your Heart

Our girlfriend Cindy felt terribly sad for years after she left her ex partly because she had never stopped loving him. She left on account of his substance abuse and related irresponsibility. One summer, four years after they had split up, Cindy found herself on a five-hour train ride through Europe crying about him to a Dutch friend. She remembers saying, "What's my problem? I can't get over M." And the friend said something to her that has stayed with her forever: "You don't have to *get over* him. You wanted to spend your life with him, you really loved him and it didn't work because of his problems. You have enough room in your heart for him and other people. Your heart is big enough." Cindy says that the idea that she could still love him even though she couldn't be with him somehow made everything okay. She relates, "The biggest mistake was thinking I had to get over him." She had put so much pressure on herself to forget about him and move on, which wasn't working, when what she needed to do was accept that she would always love him even if she couldn't be with him. Mehta expressed something similar about her ex: "There's a place in my heart where he'll always be."

Misty, Water Colored Memories

Other divorcées have discussed how, as time passes, there can be a tendency to forget about what the problems were between you and your ex and reminisce about the good parts. Andrea talks about finally moving out of the house she shared with her ex and finding all his musical equipment in the attic, reminding her of all the parties and the good times they'd had: "I can be a super sentimental fool that way . . . you forget what was wrong about the relationship, and you really have to remind yourself." Elizabeth had a similar experience when she was cleaning out an old closet and found her old wedding album: "It brought back all the goodness. I had all this nostalgia for what we were in the good days and all the good times we had. I had to make myself remember how bad it had gotten. You can forget."

Indeed, your memory can play tricks on you and sometimes present you with a one-sided picture of your relationship. The reality is that there were wonderful things about your union with your ex, and there were also deep-seated conflicts between you that couldn't be overcome. It can be hard sometimes, but it's important to hold both of these things in your hands at the same time if you find yourself romanticizing the relationship and even having feelings of regret. Both the good and the bad are part of the reality, and both are important to remember.

So, while your ex may have been out the door many moons ago, no matter how much contact you choose to have with him, he'll still be floating around in your imagination and wafting through your synapses. It's best not to fight this but rather to simply notice how you're thinking about him, what you miss about him, and what still irks you, and let it inform who you are and what you want today. Try to do what Kay's yoga teacher, Pretzel, says to do when meditating: "Simply observe the thoughts as if they were clouds passing by on the sky of your mind, and let them teach you about yourself."

CHAPTER SEVEN

Here Comes the Divorcée

Single in Society

> Marriage, as one of my relentlessly married
> friends says, is a "cover," a form of social
> armor. You can go to parties and announce,
> "this is my husband" and the world will
> smile upon you as one of their suitably
> partnered own.
>
> —Daphne Merkin,
> "In The Country of Divorce"

Divorce is an incredibly personal affair, and yet people's perceptions never fail to invade your private universe, even if just as figments of your imagination. You've gone through, or are still going through, your own private odyssey by becoming divorced, but every once in a while, you pause to think, "I'm going to be a *divorcée*—whatever that means." Despite the fact that divorce has become very common in our culture and society, many divorcées feel some uneasy mixture of embarrassment, shame, and awkwardness about being divorced. We live in a culture that so hypes the ideal of marriage and the dream of wedded bliss that getting divorced can sometimes make you feel like a social failure.

Compounding this is the fact that, if you are a Gen-Xer like us, you probably grew up with the specter of divorce among your parents or your parents' friends and may have been even more determined to have a lasting marriage yourself. Divorce was something that happened to couples like our parents in their later forties and fifties, inspired by midlife crises and affairs (like the culture portrayed in *The Ice Storm*), not our self-aware, evolved, and post-feminist generation. Despite how far we've advanced as a society in terms of acceptance of divorce, though, a divorcée is still a complicated role to play. Even if you yourself have few hang-ups about your new identity, it's likely you'll encounter other people who do.

No matter how you feel about being single in society again, our goal in this chapter is to help you rise to any occasion in your new solo status, whether it's responding to your own inner critic or responding to reactions from social circles outside of your immediate family and friends. As we encourage you to develop your post-marriage social life, we'll also offer suggestions for reshaping marriage-based friendships and navigating the difficult terrain of mutual friends and social obligations. Finally, we'll discuss positive approaches you can take to facing messy milestones like the holidays and various anniversaries.

Consider Your Divorce an Advanced Degree in Your Personal Education

Yes, divorce is a huge personal disappointment, but there is no need to see it as a failure. What you're doing takes immense courage and endurance. No matter what the particulars of your situation, you are not a bad person for getting divorced. You do not deserve any stigma you or others might attach to the process.

In all likelihood, you've endured a lot of turmoil, you've worked hard to think all of the issues through, and you're going to come out on the other side much smarter and savvier, not only about your own life but about relationships and life in general. You're amassing all kinds of new knowledge and even new skills. Enjoy this wisdom and don't let society or other people let you think otherwise.

If you are feeling uncomfortable about being a divorced woman, you're not alone. Many of the women we interviewed also felt this way initially, and recommend addressing the source of your discomfort head-on. Preempt any self-criticism you might be prone to, and consciously adopt a positive or at least neutral opinion of your status as a divorcée. Sounds like a tall order and a lot of psychobabble but basically, our operating principle is refuse to accept the baggage that others seem to want to give you, or that you seem to give yourself. Our friend Tanya said she just doesn't identify as a divorcée, doesn't feel any baggage about being one, and doesn't let other people hand her *their* baggage. She refused to engage their discomfort or let it get to her. Or, as our friend Sydney put it, "I adopted a different attitude about it and the more comfortable I became with the divorce, the more comfortably I could talk about it. It reminds me of the people I know who were Deadheads once and spent a year following the Dead but are now executives. You can tell by the way they talk about it that they're not embarrassed by their experiences. They're fine with them, they're not hung up about it."

Many of the women we know decided that they didn't want the divorce to be their main identifier, so they tend to tell people on a need-to-know basis. Sure, it's part of who you are, but it's just that—one part. And as time goes on, it will only be a smaller and smaller part of who you are. As our friend Janine put it, "Yeah, it's baggage, but it's baggage you can leave in the closet. You don't have to take it on every trip." And, as one woman now in her forties and happily remarried said of her first marriage in her twenties, "There are days I forget I was ever married before."

Plagued by the Scarlet *D*

Nevertheless, we realize you may not be capable of seeing your divorce as a badge of honor just yet. If you're like many of the women we spoke to, you may feel like you have to overcome the embarrassment factor first: embarrassment at the breakup of the marriage and embarrassment that you have made a mistake that has to become so public. Laura, for example, waited a whole year before telling her new fiancé's parents about her first marriage: "One day I decided I had to tell them, went over to their house by myself, and when they opened the door, I started sobbing uncontrollably. I didn't want them to judge me. It turned out they were fine with it, but I was so scared they would hold it against me." In Laura's case, as with so many others, the challenge was much more about self-perception than it was about external reality. There's this odd disjuncture between the prevalence of divorce in today's culture, with half the world having done it and continuing to do it, and the reality of how you can still feel tainted.

And sometimes, the very strength of the numbers sometimes only irritates you more. Erin, who is getting married again, had a hard time telling her new in-laws for this reason: "C.'s family doesn't think I should be so embarrassed, they say so many people get divorced, but I don't want to be a statistic. I don't like to be 'so many people.'" There's a sense of not wanting to be just another failed marriage, of not wanting to have been defeated by the odds.

For some women, the embarrassment factor is especially acute if the marriage was short-lasting and the wedding was a traditional, large affair with generous gift-giving. As our friend Elizabeth put it, "I was mortified at the stigma and the failure, especially with the two hundred fifty people who were at our wedding. We got everything from our registry list, and I felt such guilt and shame, I would have returned it all if it wasn't too late." Similarly, our friend Megan said, "I've felt such guilt about all my family members, especially the ones who came to the wedding, I felt so ashamed and afraid, like I should send all the wedding gifts back."

🔖 *Etiquette note*: Although one of our friends, Isabel, whose marriage ended after a few months, did in fact end up returning the wedding presents that were still boxed, it is certainly not necessary or expected that you do this. As Judith Martin explains in *Miss Manners Guide for the Turn of the Millennium,* "The rule about wedding presents is that they are returned to the sender if the wedding does not take place. Once it does, they cease to be wedding presents and become the joint property of the couple, to be given to whoever can make a better case for possession . . . or whoever has the better lawyer."

For some women, embarrassment lingers because the regret runs deep. Even though Erin's divorce is several years behind her and she's getting remarried, she says, "Even now, it's very embarrassing to me to be a divorcée. There are certain family members of C.'s who still don't know. I am ashamed of it. I still get things in the mail with my married name, and it really bugs me because it was the biggest mistake of my life. And the only way I really pacify myself is because I feel like I would not have met C. unless I had gone through what I did, and I really believe everything happens for a reason."

Sometimes, what haunts women is what they perceive as a lapse in judgment in getting married the first time around. As Maeve put it, "I had a real sense of, 'I cannot believe I made such a public mistake. How could I have married this jerk? My poor family, how could they have sat through this wedding? I am so embarrassed, you people were so nice. And on the flip side, why didn't you stop me?' " Hindsight is 20-20, of course. Remember that most other people are probably over the situation well before you are, and if they are decent human beings, they are *not* thinking "What a fool" or "I told her so!" Focus on the fact that you're giving yourself this wonderful chance to be true to yourself and start over.

One of our friends, to help herself overcome what she felt was the "Scarlet *D*," played a positive word association game. She tore out a sheet of paper and started to make a list of great *D* words to define herself: "dignity" came first, then "daring," "dream," "discerning," "dessert," "daughter," "dodge" (as in dodged a bullet), "determined," "debonair" (as in, her next man will be . . .). It was a healthy (if slightly goofy, but what exercise isn't goofy) exercise in self-actualization that helped release her from a negative mindset about her divorce. Sometimes, you just have to consciously and forcibly take on your embarrassment demons.

Rising to Social Occasions

Resuming a healthy social life is an important part of getting back into the swing of things while you're going through a divorce and after a divorce. Social engagements of any kind—margaritas with colleagues after work, dinner with friends, or just a movie with your sister—can inspire you to put on some lipstick, iron that shirt, and flex your conversational muscles every so often. Even if you're not feeling like your most sparkling, extroverted self, it can be good therapy to get out of your own head and join a festive crowd.

As social events go, attending your first wedding solo, especially if you're still in the throes of separation or divorce, may feel a bit anxiety-producing, but it can also be a great way to reaffirm your belief in love and matrimony and enjoy a good party. Sarah remembers a Valentine's Day wedding of one of her friends; she went feeling a bit like a black widow, as if she'd jinx things for the happy couple by being there. However, once she got out of her own warped head and over her fears of feeling out of place, she had a great time and was heartened to see two dear friends make the big commitment and celebrate. Seated at a table of almost all married couples, Sarah realized, "Hey, this is fine. This used to be my milieu, I can handle this. I can talk the talk, and it's great that the wives' husbands have asked me to dance." And, as cheesy as it sounds, weddings are good venues to meet people, too. Not just men (although that's particularly fun) but also other people. Weddings are often packed with potential new friends of all stripes.

Hazards of the Road

As you start to circulate, it's a good idea to be prepared for the occasional dip in the road. For example, our friend Cindy attended her high school reunion right after her divorce was finalized and found herself unnerved by an encounter there. As she recalls it, "A friend came up to me and said, 'Some guy was asking about you, but don't worry, I told him you're divorced.' It bothered me for two weeks! I felt like a scarred woman." People will make the strangest assumptions. Maybe Cindy was ready to date, maybe she wasn't; that's for her to judge. So, beware of random judgments or remarks. Correct these when you feel like it, but otherwise, try not to let them bother you. They are often a result of other people's issues.

At the opposite end of the spectrum are the people who want to set you up right away and expect you to be immediately on the prowl again. Our friend Hope told us, "I remember at a wedding someone said, 'You're next,' at the bouquet toss. I replied, 'Been there, done that,' and just walked away. I feel like I could have grown another head but as long as I was with someone I would have been fine in their eyes. It's just so offensive. At first, I had hurt feelings, but now I just laugh. I think society comes down way harder on women than on men. There's just not the same race to fix men up." Old paradigms die hard.

In many awkward social situations like this, it's helpful to bear in mind that with anyone but your closest and longtime friends, less is probably more. If you're not already, you will become adept at skillfully and subtly mentioning the fact that you're divorced to social friends, acquaintances, and random others. Sometimes necessity forces you to get good at this kind of communication. For example, about three weeks into her separation, Sarah got a phone call out of the blue from a college friend who had attended Sarah's wedding. They had seen each other only once or twice after the wedding, but this friend called to say hello and confess that she'd just realized she'd never gotten Sarah and T. a wedding present. In fact, that moment, she was "calling from Bloomingdale's, arranging to have something sent, but didn't have their address handy." Sarah felt sorry for her earnest and in-the-dark friend, and replied, "Ohhhhh, I'm so glad you called, but please don't bother, you're not going to believe this, but we've recently separated." This encounter, as awkward as it was in the moment, eventually became an amusing story and one that helps illustrate the ease and effectiveness of the less-is-more approach.

Your Elevator Speech

So, with friends, acquaintances, and random others, you'll learn to formulate a one-liner or a one-paragraph narrative (known as "the elevator speech" in marketing), and things will start to become easier. Our friend Megan told us the best advice she got was from her mother: " 'Find one or two confidantes who you tell everything to; you can bitch to them, cry to them, call them all hours of the night. Other than that, come up with a canned statement to tell the rest of the world.' Mine was 'We were just going in different directions.' "

You can sometimes try out more daring summaries like "Yes,

I made the very unfortunate mistake of marrying a complete narcissist." It can be strangely fun to cultivate your wit in the telling of your story. For example, we love the *New Yorker* cartoon that features two women on a couch drinking coffee and talking about a photo in a frame: "That's Norman. He was badly miscast as my husband." Naturally, there's no need to be a pithy Oscar Wilde all the time, but don't be surprised if you find that a pleasant by-product of your personal pain is that your sense of humor develops a new wry sophistication.

Sometimes acquaintances, colleagues, or virtual strangers, especially if they've gone through something similar, will actually seem so trustworthy that you do feel compelled to open up to them a bit more. Go ahead, have that conversation on the bus with another soul sister you've just met or the divorced man seated at your table at a wedding. The anonymity can be liberating. It's also amazing how once you start mentioning your divorce, other people will volunteer their status and stories. Sometimes, it's quite a surprise and relief to realize how many comrades you have out there.

Random Rubbernecking

The more comfortable you become with the fact and the facts of your divorce, the more comfortable you will make people feel and the less you'll be affected by their reactions. We've already established (in chapter 3) some strategies for coping with the reactions of your inner circle, but what's up with those odd comments and looks by random others? Obviously, a healthy majority of the vast public isn't going care one iota that you're divorced. It's just that tiny vocal minority that can get under your skin from time to time with the irritating but common reactions of (a) surprise, (b) pity, and (c) discomfort. Let's analyze these briefly for what they really are—usually, just expressions of ignorance.

The Surprise Reaction

This is the "*You're* divorced?" response, usually accompanied by a loud "*but*" and then a string of descriptors like "you're so young, beautiful, talented, successful," as if to be a divorcée, you have to be older, losing your looks, bereft of a career and an identity, and utterly washed up! Instead, you belong in the company of the "Young, Hot, Divorced" demographic profiled in the April 2001 issue of *Jane* magazine. Realize that these poor souls probably don't realize how they sound and are, of course, actually trying to compliment you. And remember that there can be some hidden assumptions about both men and women who are divorced. Not knowing any better, people can assume it's a tragic flaw of sorts. For example, one of Kay's book group friends, Chitra, who didn't know Kay was divorced, was about to set her up with a guy but thought she shouldn't because "he's a great guy, but . . . he's divorced." Kay told Chitra, "Hey, that's fine with me—I'm divorced too." In such instances, it's wise to take the educational approach, imparting a version of "it happens to the best of us" to your audience.

"You Poor Thing!"

Occasionally, you may find that "I'm sorry" is offered as a knee-jerk reaction from a relative stranger. This can be hard to stomach if it has the pity overtones of "I feel sorry for you." For our friend Leslie, the sympathetic looks she'd get from strangers somehow just made her feel more pathetic. Gina recalls feeling people's eyes go downward, as if she'd told them about an untimely death! This kind of thing happens because people don't know how to react, and they're simply uncomfortable themselves. We recommend showing these people that you don't feel sorry yourself by asserting a fine platitude, or elevator speech: "Yes, it didn't work out, but it was for the best." Or something slightly sassier, like "Don't be sorry—it's a good thing."

The Discomfort Reaction

This is the "Oh dear, I don't know what to say" reaction, such as Cindy encountered one day: "I was out at a restaurant with my mother, and we ran into another woman in the community. She came over to our table, started talking to us, and then she looked at my hand and said, 'Oh, I thought you were married.' And there was this pregnant pause and my mother kind of snickered and looked at me, like it was up to me how to handle it. And I said, 'You know what, it didn't work out, and I'm really happy.'" The woman's nosiness was nipped in the bud by Cindy's matter-of-fact response, turning her face a shade of red. Remember that some people are just not very good at hearing such news. Discomfort can be the hardest kind of reaction to deal with because there's nervousness. Try to act Zen-ful and unfazed. In other words, don't let their unease get to you. Remember, it's *them*, not you.

Why Others Might Feel Threatened by You

Though no one envies you for having to go through the trauma of divorce, there are people, especially married women, who may feel envious of your freedom. As our friend Megan told us, "Married women do not like divorcées; they seem to feel threatened by me. I don't know if it's because I represent this alternative that is tempting but forbidden, or if they think I want to steal their husbands, which I don't. Most of them are fat, bald, and ugly!" Most of the time, happily married and secure women will not have a problem with your new status, but realize that there may be times when you unwittingly bring out other people's issues simply by your very existence as a divorced woman. If you sense a lot of strange, uncomfortable vibes from someone, it may be best to simply avoid hanging out with them. Many times, people who have these feelings don't even know they have them, so they can't even talk to you about them to clear the air. If they're solid friends, of course they'll get over these problems eventually.

In the meantime, you're better off taking a break from their company.

Fear may be a factor in a married person's reaction. This is the "if it happened to them . . ." response. As our friend Caitlin recalled, a good number of her married friends, upon hearing of her divorce, suddenly felt vulnerable in their own marriages. And as our friend Trudie remembers, "I had a hard time telling old friends who saw us as the perfect couple. They said things like, 'Oh no, you can't divorce, you guys are my only hope that a marriage can work.' " Your decision to dissolve your marriage might also make others nervous, nervous the way one becomes paranoid upon hearing about someone getting cancer. For a lot of people, divorce can seem contagious! As Megan experienced, "Most of our friends just thought of us as the greatest couple, so they had this feeling of 'if the two of you can't make it, I can never get married.' " So, remember: anyone in your life, married or single, may be selfishly upset that your problems might become their problems, or feel like the news you're sharing shakes up their sense of certainty in the world. As writer Daphne Merkin tells us, marriage is a cover of sorts, and by getting divorced, you've in effect blown the cover.

In its extreme forms, discomfort among other people, particularly the single/never marrieds can make you feel like you're a threat to homeland security. You're suddenly competition again, competition of a special kind. Let's think about this: having been married once means we've lived with a man and done battle with a man we called husband, *and* had the maturity of mind to get out of a bad situation. "Divorcée" will therefore suggest to some people that you have attained a level of emotional and sexual experience that the never-married woman has not. Most divorcées we interviewed felt that they grew up fast when they got divorced. And, conversely, a single friend of Sarah's once joked to her that, having never been married, she felt "behind in life" compared to Sarah, who had gone around the proverbial block once already.

Who Gets the Friends?

One of the biggest challenges of getting divorced is navigating and often reconfiguring your base of mutual friends. In most cases, divorce forces you to re-create or divide the mutual friendships you and your husband developed over the years. As a result, most women we spoke to admitted that, in this department, they had to endure a few friendship casualties. For some, the loss of mutual friends can rank among the greatest costs of divorce. Others are able to maintain a few good friends from their marriage but will admit that, initially, it takes some work and discipline to sustain these relationships.

Even though some of your mutual friends may need some time to adjust, it's also a good idea to take the initiative with the ones whom you want to preserve from the marriage. To some extent, this calls for putting your blinders on and seeing your formerly mutual friend in a new light, divorced as it were, from your husband. Invite these friends to do new things with you. For example, go to a book reading or a concert or some such, so that you build fresh reference points with them. Introduce them to your new beau only when you and they are ready for that.

Generally, it's a good idea to realize that they may feel as uncomfortable as you do about the situation and may be waiting from a cue from you. So, unless mutual friends make it clear that they want some distance from you, you shouldn't write them off if you don't hear from them right away. If you feel like it, reach out to them. As the therapist-writer Anne Newton Walther puts it frankly in her book *Divorce Hangover: A Successful Strategy to End the Emotional Aftermath of Divorce*, "It may not be fair that you have to make the first move when you're already struggling to stay afloat . . . but you are the one with the most to gain or lose. If you want to keep these relationships intact or at least give them the best possible chance of surviving, you have to take charge and direct the action."

The Politics of Sharing:
A Few Best Practices

Some friends manage to maintain dual allegiances to you and your husband, and it's wonderful when mutual friendships can overcome the strain of your divorce. You'll want to make mutual friends feel as comfortable as possible with the new situation. This means trying your darnedest to avoid putting them in the middle as a communicator or spy, and trying not to vent to them about your ex. Instead, rely on *your* friends for those deepest of confidences, for those times when you need to be catty. No matter how hurt you may have been, resist the temptation to win someone over to your side. With your mutual friends, you may have to consciously develop some new habits in order to preserve the neutral ground. For instance, tell them you will handle figuring out who will come to a given event of theirs to which you're both invited.

Indeed, there are bound to be a few social occasions hosted by mutual friends that might bring you and your ex together again: the cocktail parties, the weddings, and even the funerals. Unless you and your ex are blessed with a remarkably amicable arrangement, or you now live in different cities, these decisions about whether to go can be trying. For a couple of years, Sarah decided it just wasn't worth it to go to parties where she knew there was a good chance of seeing her ex-husband. Even when there wasn't a whole lot of bitterness between them, she knew she wouldn't be able to completely relax with him in the room, so she tended to decline party invitations from mutual friends and instead follow up with those friends one-on-one for a meal or drink.

During the first year of their separation, Kay and her ex took a more creative and collaborative approach to such situations. They had no trouble being at the same event if it was just the two of them, but if he wanted to bring his girlfriend, they would agree to split time at a party (i.e., you go from five to six and I'll go from six to seven). The arrangement was indeed somewhat odd, but they and their friends made light of it. One note of caution: as tempting as it may be, be careful of involving your host or hostess too much in any trials and tribulations in this department. They may have wondered a bit themselves whether you two should both be invited, but if they went ahead and did so, don't make them think twice about this by asking, for example, whether your ex has RSVP'd. Either ask him directly if he's going, don't ask him and take your chances, or don't go. If you go, psych yourself up to handle an encounter gracefully.

Obviously, there will be times when you cannot do a timeshare approach and when you cannot sit something out. For example, the funeral of a mutual friend brought Megan and her ex-husband together. He was there with his new girlfriend, which was an inherently awkward thing, but Megan could see the two were in as much pain as she was, so she went ahead and introduced herself to the girlfriend, acknowledged the sadness as well as the awkwardness of the situation, and thereby put everyone at ease. A few weeks later, she ran into the girlfriend, who thanked her profusely for being so kind. Of course, this kind of situation *should* bring out the best in everyone, but it doesn't always happen that way. Remember, you're usually really glad when you do not stoop to your lowest self, but instead rise to the occasion.

Inevitable Attrition

Of course, mutual friendships aren't just simple custody issues and attrition tends to happen pretty organically. Sometimes, one of you just ends up being closer to one friend or another. Or the friends themselves may even find it hard to maintain ties with one or both of you for a number of reasons.

They're Feeling Their Own Loss

Recognize that they are probably sad for themselves that they're losing you two as a couple. Over the years, they've become accustomed to your couplehood and they may be grieving this loss for a while. Even the most privately troubled husband and wife can make a great team in public, whether it was being entertaining dinner companions, moviegoers, or marathon runners. Give these friends who were close to you as a couple some time. If they can't come around to appreciate you as an individual, it's their loss.

They May Have Heard Only One Side of the Story

As our friend Patti recalls, "I didn't want to be caught up in the 'he said, she said' thing, so I let him tell all of our mutual friends. To this day, I have only one friend from our marriage." Of course, it doesn't need to go this way, but depending on how things happened, it very well might. Also, people are naturally going to hear more from the person they know best, potentially biasing them toward that person.

Maintaining Ties to One of You May Seem Like Disloyalty to the Other

Very close friends may still care about both of you but feel that if they are close to one of you, it would be strange to also be close to the other. Taken to the extreme, this can mean that some friends may drop both of you. For example, as Hope describes, "When we separated, we were still working together at the same small school, which was less horrible for us than it was for other people. No one wanted to choose sides, so no one wanted to hang out with either one of us, leaving us stranded. We'd go out to the movies together because there was no one else to go with!" Of course, Hope's case is unusual, but in general, your friends may need some time to adjust to the new situation, and you may need to communicate to them that they're not being disloyal if they also maintain a relationship with your ex.

Find Your Inner Diplomat, Especially with Mutual Friends

There may be times when you get that urge to tell your side of the story to the friends you and your ex shared. That impulse is perfectly normal, but we do advise that, as much as possible, you try to avoid bad-mouthing your ex in such a context. As Valerie put it, "The one thing I regret is that I went out of my way to make sure that everyone knew he was at fault. It's kind of embarrassing to look back on that." Why not bad-mouth him? You might feel a short-term satisfaction, but you risk making others not only feel uncomfortable, but also perceive you as bitter—not a good thing. Nine times out of ten, you'll feel a tad emotionally hungover and regretful the next day. If you want to preserve these friendships, it behooves you to be sensitive to people's relationship with your ex.

Discussing Your Ex, Gracefully, with Mutual Friends

Whenever possible, try to use neutral words and speak in the passive voice, or use "the marriage" as your subject, so that blame is not assigned. For example, "The marriage had become joyless," or "Counseling revealed some basic incompatibilities," or, if you have to, "The decision was not mine." We advise these tactics because no matter how good dissing him may feel in the moment, we promise it can leave a yucky taste in your mouth for weeks. There may be times when you can use an ironic twist of expression to get your point across, without revealing the exact data. For example, wasn't the late Princess Diana all the more admired for the way that, rather than state the obvious, she carefully asserted in the famous BBC TV interview, broadcast on ABC on November 25, 1995, "You see, there were three of us in the marriage . . ."

Sometimes, of course, you just don't have control over the way the news travels to your mutual friends. If you've been the one to initiate things, and your husband decides to be loose-lipped, the grapevine can feel pretty strangling. Our friend Greta, for example, who became involved with someone at her company when she still was married, relates her story: "People started to hear about it in the most spectacular fashion . . . One of my bridesmaids, who worked at my company in another division, ran into G. [Greta's ex] and he told her the story from his perspective, according to which, I was just this evil person. The next thing I know, it's all over the company. So, she dropped off my Christmas card list." If you find yourself becoming the topic of gossip, try to take a leaf out of Greta's book. You can't control the way people react, but you can control the way you feel about it all. As she put it, "I recommend one really good scandal in every girl's life. You haven't lived until you are the center of a scandal." As horrible as it is, things will get better. People will move on as the news gets stale, and you'll have lived something most people only read about in novels. Chalk it up to some true character-building.

Beware the Ventriloquist Impulse

If you're curious to get the occasional report about your ex, it can be tempting to inquire about him with mutual friends. This is only natural, and here and there, it's okay, but you don't want to abuse the privilege. Sometimes, a good friend will find a way to offer an update on the things she knows you'll be most curious about—your ex's new girlfriend or wife, for example. If you must find out a detail, ask what's on your mind, but try to do so with as disinterested or spontaneous an air as possible, so that the friend doesn't feel overly obligated to give you updates on your ex every time she sees you. No one wants to feel like the go-between.

Likewise, you'll want to be cautious with what you say to your mutual friends about your ex. Word may get back to him and, as we all know, third parties are not the best vehicle for communication. You may not even be conscious of your impulse to talk about him to others. Often talking about him in not-so-complimentary terms is a veiled effort to communicate with him. Check yourself to make sure that you're not doing this; as a strategy, this is neither very effective nor satisfying in the long run. If you've got something to say to him, it's much better to examine the message first and then decide whether to address him directly or whip out your journal and write him a letter you'll never send. As Sarah's closest confidante would say to her on such occasions, "But, Sarah, what's your objective?" Learning to answer this question honestly can be hard, but it will help you get to the root of your impulses and figure out if what you want to say is really worth it.

If You're the One Who Left

If you're the one who left, particularly if there is someone else in your life, it's inevitable that some friends may have a tough time sticking by you, especially if you had an affair. If this is the case, be ready for the fact that people may take your infidelity personally, as if you were unfaithful to *them*. As Greta put it, "I was definitely the bad guy because I had the affair."

Some women are really taken aback by the force with which their husbands try to turn their mutual friends against them in such an instance. Our friend Nancy, who was with her husband, N., for ten years, remembers, "Initially, everyone was really supportive, but N. really made people choose sides. He really spiraled out of control. I stopped speaking to any members of his family, and our mutual friends stopped speaking to me. And really, the only friends we had were mutual friends. It was horrible." To some extent, sympathy with the one who's been left is only natural, but if their sympathy for your husband turns into animosity against you, walk away from that friendship, even if it's a longtime one. It may sound trite, but if they can't forgive you for your role in the divorce, you really are better off without them.

If You're Not the One Who Left

Generally speaking, if you weren't the one to initiate the divorce, you may find yourself with a windfall of the mutual friends. Even when a split is reasonably amicable, there is still a tendency to side with the person who's been left. Maybe people liked you better than your husband, anyway. In this case, they may feel free to tell you what they always thought, and sometimes, this will yield insights that *can* be helpful if offered in moderation. After all, they've seen you two interact, and they've gotten to know you both over the years, and they are actually in a position to help you piece together the puzzle of what happened.

For some women, the transition from married to singleton is actually pretty smooth because of the lack of mutual friends. For example, as Maeve put it, "There was not a one [a single mutual friend] that we shared, which really should have told me something. On the other side of marriage, you realize how unconnected you really were."

Letting Nature Take Its Course

Often who retains which friends is nothing you work at consciously. It just happens depending on who's closer to the friends, who knew them first, and where each of you is in your interests, professional life, and personal needs. Because Kay and her ex had been together for almost nine years, a huge number of their friends were mutual. Since splitting up, Kay and her ex have shared several friends, but without being intentional, they have de facto split the remainder of the friends based on who was historically closer or had grown closer to the friends since their separation. Our friend Andrea took a charitable approach, detaching herself from their mutual friends because her ex-husband really had no other friends, whereas she had a great group of her own and a supportive family. But what goes around comes around, and in the end, these folks are back in her social circle. If she hadn't graciously let go the first time, who knows if she'd be friends with them now. Again, sometimes it pays to be generous.

Transitioning from Smug-Married to Swinging Singleton

At the risk of stating the obvious, unless you were like Maeve and really had no mutual friends, the way you socialize when you are married is different from the way you socialize when you're single. Married life usually brings with it dinner parties, double dates, and weekend trips with other couples. But what's important to realize in making the transition from being part of a couple to being on your own is that you can preserve much of what you enjoyed as a couple, only with greater freedom. For example, when Sarah and her husband separated, she realized she missed entertaining. But once she got used to throwing open her doors alone or cohosting a party with another girlfriend, she found entertaining sans husband had its own great pleasures: her own decision-making power on the music, the menu, and most of all, the guests.

Take a proactive approach, especially with single friends. They need you as much as you need them. If you're at all like us and the women in this book, you'll find that your friendships will blossom with your new status if you just give them a bit of energy. Cultivate and maintain good girlfriends at this critical time by reaching out and setting up drinks dates, movie dates, etc. Whether or not you have a man in your life, these friendships will be a tonic to you, even when you start to feel better and get distance from the darker times.

Planning vacation time by yourself or with a girlfriend or two can be a wonderful way to explore new places and create new traditions. Even if you're feeling financially stretched, you really should try to make room for those "investments in yourself." Such investments might be as simple as joining a new health club or as big as going to a beach house in the summertime or a ski house in the winter. The change of scenery and introduction to new people can do wonders. The summer after Sarah and T. separated, Sarah joined a group of people she really didn't know too well in a summer house on the New Jersey shore. No one except for one close friend knew she was going through the healing process post-divorce, which was liberating in itself (no need to talk). She remembers getting off that train and the smell of the ocean was instantly restorative.

Divorce Showers
According to a few sources, a growing trend among the recently divorced is a phenomenon known as "the divorce shower," parties where guests bring items to help you outfit your new home or your new self in general. In some ways, we suppose it makes logical sense. After all, after your ex has left your life, you may be missing some key items in your household and have to replace them. In an article called "Shower Power" by Jeffrey Cottrill in the January 2001 issue of *Divorce* magazine, Dan Courvette, the publisher of the magazine, put it this way: "A divorce shower, or party, is a great idea: psychologically, it's a good way to complete the past and start a new life; practically, it allows friends to offer moral support and/or gifts to help you through a difficult time." While we can't quite fathom asking a friend to host a "shower" (especially if you had a wedding shower only a few years ago), we could certainly see getting the same benefit out of a housewarming party that you host yourself, or that a friend helps you with.

Any excuse to crank up the Aretha Franklin or Gloria Gaynor and pop open some bubbly is fine in our book.

Happy @#$%&* Holidays!

Holidays are the classic time to get mired in sad memories, so it's doubly important to plan ahead, and rock out a new tradition. If you used to celebrate holidays privately with your husband, you may find yourself with your own family again. If home means stress in any way, consider going away for the holidays. Encourage your family members to go somewhere exotic. Kay and her mother couldn't bear the thought of Christmas in San Francisco, which used to be their tradition with Kay's ex, so since her divorce, they've gone to Mexico, New Orleans, and Amsterdam during Santa-time instead. Or celebrate with friends. Orphan Thanksgivings where everyone pitches in can be really fun. Sarah used to think of this process of creating new holiday memories as writing a word document, and hitting "save as new file" over the previous year's memories.

Get a copy of *Holidays on Ice* by comedian David Sedaris and realize you are not alone in having a hard time during these seasons. Allow yourself the occasional ironic laugh at holiday time. When Sarah realized she didn't have to worry about gifts for her in-laws, and that her Christmas card list was a bit shorter than it used to be, she felt ridiculously giddy about her freedom from the old obligations associated with T.

Then, of course, there are all of your personal holidays that can crop up to unsettle you—your wedding anniversary being one of the biggies. If you're having trouble with the symbolism of the day, definitely reach out to friends and family. If possible, schedule something fun for yourself to create new memories on that day, so that it becomes "July 16, the day Mom and I went to the spa" or "November 1, when I took my first sky diving lesson." As the anniversary or whatever personal holiday recedes in your memory—and it will, we promise—you'll have new associations and new connections.

Stigma, Be Gone

One of the upsides to the experience of being a divorcée is that you'll probably find yourself becoming less judgmental of other people; you've developed a more liberal lens on the world. As Caitlin said, "Before it happened to me, I remember some of the stigma I'd place on other marriages that had ended in divorce. I'd sometimes have a snide or sarcastic comment; I'd notice other people doing the same at dinner parties." Sarah felt the same way. After going through her own saga, she realized that marriages (and divorces) come in all shapes, stripes, and sizes, and you can never know what's going on in your neighbor's life. People will be learning lessons from you too, so be patient with them and with yourself. In the early days, it really is a major accomplishment to go into social settings without the armor and cover you were once accustomed to; but as you revise and expand your network of friends, be assured that your sense of self will emerge more authentically than ever before.

CHAPTER EIGHT

The Dating Scene — Take Two

When you first turn your attention from
your husband, your judgment is wild and
you can't potentially tell suitable people
from entirely wrong ones . . . there are
days when almost any man (or woman) in
the known world looks like a real
possibility.

—Jane Shapiro,
"This Is What You Need for a Happy Life"

You never thought you'd ever date again, let alone kiss another man and climb under the covers with him. Your life
was settled in the love department, and you'd retired that messy
arena known as dating. You listened to your single girlfriends
telling hilarious tales of the dating world like a spectator in nose-
bleed seats. You had taken a big sigh of relief and moved on to
more important matters such as who was going to take the
garbage out and whose parents you'd visit for the holidays.

And, then, ta-da! Everything in your life turned upside down and you became single again. It's a big shift in identity, behavior, and priorities, and it takes some adjusting. To boot, you're not just any single woman . . . you're a *divorcée*, which comes with its own particular joys, pitfalls, and, above all, potential.

We are going to encourage you to embrace the wonder of this unexpected fate, to see the amazing possibilities of this chance to start your love life over. We are also going to try to save you some of the grief we and our girlfriends experienced when reentering the singleton universe, while also realizing that you may need to learn some of these lessons in your own way and in your own time.

The Early, Somewhat Spastic Phase

Everyone's "early phase" lasts a different length of time. Generally, the longer you were married, the longer it will take you to regain your bearings in the realm of romantic relationships. Naturally, it's also a matter of individual personality. For some people, no matter how long they were married, it takes years to imagine being with anyone else again, while others find their new soulmates soon after the divorce. As we'll see, though, many divorcées go through an initial wacky period of six months to two years that can be filled with delicious novelty and exploration but also some loneliness and confusion.

Note to Self: Proceed with Caution

We hate to sound boring—we really do—but it's only wise, kind, and right for us to recommend that you be careful and handle yourself with kid gloves during the early period. Don't worry, we know you won't always follow this advice, and we didn't always follow it either in the early phase. We're just trying to make the journey a wee bit smoother for you. With this goal, we've collected a few brilliant insights to help you make better rather than worse decisions *most* of the time (after all, we're realists).

Brilliant Insight #1: You are phenomenally vulnerable, possibly only as vulnerable as when you were a gawky, tortured teenager. For this reason, you'll want to try to be as self-protective as possible. You may feel strong, but we promise you, this is a very cunning illusion. Once you're beyond the early period and strong in a real way, you'll look back and see just how off-kilter you were.

Brilliant Insight #2: You are still getting over your ex. It doesn't matter how "over it" you feel you are or how much you wanted the Big Split. You are still processing what happened in that relationship, and it's still informing the way you approach new ones. The more you face the demons of your past straight on and learn from them, the more likely you are to propel yourself into a happy future.

Brilliant Insight #3: You are unusually hungry for connection and acceptance, especially in the areas of your identity that were rejected or squelched by your ex. On the one hand, this hunger can encourage you to meet lots of exciting, new people and feel an exhilirating openness to humanity. On the other hand, you can find yourself needier than usual and supersensitive to rejection. Try to balance out time with thrilling new acquaintances or lovers with time by yourself and time with good, old friends you can trust.

Brilliant Insight #4: You are a dating novice again. You are learning all over again, or maybe for the first time as an adult, what it means to traffic in the world of uncommitted relationships. Take things slowly whenever possible, and get a lot of advice and support from your other single friends.

Now, with these gems of wisdom under your belt, you will likely lead a flawless life, making no mistakes and generally amazing the world with your exquisite grace and perfection under duress. *Not.* But perhaps keeping these things in mind will grant you a measure of self-awareness that might help with some of your choices and give you some perspective amidst the tumult.

You'll notice that while we counsel you to be self-aware and cautious, we do not advise you to postpone all dating activity until you're totally together, stable, evolved, and perfectly mended. Many people will kindly tell you not to get involved with anyone until you've gotten over the separation/divorce. Of course, this is highly sensible and rational counsel and is meant to be in your best interest. However, such advice is, in the words of our girlfriend Leslie, "utterly Victorian and unrealistic," not to mention no fun whatsoever. Given that you have just experienced a huge loss, it is only natural and understandable that you'd want companionship and someone to hug at night, even if you just met him at a cheesy club. So, on the flip side, do not lambaste yourself for engaging in some blatant rebound behavior or hooking up with someone too quickly or whatever shenanigans strike your fancy. You are a person recovering from a major debacle, and it only makes sense that you'll want to start fishing again and find reassurance that the sea really is pretty plentiful.

A Tendency Toward the Extremes:
Ice Queendom, Boy Mania, and Insta-marriage

In conversations with other women (and, yes, in our own lives), we've found that in the early period, women tend toward three different extremes. The first extreme involves becoming a somewhat aloof, asexual being, the second a boy-crazy freak, and the third a wife all over again, just with a different man whom you haven't yet married (and may not particularly want to).

"I am the Ice Queen"

Some women do not feel much like interfacing with XY-chromosomed creatures for a long spell after the big breakup. In fact, the thought might be utterly repellent. Especially if a woman

Not Your Mother's Divorce

has gotten very hurt and faced a huge betrayal in the divorce, she may tend to avoid relationships altogether and seal herself off emotionally and physically. Such a reaction is totally understandable and probably necessary before opening up to someone again. Sometimes we need to regroup and find our strength before we can even think about intimacy again.

For over a year after her separation, Delia said that whenever she met eligible men, she would feel that "you're all very attractive here, but I am in the fridge being an ice queen right now." Valerie voiced a similar sentiment: "I remember not being remotely interested in dating . . . I'd go out with friends, do the bar thing, and it was fun, but I never gave any guy my number. I just wasn't ready." It took Valerie time to reawaken her interest in men. She had some tickets for a trip she and her ex were supposed to take to Italy before they split up, and she took a girlfriend with her instead. The casual attention from the Italian men, as clichéd as it was, was enjoyable and her healing process began. Later, after dating only casually, she reconnected with an old guy friend whom she really trusted, and they eventually fell in love and got married.

If you're in the ice queen mode, don't feel down on yourself or push yourself to date before you're ready. Why rush? You can spend this time exploring what you enjoy, taking Thai cooking classes, Tae Bo classes, tie-dyeing T-shirts—whatever floats your cruise ship. You can go out and socialize with girlfriends, with guy friends, or in groups. You can be open to new people in this state of mind without needing to get involved with anyone. What you want to avoid is crawling into the cave of yourself, wallowing in the darkness there, and abstaining from *Homo sapiens* contact entirely. Get out and engage in the world, and eventually you'll feel ready again. As Leslie said in her interview, "Sometimes there's just no substitute for doing the time."

Boy Mania

Women who fall into this camp experience a period of incredible liberation and sexual exploration, even if they're sometimes on the verge of a nervous breakdown. They feel like teenagers again but with the hormones of a thirty-something woman in her sexual prime. Especially if your desire had died for your ex and you'd forgotten what lust felt like, you might find yourself in this mode. Enjoy it while you can and don't worry, you won't always be this randy.

Sydney reports, "I dated a lot. I was totally wild for about a year, dated a total babe from Holland and had a fling with a guy in England while I was there. I could not go a month without meeting someone and diving into a relationship with them." Maeve says about her early period, "I had the time of my life. I had never felt more beautiful, I had never felt more intelligent, I had never felt more sexual. I just loved boys."

One of our girlfriends, Trudie, reports, "I really got in touch with that part of me that when I was married thought, wow, I'm never going to sleep with anyone else." The dynamic with her ex-husband had been to be antisocial, so she started going out every night. She describes this period as "fiery and dangerous." She had "crazy email flirations" with guys she'd met only briefly. She says, "I just wanted to date all these people. I was incredibly open to new connections. When you're married, you can't stay and talk to a guy you meet at a party until 3 A.M. if you're enjoying it. When you're not married, it's all open, it's so wonderfully uncircumscribed. I felt like a kid again, like a child with this whole amazing world of people to explore." She warns, though, "You're dangerous to yourself and others when you're so open. You really don't know what you're doing, and you do stupid things. You're in a wild vortex of emotions." She feels her saving grace was that she also developed really strong girlfriend connections during the early phase: "I don't know where I'd be without the girl gang."

Many formerly married women, then, experience something of a romantic and sexual renaissance once they are single again. If you find yourself in this boy-crazy mode, just know that many of the connections you make during this time may be intense but short-lived and may not always leave you feeling fabulous. Your close friends, especially other single girlfriends, and family members will help you keep your feet somewhere near the ground, so stay in good touch with them between dates and nights out on the town.

After a period of time, you will likely find yourself tiring of the merry-go-round of guys. Caitlin commented about ending a long dating spree that had followed her breakup, "Suddenly, I felt too old to be doing this." Kay also remembers something clicking inside her after a rather wild New Year's Eve and realizing she wanted her life to return to normal and wanted to be in something serious again. Often, after the insanity dies down, you may find yourself facing some of the more difficult feelings left over from the divorce. And while they don't always feel good, processing them is the first step toward calming down and truly moving forward.

Insta-marriage

In the third scenario, women dive into a relationship with someone immediately so as to have a kind of ersatz husband. This response to your separation is entirely normal; after all, coupledom is all you've ever known in the most recent portion of your life. Our girlfriend Leslie says, "I got involved with my best friend, the guy who got me through [the breakup], it was classic. But I didn't really want to be with him, so I ended up hurting him badly." Indeed, many divorcées find they have fallen into something that is not viable for the long term. And while a warm body can ease the pain at times, it eventually leaves you feeling lonelier than ever.

Another girlfriend, Laura, also became involved with a guy friend from work who helped her through the breakup. On some level she knew he wasn't right for her, partly because he was quite a bit younger, but he was incredibly kind and totally there for her. She feels she needed someone like him to make it through the trauma of the divorce. She recalls, "I was kinda crazy in the relationship, very demanding . . . I will never act that way again. I wanted him to be there whenever I asked him and was very needy." Laura thinks that by throwing herself into this other relationship, she wasn't dealing with her feelings about the end of her marriage.

And that's the trouble with such insta-marriages. They make sense in the short run because they provide much-needed comfort and companionship, but they are usually not long-term solutions. Immersing yourself in a new relationship right away often means you are putting off the hard stuff, in other words, avoiding some necessary time grieving and learning to function on your own in the world. Only when you have spent some substantive time alone getting over the divorce and rediscovering yourself as an autonomous being will you be strong enough to make wise choices about who the right companion is for you.

Of course, we don't mean to suggest that it's an either/or scenario. It's entirely possible to be in a relationship with someone new and still be locating the black box of what went wrong in your marriage. People do it all the time; think of it as emotional multitasking. But if you do find yourself in a serious relationship soon after splitting from your ex, it's a good idea to safeguard some time by yourself, with family and friends, and perhaps with a counselor to make sense of your past and move more consciously into your future.

Beyond the Extremes and Out on the Scene: You're a Dating Spaz

Once you've migrated away from one of these extremes, or if you never embraced one, you'll find yourself in that absolutely fascinating and utterly perplexing new landscape known as "the dating scene."

Theoretically, you should know about relationships better than anyone. After all, you've been married. You've done the *real* thing. You have vast amounts of experience with intimacy, living with someone day in and day out, and long, hard conversations until early in the morning. Dating, however, is an entirely different world of relating. And it can take some time to figure out what the heck is going on out there in dating country after having been cocooned in a marriage (and probably a serious relationship leading up to the marriage) for any number of years.

Recall Brilliant Insight #1: your judgment right now is definitely questionable. You can potentially be very needy or very closed, and you can get hurt or be hurtful, depending on how you're dealing with the divorce. We're not sure you can totally avoid going through these things, but it's useful to keep your altered state in mind and possibly alert those with whom you're involved.

The World Is Your Petri Dish:
"Experimental Dating"

We encourage you to approach the dating scene with an attitude of experimentation and openness. You're in a period of redefining yourself and you're somewhat protean; different kinds of relationships can help you figure out who you are and what you want. *The Complete Idiot's Guide to Surviving Divorce* calls this "experimental dating," defined as "dating many different kinds of people casually without any deep involvement or commitment."

Don't necessarily focus on Mr. Right but on Mr. Right Now. Embrace the "transitional figures," those men who you know won't last long but who make for excellent company for a spell because they make you feel good about yourself or introduce you

to something new. Our girlfriend Maeve says she got some wonderful advice when she first started dating again: "If you don't
know what you want, date everyone." She took this approach, accepting every date she was offered, and realized, "There's a wealth
of people out there I never would have picked for myself." She
later ended up marrying one of those guys she never would have
picked for herself and finds herself incredibly happy.

Think of the dating process as just getting to know people
and figuring out what works for you and what doesn't. Gina advises, "Just be open and see how it goes. A date can end up being a friend or a lover or whatever. The goal is not to make a
guy your husband but to discover him and have him discover
you." Several of the women we spoke with became friends with
several of the guys they casually dated and met other people
through those guys. Of course, you will have your standards and
will need to rule guys out when necessary, but stay open to the
unexpected and don't be too goal-oriented or picky. As Tanya
says, "You may not like the guy but maybe you go to a party
with him and you like his friend or his cousin or his roommate!"
In other words, get in touch with that opportunist streak that
lurks within us all.

Sometimes the experimentation might become too much
and take you places you don't want to go, and you may want to
mellow out or focus inward for a while. For instance, Sarah had
been on two dates with D., who was about fifteen years her senior, when she accepted a third date to go turkey hunting with
him. There she was, in a camouflage jumpsuit, stalking turkeys
in the woods with a strange man who had a shotgun in his
hands. It sort of makes her shudder to think about it now, just
how open she was to new experiences. You will have to gauge
when you have gone overboard, and you'll know it when you
have. The hilarious stories from the dating world can make you
a great raconteur, for sure, but they also teach you about what

you enjoy and what you don't, what's in your comfort zone and what's *way* beyond it.

Defy the Checklist:
Rediscovering Your Type

Many of us think we have a "type." You hear women say, "I only like tall guys." Or, "I only like dark-haired guys." Or, "I only like really artsy guys." This is what you think you want, your ideal, which is not necessarily what would really make you happy or the only thing that could make you happy. In fact, your ex-husband may have had many of the qualities of your ideal type and well, we hate to remind you, but that didn't work out. Having really strict criteria for men, especially superficial ones, may also be a way of avoiding intimacy by dismissing potentially amazing guys before you even get to know them.

We recommend you jettison the checklist, get out of your head, and experiment with what really makes you happy (or makes you gag) so that you're living in reality and not some myopic fantasy land. Kay had mostly dated guys over six feet, and her ex-husband was 6'2". At first when she reentered the dating scene, she only liked tall guys. Eventually, though, after being attracted to several men under six feet, she realized it wasn't that important after all. Plus, with guys under six feet, she no longer had to stand on her tiptoes to hug a man (she's only 5'5"), which ultimately was far more comfortable.

Before she was married and divorced, Gina tended to write off "nice guys"; she thought she had to be with a tough guy who could handle her sarcasm and strength. Now she's experimenting with guys who are expressive and emotional. Her ex-husband had also been very money-oriented, and she thought that she needed someone who could be a serious breadwinner. Since her divorce, she's dated guys who have no money and are totally unmaterialistic. In this whole process, she's realized what really matters to her: she likes people, including men, who are passionate and alive, open-minded and solution-oriented. Her criteria have changed entirely, and she feels like she now knows what she really wants and what makes her genuinely, deeply happy.

Doing a 180

One form of defying your checklist is being attracted to or getting involved with guys who are pretty much the opposite of your ex-husband. Human nature being what it is, sometimes we need to swing from one extreme to the other to make progress. For instance, our girlfriend Leslie didn't find her ex-husband intellectually challenging enough for her, so she reports, "Every guy I've been with since him is off-the-charts brilliant." Trudie feels her boyfriend, A., who is extroverted, happy, and easygoing, represents a pendulum swing away from her ex-husband, who was introverted, depressive, and dark.

If you find yourself getting involved with someone strikingly different from your ex-husband, don't be surprised. Use it as a chance to figure out what works for you. A 180-degree pirouette away from your ex may be just what you need, for now and in the future. One thing dating someone other than your ex-husband teaches you is that there are wonderful and difficult things about every relationship and every combination of people. You may find yourself missing some things about your marriage even while you are very happy and maybe even more happy with a different kind of guy. There is no such thing as perfection. Rather, there is better/happier and worse/unhappier. And there are different ways of being in love and loving someone. Dating someone other than your ex-husband is a lesson in relativity and in how different the dynamics can be between two people. And, if you haven't already, you're probably shedding the notion that there is or ever was a single "one" for you.

Dating for Dummies . . . Uh, Divorcées

Both of us and many of the women we spoke to acted somewhat oddly after emerging from a marriage and reentering the sometimes confusing world of dating. You must face the harsh truth: you're a dating dork. Don't worry, you're not doomed. You just need to keep some things in mind and recognize that you have been out of practice for some time. Here are some basic pointers we can pass along after having spent some time in this new land and talking to other divorcées about their travels there.

It's One Big Process of Elimination

An important thing to know is that a guy you meet or go on a date with does not have to ever get in touch with you again. You're used to someone who (at least at one time) you could rely on to call you back and who you could call anytime. In the dating world, there is no obligation for either party to call each other after a first, second, even third rendezvous. If a guy doesn't call, he's not interested, he's commitment-phobic, whatever. Don't fool yourself that he's busy, traveling, and so on. Someone who's interested will be in touch. Elizabeth says she was shocked when a guy she'd been set up with by her sister didn't call or return her call after what had seemed like a successful first date. She "just didn't realize people could or did operate that way." At first, Gina would feel bad when a guy didn't call back and think, "I'm too old, I'm too fat, etc." She says, "But then I learned not to take it personally and realized it's a weeding-out process. You don't want to be with someone who doesn't want to be with you anyway. And you're weeding people out too." Right on, sister!

Avoid Inadvertent Stalking

Be careful not to engage in premature couple behavior just because it's what you know best. If you like a guy, it can be tempting to treat him as you did your husband: call and email all the time, include him in everything in your life, or have sex right away. Especially if you think he has a lot of potential, go *slooowly*. Jennifer Aniston is rumored to have waited nine months before having sex with Brad Pitt (now that's discipline!). Our girlfriend Sydney says that after jumping into things with numerous guys in the early period after her divorce, she took things at a snail's pace with her now-husband: "I didn't fall into my old pattern of acting married right away. I didn't rush in at all. I didn't expect anything." We don't recommend the slower approach because we're Victorian or scheming devotees of *The Rules: Time-Tested Secrets for Capturing the Heart of Mr. Right*. We recommend it because you don't want to ruin something good by overwhelming the guy and yourself before you even know what's there. You want to make sure he is as great as you think and, if it is a wonderful thing, you want to savor and enjoy that initial ga-ga period.

Shadow and Gesture

Nuance is the language of dating. You know how marriage counselors always talk about being direct in your communication and not sending messages passively or obliquely? Well, throw all of that information out the window and forget it for now. When you are dating, you enter into the world of subtlety and suggestion. Each of you makes small advances and retreats, sending messages to the other without explicitly pronouncing "I really like you right now" or "I'm really not sure about you right now" or "I need some space." Until you've developed deeper trust and intimacy with someone, these more indirect forms of communication often make sense. The reality is that it will likely take you a little while to figure out how you feel about the person, and you want to allow some ambiguity on both sides while you do this, so send and read messages without worrying too much over what any single message might mean. Time will always tell how you or someone else really feels, and if you ever get serious, you'll likely get more direct as well.

To Thine Own Self Be True,
Without Oversharing

Before confiding in someone, make sure they are trustworthy and someone deserving of your intimacy. Be yourself, but don't spill your guts. It's very important to try to be true to yourself as much as possible when on dates or dating someone. Pretending to be someone you're not won't get you very far. In fact, a good barometer of how things are going with a guy is if you feel comfortable to be yourself around him. After being nervous and shy on a number of dates, Gina realized, "Now I'm just going to be myself and see how it goes. It's a favor to find out earlier rather than later whether it's going to work. Be yourself and attract the right one versus a handful of bad ones." The caveat is that "being yourself" does not mean revealing every one of your deep dark secrets before dessert. Whether you view it as "being mysterious" à la *The Rules* or honoring your own privacy, going slowly on the information front means you are confiding in a guy only once you are ready and know he is worthy—an important measure of self-respect.

Safe Sex or No Sex

We hate to sound like the teacher in a Peanuts special droning on about something you already know, but having sex in the singles world comes with some pretty serious risks, and divorcées can be somewhat oblivious to this reality after having been in a monogamous relationship for years. You're used to unprotected sex with someone you trust, and you're out of practice having sex with someone whose sexual history you barely know. First off, as we discussed above, although your instinct may be to rush into things sexually because you're used to a high level of sexual intimacy, you want to venture into this realm as slowly as possible. There are many things that can happen before intercourse, and you may want to explore these for a while first. Once you do get to the act itself, you absolutely must insist on a condom—without an ounce of equivocation. Any guy worth his salt is going to know it's the best thing for him and may even suggest it first. If a guy balks or refuses, this is a very bad sign about his judgment and general intelligence. You can say, "Look, you don't know who I've been with and I don't know who you've been with, and it's not worth the risk for either of us." If he really hates condoms or has technical trouble with them, you two can enjoy yourselves other ways. But you must be strong in this regard. Not only is it incredibly important for your health, it's also, once again, an important assertion of self-respect.

Going with the Gut

In our experience, you'll usually know by the second or third date whether you're vaguely interested in a guy. If you're not looking even slightly forward to the date by the third date, you're probably not into it. Kay often experienced a "first-date rush" whereby she would find most guys handsome, engaging, and promising on the first date but then by the second or third, felt no more spark. We're not saying you'll know if you want to marry the guy, we're saying you will know whether you want to explore it further. Sometimes it's just a little hunch that keeps you going. Sometimes you know the guy isn't your next big hearthrob, but he's good company and likes to do the same things you do. But if hanging out with a guy seems like a chore, stop arranging new dates with him and wasting his and your time. Sarah knew it was time to stop seeing B. the tennis player when doing her laundry seemed more compelling than watching the U. S. Open with him. We know it sounds obvious, but don't date someone out of obligation—you're really not doing anyone a favor.

Nipping Things in the Bud

When you've had only a few dates with a guy, it's often easiest to show your lack of interest by acts of omission: not calling back, not returning email, and cancelling dates without rescheduling. Sometimes it might make sense to be more direct, as in the case of someone you were set up with by friends, someone who doesn't get the subtle hints, or someone you'd really like to have as a friend but have no interest in romantically. Your common sense and decency should dictate when a situation deserves more formal closure, but in many of these cases, email can be a good modern option. You can write and say how great it was to meet him and then use any number of excuses: "I'm not ready to date right now," "I'm really busy at work and can't manage a love life right now," or "I met someone about the same time as you and want to explore that relationship so am not available right now." Finally, the divorce can be an excellent excuse: "I'm still getting over it," "I'm emotionally unavailable," etc. Valid or not, no one is going to press you on it.

Of course, there are no set rules to dating or any of the other important things in life. Most of what matters in dating will pertain to specific instances, and your single girlfriends, especially those who have been actively dating, are your greatest asset in this regard.

Finding Your Inner Flirt

After having banished her to the attic or the basement for the time you were married, now's the time to reacquaint yourself with your "inner flirt," that part of you that enjoys the thrill of getting to know a new guy and wowing him with your snazz, pizzaz, beauty, brains, and more. Flirting is a state of mind. It's about engaging in a sense of play about human contact and connection. It's about charming someone and letting yourself be charmed, about delighting in someone's vitality and having him delight in yours. It's frothy and joyous, not deep or serious. It's about instant gratification, not long-term goals. Again, it's a mind-set. It's not about looking for your next husband, it's about savoring interaction with great people, including men.

And, although you may not know it, you're most likely more desirable than ever with the newfound confidence you've gained from going through something as monumental as a divorce. In our experience, exuding an inner strength is much more compelling to the opposite sex than an hourglass figure. Many divorcées find themselves getting more male attention after their divorce than before they were married. So, use the divorce as a chance to meet different men and see what works for you and what doesn't. The chance to flirt may not last forever, so enjoy the freedom while you can—flirt 'til it hurts!

Places to Go Hunting and Fishing

Sometimes you're ready and interested in dating again but, having lived a coupled life for so long, it's hard to know where to start. You can feel the occasional pang of despair and mild desperation of, how the heck am I going to meet single men who are vaguely in my ballpark? Where do they go? Is there one bar in town where I will find them all? We haven't yet located that watering hole where the single dreamboat guys hang out, but we do have some tips on how to get yourself out there to increase the chances of meeting someone you like. As our now-married friend Barbara said about her many years of being single, "It's a numbers game, and you gotta increase the numbers to increase the odds."

Blind Woman's Bluff

One of the best ways to meet guys who might share similar priorities, lifestyles, interests, and outlooks is through good friends.

Let friends know you are open to being set up. You can give some parameters, for instance no one under thirty or only someone who's interested in a serious relationship, but try to be adventurous and "game" to the whole experience. Sarah had a policy of refusing no setups and eventually met her second husband on a blind date.

Many of us who were married have never been on blind dates and may have to swallow some pride and anxiety about going on one. But once you relinquish the natural hang-ups about this whole genre of dating, it can actually be a fascinating experience to see who friends think might be your type and to try to get to know this virtual stranger well enough to know if you're interested.

An alternative to the standard going-out-to-dinner approach is doing something together, such as going to an art show or taking a hike, so that your focus isn't totally on staring into each other's souls. Another approach is to go out to dinner or drinks with the friends who are introducing you. This kind of situation is somewhat less high-stakes than a one-on-one blind date because you don't have to focus solely on each other and, if there's no spark, both of you can walk away fairly unscathed by the experience. You also get to see each other interact with other people, which can be revealing.

Of course, if the setup is not a hit and you're not interested, you'll need to handle the hosing of the guy (if he's still pursuing) very gingerly and tactfully because you don't want to jeopardize your relationship with your friends. If your friends are truly friends, they won't be bothered at all if it doesn't work out. Any rational person knows that although love may be blind, you don't always find it on blind dates.

Accidental Boyfriends

Sometimes what you're looking for is right in front of your eyes, it's just so obviously placed that you can't see it. We and several of our girlfriends had the experience of rethinking some of our guy friends after becoming single again and finding them a tad more interesting as potential romantic mates than before, especially because the trust and mutual history was already established. Sometimes friendships evolve nicely into relationships, and the experience can be much more relaxed than dating someone whom you're meeting for the first time.

However, you'll want to tread somewhat carefully, because if the friendship is important to you, it can become strained or damaged by romantic involvement. For instance, after getting separated, Kay had a flirtatious friendship for a while with a longtime guy friend and then when he wanted to cross the line (and she realized at that moment she didn't), the friendship fell apart. Take it slowly and gauge your feelings carefully so you're sending only the signals you want to. And if it doesn't work out, it may take some extra effort to rebuild the friendship.

Like guy friends, old boyfriends or crushes can have a way of coming out of the woodwork when you tell them or they learn about your new single status. And, like a friendship that transforms into a romance, renewing these connections with these guys is only natural because you have some level of trust and familiarity. This scenario is especially common if you're in the thirty- to forty-something set. Maeve said about the period after her divorce, "At this age, a lot of men are doing the recycling program. Every one of my ex-boyfriends called. They were either getting divorced or hadn't been married. It was that last scamper. It was fun." Elizabeth reconnected with an old flame from college after her divorce, and they went out for several months. So, whether it's with an old guy friend, boyfriend, or longtime crush, your new singledom creates a window for you to reconsider romance with guys you never thought you would.

Cyber-Romance

These days many people are turning to the Web to meet people. If you think about it, going to a dating site is like going to a singles event but without the excruciating embarrassment of actually having to attend. Like singles events, dating sites have an advantage over most other places you might go to meet someone: they are filled with single people *looking* to date. If it's a numbers game, the numbers are very good online. From our anecdotal experience, there are many more guys online than women, so it's not hard at all to get dates this way. We have several good friends who met their now-serious boyfriends on sites like www.match.com and www.nerve.com, so don't dismiss the idea completely. Both of the sites mentioned have good tips for how to create ads, reply to ads, and protect your personal safety. Most of it is common sense, but we still recommend apprising yourself of some of the norms of the online dating scene before venturing into it.

A Few Pointers About Online Dating

Online dating seems like a low-maintenance thing to do, but according to many of our girlfriends, if you take it seriously, it can be somewhat all-consuming. In any case, it can take *a lot* of time and energy, so you'll need to assess whether you're up for it. You'll be opening up the floodgates to hundreds of potential callers, and the question is whether you really want to swim that hard and fast. If you do end up diving into the torrents, you'll find yourself constantly checking who has written you or written you back, not to mention all the phone dates and real-live dates that emerge from all the e-flirting. Basically, it can become your life. Our girlfriend Angela found herself canceling dates with friends and leaving social engagements early because she had to get home to check her overflowing Inbox.

Many women take the approach of simply posting an ad and seeing who expresses interest. If you put a picture in your ad, as long as you don't have two heads, you will get lots of responses. Our friend Stella created an Excel spreadsheet to manage all her e-suitors, with lots of notes to herself so she could remember them, things like "studly picture, weird email about crystals." It's a rigorous process of elimination, and you'll want to read people's profiles very carefully to figure out if you even want to engage in any communication with them. Then, after you've separated the wheat from the chaff, you'll want to try to get to know the ones whose profiles you liked better by email and then possibly by phone before actually meeting them face-to-face. Don't waste precious hours of your days and evenings with guys you could have eliminated with a few more email exchanges.

Some women prefer to find the men instead of having men find them. Tanya would identify men she might be interested online and then email them with a link to a website with her pictures and profile. She says she knew she was asking for a lot more rejection but she felt this approach was safer and more efficient. She was going after what she wanted as opposed to having lots of unsavory or inappropriate guys come after her.

Although the numbers are good online, it's still a numbers game, and you may need to interact with dozens of men before you find one even remotely suitable for you. Angela says she sorted through countless men and went on dates with over twenty before finding her present husband. It's best to take a very rational approach and try to just move at a quick clip through as many people as possible until you land on someone you might actually want to date. Although at times it can be discouraging to encounter so many people you don't click with, we promise that you are learning more and more about what you *do* want so that when the right one comes along, you'll know to press Save instead of Delete.

Get Thyself Out the Door

Aside from some of these more deliberate approaches to meeting men, the best way to rack up the numbers and make yourself available is to get beyond your doorstep and out where there are people, particularly people you haven't yet met. Sitting on your couch watching TV or reading a magazine will not get you anywhere in the realm of romance, nor will hanging out with old friends night after night. Of course, sometimes these things are what you feel like doing and that's fine, but if you want to date, you need to get out into the world. Accept every invitation you get for a party, brunch, happy hour, and wedding (it's a cliché but weddings are often great places to meet people). Walk your dog places where there are other dog walkers. Bring some work to a café and glance occasionally at the cute guy with the laptop. Take classes in things you're interested in, engage in volunteering, and join groups that hold events you might like to attend, for instance a museum that has regular openings or an outdoor adventure group that has regular trips or hikes.

Bars are also possible venues for meeting someone for the simple fact that they are filled with men. While many of the men may not be the most appropriate, lots of good guys go to bars too. Of course, you'll want to choose tasteful bars with higher percentages of acceptable blokes and avoid the seedy ones. Kay actually met several men going out in San Francisco with her friend Jackie. They found that if they simply planted themselves at the bar, guys would come and talk to them. Sitting at the bar makes you open and approachable—a guy can always use the excuse of ordering a drink—whereas sitting in a booth or at a table makes the stakes generally too high for a guy to approach you.

Singleton Girlfriends: Your Greatest Asset

If you don't already have girlfriends who are single or have recently been single for a significant period of time, find them.

These women will be an incredible resource for you both because they are in a similar phase of life and because they know the ropes of the dating world better than you. As Gina says, "Talk to your single girlfriends who have been doing the scene for a while, *not* your married friends, since they haven't dated for a long time and generally have no clue since they are in a long-term commitment mind-set. Anything they may have known at one point, they've forgotten!"

After having been in a long-term relationship for almost nine years (and married for four of those), Kay discovered that she had almost exclusively married friends, many of whom had children and none of whom were interested in going out to drink lemon drops and scope out the guys. Through one very social single girlfriend, she developed a whole new group of single friends who have been invaluable sources of insight and support. In the beginning of your new single life, you may want to actively cultivate your few single girlfriends and make an effort to meet their other single friends. Or, if you don't have *any* single girlfriends, take classes or join organizations where you might meet new people. It may take some time and energy to meet women you really like, but good single girlfriends are absolutely critical for thriving in your new single life and surviving the perplexing and sometimes vexing world of dating.

Discussing the Ex and the Big D on a Date

There are different approaches you can take to broaching the subjects of the ex-husband and your divorce with romantic prospects. One thing seems to be true: the more comfortable you are with the fact of the divorce, the more comfortable your communication will be and will likely make the other person.

One approach is to be discreet about the divorce and simply call your ex-husband "my ex" and not discuss the divorce until you're somewhat more serious with someone. With this approach, you're not hiding the information, rather you're simply not making a big deal out of it and treating the marriage as an important, long-term relationship without mentioning the marital bit.

If you've been set up on a blind date, of course, it's likely that your mutual friend or acquaintance has mentioned the fact or has asked permission to tell your blind date beforehand. This can be a relief because your divorce is a given and you don't have to gear up to broaching the subject.

Some people feel dishonest if they don't reveal the fact that they were divorced early on. Our girlfriend Tanya, for instance, mentions her divorce matter-of-factly in the first couple weeks of a relationship, because she doesn't want to give the impression of hiding something. She also makes clear it was five years ago and is not a big deal to her anymore. She says it's never been an issue with anyone she's dated, and she thinks that's because she's very much over it and comfortable with it. Indeed, many men are more comfortable with your divorcée status than you might think. The commonality of divorce in today's culture means that most guys are okay with the idea, at least in principle. Gina actually took an informal poll of her guy friends and asked whether they thought it was worse for a woman to be divorced or to never have been married at thirty-three (her age at the time), and the majority of men said the latter was worse! So, if you don't treat it like a stigma, your date probably won't either.

Sarah actually felt that her divorce somehow gave her an air of mystery and experience with other men and that it sent the message that she wasn't desperate to get married. Like Sarah, many divorcées feel much less panicked about actually getting married than many women who have not yet tied the knot, which can be a very attractive quality to the eligible bachelor. In any case, if you look at the divorce as a positive or neutral thing, you will likely communicate this as well.

If, on the other hand, you find yourself feeling shame while disclosing the information to a date, it may be a signal that you have some work to do before coming to terms with the divorce. As Gina says, "Until you feel good about the divorce yourself, other people's reactions will bother you, so if you focus on getting comfortable with the divorce yourself, dealing with others will follow."

How a guy reacts to the news is also revealing about his emotional maturity and makeup. Leslie reports that learning about her divorce, especially the fact that she had left her husband, scared several of the men she dated. She says, "All guys want you to be emotional virgins; they don't want you to have loved or married anyone else." Her present boyfriend, though, is very different; he's very confident and it doesn't bother him at all that she's been married.

On the flip side, a blind date once asked Elizabeth how her divorce happened, so she told him in a very terse and matter-of-fact way, and then after the date, she never heard from him again. He later told their mutual friend who had set them up that Elizabeth's explanation of the divorce just reinforced his fear of commitment (he had been engaged twice and broken off the engagement both times). So, communicating about your divorce is an opportunity to see how comfortable *both* you and the guy are with the fact of your previous marriage and with the whole institution of marriage.

Desperado, Why Don't You Come to Your Senses?

A word about that awful, nauseating feeling known as desperation that can befall you after months or years on the dating scene without any quality prospects, or after yet another relationship that doesn't work out: you need to fight it with all the moxie you can muster. Like a mantra, you need to keep telling yourself—because it's true—that one day you will meet someone right for you and that it's just a matter of time and effort. You absolutely need to keep your chin up and conjure up faith from the depths of your spirit—and catch yourself if you lapse into doomsday thinking. You need to have persistence. Namely, you need to keep getting out there and meeting people in whatever ways work for you, and recognize that dating is not always fun. In other words, it may take a good bit of work to find someone right for you.

You also need to be patient: accept that it will take time and manage your anxiety about your age or how long it's taking, because anxiety really doesn't do you much good and it's also highly unattractive. Having patience allows you to keep your standards high, which they should be since we're talking about your *life*. Wait for someone you feel really good about and who feels really good about you. You want to avoid or get out of "better than nothing" relationships. They are a colossal waste of time. It's truly better to be alone than close yourself off to other possibilities by staying in a mediocre-to-bad relationship. You will meet someone right for you, we promise. Your job is just to keep hope alive and keep catapulting yourself out of your apartment.

Slouching Toward Serious

You might wake up one day and find yourself in something bordering on serious, in something that could legitimately be called "a relationship." After having been married, it can be strange to be in a real and bona fide thing again with someone else. Your marriage is probably still your primary point of reference and you may find yourself comparing and contrasting your new relationship with your marriage to your ex. Overall, becoming serious with a new person can be amazing, teaching you about a different kind of love and about yourself as a different kind of person in a relationship. There are also, of course, some particular issues that come with having been married before that are useful to keep in mind as you find yourself wandering into intimacy again.

The Residue of the Divorce

Unless your divorce was a loooong time ago or you have super-human capacities to get over things, there is a strong chance that the demise of your marriage will inform your feelings, reactions, and behavior in future serious relationships. This is not to say you are destined to repeat past mistakes or fated to be forever plagued by the issues brought out by the divorce. It just means you may need to acknowledge and tackle some of the ways the divorce still affects you in order to make conscious, smart choices in a new relationship.

What Me, a Commitment-Phobe?

You've been married, so how could you have commitment phobia? You made the biggest commitment one can make in the realm of love. However, people who have been very committed at one point only to have that commitment go sour, let them down, or compromise them in some way can develop such a phobia, even if they really believe they're not the type.

Gina dated a wide assortment of men for a while and didn't get serious with anyone. Now she's met someone, but despite how much the new relationship delightfully surprises her, she says, "If I think about him for the next few years, I shake in my shoes. If I think about him for the next three months, I'm okay. If I think about him for the next week, I'm great. Right now I'm just taking it one day at a time until I feel like it's not going to freak me out. I lost my individuality in my marriage, so now it's very important to me to maintain it."

Some divorcées, then, find it difficult to commit again once they find someone they feel more serious about. In some cases, it's fear of failure, fear that the relationship might end like the last one. Other women, like Gina, have trouble committing because last time they did, they lost themselves and they never want that to happen again. If you find yourself experiencing commitment phobia, you'll want to be aware of it and guard against it under-mining a relationship that means a lot to you. You may even want to share the sources of your commitment phobia with your part-ner so he understands your behavior and doesn't necessarily take it personally.

Overcorrecting and "The Negativity Bias"

Especially if you feel that you made a pretty fundamental mistake in marrying the person you did, you can find yourself hyper-vigilant about not making a mistake again. This means that once you become involved in a serious relationship, you are hyper-aware of all the problems and all the ways things could go wrong down the road. Our girlfriend Leslie calls this "the negativity bias," the instinct to extrapolate from every little thing that goes wrong to a problem you are going to have for the rest of your life. Positive things that happen in the relationship, on the other hand, are only wonderful exceptions.

Leslie has been living with O. for over a year. Originally, they fell madly in love and felt that they had finally met their true equal. However, they have hit some stumbling blocks, and she feels she overreacts to them because of her divorce. "I didn't see any of the potential issues with my ex-husband or with the mar-riage and went into it kind of blind, without any idea of what I was getting into. Now I see only problems and have a hard time believing it can work. I can feel helpless, out of control, over-whelmed, and plagued by the fear that it won't work out."

For some time after her divorce, Sarah had a negativity bias, too, overcorrecting for the mistakes she made in her marriage. Men she dated after her husband were viewed through a much more critical lens. She had been so willing to overlook faults in her first husband and flaws in their relationship, that she was stu-pidly tough on some comparatively minor issues in her next big relationship. About dating after her divorce, Valerie also says, "I became incredibly picky. Usually, I'm able to overlook some things, but it was like everyone's faults were magnified."

If you find yourself tortured by the negativity bias, you'll have to work to counteract it so that you don't let an underlying pessimism, sense of disappointment, or fear stemming from your divorce kill a promising relationship. Try to remind yourself, either mentally or by making an actual list, of what you find attractive about this person and what originally drew you to him. Also think about how this person meets needs that did not get met in your marriage. There may indeed be problems in the relationship, but you need to acknowledge there are differences in every union and it's not a question of whether they exist, but whether you can live with the ones that exist in this relationship. And that's the operative word—*this* relationship. You need to regularly remind yourself that you are dealing with a different person who is not your ex and that this new relationship is not at all destined to repeat the problems of your marriage, especially if you identify what they were and take responsibility for your part in making them happen.

Dealing with Guys' Insecurities (Not That They'd Ever Call Them That)

As we've discussed, you may have baggage that you carry in from the divorce, but the reality is, the guys who come to care about you a lot may bring their own Samsonite into the situation.

As Leslie expressed earlier, guys can want you to be "an emotional virgin" who has never loved or married anyone else. They can feel threatened by the very serious relationship you had with another guy and they can even feel competitive with him, wondering if they are being as good of a lover, boyfriend, provider, etc. to you. Greta laughs at how her longtime boyfriend will say about her ex-husband, "Bet he never made you waffles." Kay's first serious boyfriend after her divorce would mock funny clothes on other men, saying, "That's like something F. would wear, right?," effectively making a jab at her ex-husband, known for his unconventional sartorial style.

Both of these men had insecurities but kept them under control and made light of them through humor, a great way to normalize any residual tension over your ex. Some men, though, can get so scared by the ghost of your ex that they run away. One of our girlfriends, Gisele, fell in love with R. while her marriage was disintegrating. They were happily dating when she received a letter from her ex one day and started crying. R. broke off the relationship very suddenly, explaining later that he was "freaked out" by her strong emotional reaction to the letter.

It takes a man with a good dose of confidence to accept the fact that you have been married and may still be grappling with some feelings about your ex and the relationship. Give a guy who can cope with these things a lot of credit and realize that it may not always be easy to hear about your ex. Put yourself in his shoes, hearing about a woman he was serious about, and you can imagine how he might sometimes feel. Recognize the insecurities he has that aren't stated explicitly but come out through humor and, without being explicit about it, reassure him of the ways he's great for you. And, if a guy can't hack the reality of your past, there's not that much you can do about it. It may be a sign of pretty deep insecurities on his part that don't bode so well for a long-term relationship anyway.

Love Life—Take Two

It's never possible to truly start your life over, but it's certainly possible to get a new lease on life and reinvent it quite radically. In fact, it's rare in life that we have this chance to take another pass at a huge life decision. If you try to view your divorce in this way, you're likely to enjoy the wild world of dating and the fascinating and enlightening experience of getting serious with someone other than your ex.

Sometimes moving on may mean taking some steps back to

tie up loose ends and achieve more complete acceptance and peace about the divorce. Mehta was totally convinced she was over her first marriage when she went through a self-help course that brought up a lot of emotions, including guilt over leaving her first husband. She called her ex-husband sobbing and said some things she really needed to say. She feels that experience freed her up to truly close that chapter and open a new one with her second husband, J.

One thing a lot of divorcées reported is that when they exited their marriage and entered the dating scene, they were different people than when they got married. They were more confident, more comfortable with their bodies and sexuality, and more truly themselves and true to themselves. Women who divorce young have a chance that many women who are married don't have—to go out into the world at an age and time in their lives when they are more fully evolved as people and more likely to make a wise decision about who to share their lives with. You are powerful now—all the more strong, resilient and wise for having gone through the divorce—and, if you make sure to learn the lessons of your divorce, you have a high likelihood of creating a fabulous new love life and choosing a companion who makes you genuinely happy.

CHAPTER NINE

Retying the Knot—Or Not

Love is lovelier, the second time around.
Just as wonderful, with both feet on the
ground.

—Sammy Cahn and
James Van Heusen

So, what's a chapter on marriage doing in a book like this? If you're anything like us or the women in this book, it's quite likely that in the early stages of your post-divorce life, and even many years later, you might not feel particularly enthusiastic about marriage. Your trust might be shaken. Along with Bridget Jones, you might be mystified by those smug-marrieds that seem to be everywhere and cannot imagine being one of them again. Maybe you feel no bitterness about *the idea* of marriage per se, but it just doesn't seem to make much sense for *you*, particularly in to day's more progressive world. This chapter is for those of you who might be sorting out and redefining your feelings about love and commitment, as well as for those of you who do picture yourselves getting married again. One day. Maybe.

Not Another Statistic . . .

A high proportion of our demographic does eventually take the marital plunge again. Even Valerie, who swore she'd never tie the knot again and thought she didn't need to get married "in this day and age," did get married again, and much sooner than she or any of her friends expected. There's a pretty strong contingent of divorcées of our generation who still basically support the idea of marriage, despite some personal ambivalence about its lastingness. As our friend Delia said, "I liked being married a lot. I don't feel like I'm against the institution. But I did grow up feeling like I couldn't count on it—marriage—because of my parents' situation. Marriage was never a life-defining goal for me."

Even if it's not a life-defining goal for you, chances are, you may give it another try sometime. In her book *Marriage Shock: The Transformation of Women into Wives*, Dalma Heyn cites the statistic that five out of six men and three out of four women remarry within four years of their divorce. Now for a more sobering factoid: second marriages are alleged to have even higher failure rates than first marriages: 60 percent compared to 50 percent. But before you despair, here's the heartening reality: this statistic is most applicable to second marriages where there are children involved from the first marriage. Apparently the stress of building Brady Bunch–like blended families can be really hard on couples. Actually, when it comes to remarriage for our demographic, the stats are good. Research shows that marriages made when couples are post-thirty have a much stronger survival rate than those unions made in earlier adulthood. If you're wondering whether to take the plunge again, remember that you're approaching this new venture with much greater self-knowledge than you did the first time around, and that you're unburdened by kids and the stresses of having to maintain a connection to your first husband. From personal experience, Sarah believes, along with Shalamar, that "the second time around is better than the first."

The Philosophical You: Developing a New Perspective on Marriage

One of the benefits of having been married once is that you probably have a different, more mature view of matrimony than you did when you first got engaged. For many women, getting divorced meant dispelling the fairy-tale illusion of marital bliss that they once entertained. There's a refreshing reality and equality to the way almost all of the women we talked to redefined what they thought a marriage should be. As our friend Hope said, "I'd be more realistic about it now. My white knight was coming on a steed the first time around. If I remarried, my marriage would be much more about partnership." Gina echoes this sentiment: "The question should be, who's going to join me versus who's going to save me or be my prince?" Similarly, when asked about remarriage, our friend Caitlin realized, "I think I'd be more interested in being an equal partner, rather than in trying to please someone. I know what I like and don't like in terms of daily life. I guess I'm both more independent and able to share." Indeed, as many experts say, sustaining this balance between individuation and intimacy is the mark of a great romantic partnership, and it's something to strive for when you meet someone who's worth taking a second chance at a lifelong commitment.

Figuring out how you feel about getting married again may take some time. Your views on the subject will probably evolve a good deal in the first months and years post-divorce. Be comfortable with these changes and realize that your uncertainty or skepticism about the institution is not only natural, but probably very healthy, too. Many women, after enduring a less than satisfying first marriage, find that their standards have become pretty high.

This is a good thing. After all, you deserve someone and something fabulous. Take advantage of this time to reexamine what you want in a relationship, whether it's marriage again or not.

Unlike your never-married counterparts, you have a unique, firsthand knowledge about what can go wrong, and you bring this to bear on your next commitment. You know the risks, and you want some assurance that the potential for reward is going to be pretty great. As Megan put it, "My feelings about marriage change every day. I feel the same way about remarriage as I do about kids. I am only going to do that if it's for the right reason for me, if it's creating something really wonderful and right. I am not going to settle. It wasn't fair to my ex-husband and it's not fair to anyone else. I'm not sure if I believe anymore that there's a Mr. Right. I feel like I'm still figuring it out."

If you're at all interested in a second union, or even a second big relationship, it's important to think about what's most important to you in marriage. Experts say that couples who have similar visions of what partnership means in marriage, and couples who share similar expectations, dreams, and realities, have much better survival rates than couples who haven't thought these things through. As our friend Patti reflects, "I don't think you marry just for love anymore. I think you've got to have the same core morals, the same core beliefs, you have to want the same thing. And don't get married expecting to change someone." We once-marrieds are full of lessons learned, aren't we? The challenge, of course, is in taking them to heart and applying them.

When You Just Can't Imagine "Forever"

Maybe you're in a long-term relationship but having trouble visualizing saying those vows again. Maybe you're thinking that you'd prefer to be among the 25 percent of divorcées who don't remarry. As we said in chapter 1, the economic and societal benefits of being married are not as compelling anymore, so it's really a question of determining what *is* in it for you? Security. Companionship. Parenthood maybe. It's entirely possible that you may feel that you can attain all of these things on your own or with a partner whom you don't call husband. Maybe your life is starting to feel so full right now that you just can't fathom making the accommodations that you know marriage requires. Relax, you've got good company.

Our friend Greta, whose boyfriend K. would very much like to be her husband after many years of being together, has real doubts about getting married again. As she put it, "It's just like that line on *Sex and the City*—I just can't imagine 'forever.' All I can see is the foreseeable future, and why should I be taking vows for the foreseeable future? I know there's an end to a marriage. I feel like if I got married to K., I would be getting married knowing there's an end. I don't know if that's because I've been through a divorce, or because he's not the right one." After many years of living in separate cities, Greta and K. have now bought a house together, where they spend 75 percent of their time. Her views on marriage haven't changed, but she does feel that her level of commitment to K. has only deepened with time.

Like Greta, Trudie believes she does not want to remarry. For Trudie, marriage had a stultifying effect on her, so she worries a lot about what it does to a couple; she and her husband got so introverted after they were husband and wife that she just can't fathom that loss of self again. Though she's now in love with someone she has been living with for a while and does think about having children with, she's anxious about what the marital bond might do to their relationship. She often asks herself, is it the institution, or is it the two people who make the institution?

Your ambivalence about marriage is perfectly normal, as are any doubts you might be feeling about your own ability to judge someone's suitability for you. Obviously, every situation has its own unique stresses and everyone has their own timetable. If your current beau is the one for you for the long haul, you will eventually figure that out.

Sometimes when you doubt a really great relationship it's really more a question of getting over your divorce hangover. Sarah met her present husband, H., after she'd been separated from her ex for a little over a year, when she was about three months shy of her official divorce. After a string of bizarre dates one week (including the turkey-hunting episode described in chapter 8) she was set up through work friends with H. Right away, there was a love connection, though she was still processing a fair amount from her first marriage. H. had been married before too (which made things easier in some ways), but the ink on his divorce papers was a good three years dry. Hence, he was ready to really talk about getting married again much sooner than she was. Two years into their relationship, a tad frustrated with the pace, H. moved out west for a while but the distance proved to be clarifying. Sarah realized that, even if she didn't feel *entirely* ready, she definitely wasn't ready to go through life without this amazing man. One book contract, a dozen therapy appointments with the aptly named Dr. Shrinkman, and a trip to Barbados later, they were engaged.

No Husband, No Problem

Maybe you are thoroughly enjoying your glorious single status and really don't see yourself getting married again. Or perhaps you *would* like to get married, but the right guy just isn't anywhere in the picture. Try, try not to succumb to the desperation impulse; it's not becoming, and it only feeds on itself. Instead, be patient, keep your standards high—not impossibly high, but reasonably high. If you want it again (marriage), it *will* happen. Have faith that if you keep doing what you love doing, something is going to come your way. Sarah's colleague Bridget is a good case in point. She wanted to go hiking in the Himalayas, an adventure she didn't want to do alone, but none of her girlfriends was interested in such a rigorous vacation. Bridget placed an ad on the bulletin board of her gym to see about possible partners (male or female) and the first person who responded was this great guy who would become, ten months later, her fiancé. The moral of the story is, stay open to the possibilities around you every day, and in the meantime, concentrate on all kinds of other goals for yourself. The irony is, it's only when you're at ease being alone that you're most attractive to others. And only when you know you're fine alone are you most ready, willing, and able to attach to someone else.

But What About My Biological Clock?

If you don't see yourself saying "I do" anytime soon (e.g., you want to stay single or you want to get married but there aren't any candidates in sight) but you know you want children, take heart in the fact that society has evolved enormously, even just in the last decade. And while single momhood isn't exactly celebrated (unless you're Calista Flockhart, Jodie Foster, or Elizabeth Hurley), it really is becoming increasingly more acceptable and more mainstream. In other words, don't let the damn biological clock push you into a less than satisfying marriage or commitment with someone.

The critical thing to figure out is, what are your priorities? Is finding the right partner your chief priority, or does motherhood actually come first? Do you know whether you could handle being a single mom? Or do you know that you'd prefer to share parenting, and hence, would be willing to wait for The One? Kay, for example, has made the decision that she cares more about finding the right guy and having the right partner than having her children biologically. Because Kay doesn't want to raise children on her own, the partner comes first.

If being a mother has more urgency for you than finding a partner, then you can think about alternative approaches to the traditional married woman's method. First, consider the fact that technology is on your side if you prefer to have a baby biologically. Artificial insemination has become common practice these days for women who want to conceive but don't have a partner. Second, adoption is always a possibility; in this department, know that you have so many more options than your parents' generation did, with international as well as domestic opportunities. In starting your research for being a mother, talk to friends and friends of friends who have gone the sperm bank route or who have adopted; get online or go to your library and do some fact-finding. You may discover that parenthood is very much within your grasp, and that you've got a lot of company out there.

Finally, if you're feeling occasional pangs of wanting to be a mother, but you're not totally sure, consider taking some intermediate steps in this direction: feed your nurturing impulses by volunteering in the nursery of a hospital. Baby-sit the offspring of your sister or friend for a day. Sometimes, spending a few hours with a child can be quite instructive in that it can alleviate your mommy fantasies really fast, as you gleefully return to your calm, independent existence. As Kay friend's Jill likes to say when she sees a screaming infant, "MYTT," in other words, "makes you think twice!"

Looking Before You Leap

If and when you begin contemplating remarriage, we know you don't want to repeat history. Therefore, we'd like to underscore the importance of taking the time you need to think through what happened in your first marriage. As Abigail Trafford puts it in her seminal divorce self-help book, *Crazy Time: Surviving Divorce and Building a New Life*, "Successful remarriages are based on successful psychological divorces." This means not so much questioning your choice of mate in the first place (though that's natural), or blaming him inordinately, but rather, figuring out what your role was in the breakdown of the marriage. In other words, you need to get to the point where you can accept some responsibility for the course of events and recognize what the pernicious patterns were in your old relationship. An equally important part of this, of course, is figuring out who you are by yourself and who you want to be with your next mate. This step is the old "What did I learn, and what will I do differently in the next relationship?" But it's also "How do I make myself happy?"

You might not be entirely ready to go there yet, and that's okay. This process is definitely not a short essay exam; think of it instead as a research paper on a special topic in your life. You are in the process of cultivating new habits of mental note-taking. Eventually, you'll amass enough notes that you can take a stab at a thesis statement once in a while, and even revise your previous assumptions. But it can feel really gratifying to get clarity on what your issues are, why things didn't work out the first time around, and what matters to you going forward into the future. It's only then that you can really fully attach to someone new and begin to think about what you would do differently in your next serious relationship.

You can start by trying to gauge your readiness for a new commitment. Be willing to try out some hard questions on yourself, like,

- Have I not processed and moved on from my first marriage?
- Am I still experiencing strong waves of grief or sadness?
- Do I still feel a lot of anger when I think about my ex?

If you answer in the affirmative to any of these questions, then be glad you're honest with yourself, and realize that you need more space and time to heal before you completely hook yourself to someone new. If you answered "none of the above," we're impressed—we know how challenging committing again can be.

Here are some other questions to contemplate as you think about partnering up again:

- What are the two or three things I really need from my next mate in order to be happy?

- What degree of independence do I require?
- What kind of emotional support do I need and want to give?
- What do I need from myself and my world so that I can thrive?
- What do I need to *do* to get what I need and be fulfilled? (Change jobs? Take frequent vacations? Spend time regularly with my girlfriends or family?)

Most women who remarry or reattach successfully say they knew they were ready when they had (a) really come to terms with the issues in their first marriage; (b) forgiven themselves and/or their exes; (c) become happy, highly functioning and self-fulfilled people again; and (d) last but of course not least, found someone with whom they could be completely themselves *and* in love. Most women say that, as a result of having thrived on their own for a while, they approach their next relationship with much more wisdom about themselves and their life goals, and generally, more confidence that they can make it work.

Money Matters

It's been shown that one of the big stressors in second unions is money. So, before you consider hitching yourself to someone else again, you'll want to spend some time making sure that you and your partner are on the same page not just about lifestyle expenditures in general but, specifically, that you know whether you're going to keep finances separate, commingled, or, as most encore couples do, some combination of the two. By the time you're ready to live with someone again or get remarried, you've probably fought hard to get your credit and assets back on track, and you may have a natural and healthy tendency to protect yourself when it comes to money. In general, it makes sense to keep any assets you acquired before your second marriage separate. So, if you have certificates of deposit, savings accounts, mutual funds, and so forth, keep these in your name. It's absolutely nothing against your new husband or partner, rather it's good for your relationship if you have some financial autonomy.

In starting a new shared life, you will of course have shared expenses, and for these, it makes a whole lot of sense to open a joint account. An approach many money advisors encourage is to have couples each put in the same percentage of their incomes into this account, and/or into their joint savings. This way, even if you're not making the same amount, you are contributing the same percentage, which is an equitable and psychologically healthy way to go. Keep up the good habits from your single days, watch where your dollars are going, and know where the various statements are. Most important, learn to talk about money with your new partner. Be direct, be forthright when you have questions and be aware that it's a tough, tough topic for most couples. It's always linked to the emotional issues, so go easy on yourself when it feels awkward or uncomfortable. Finally, prenuptial agreements, as horrible as they sound in theory, might be worth exploring if you've got significant assets. In general, it's just a good idea to make sure you've covered this territory before deciding to tie the knot.

Not Another Learning Experience . . .

Even when you've fallen in love again and your ex-husband seems the furthest thing from your heart and head, don't be alarmed when old memories and habits of his come back to haunt you. The important thing to do in these instances is to greet the remembrance of things past in the spirit of "Oh, hello, first marriage, what are you here to teach me today?" But beware the projection impulse: it's all too easy to impose on your new mate the trespasses of the old.

Maybe your second husband has a habit that reminds you of your first husband and it's creeping you out. Be careful of reacting to your new man as if he were your ex. There could be a trace, even ever so faint, of some anger floating in your blood-

stream, barely detectable, but there. Obviously, some repeated be-
haviors should be taken more seriously (drug addiction, abuse of
any kind) but if it's a relatively minor habit of his that's annoying
to you, just realize that you're probably fairly susceptible to some
triggers. For example, right after they were married, Sarah blew
up at H. when she came home from work one day and the apartment was untidy. The specific (egregious) offense was that the bed
wasn't made. She soon realized that her overreaction to this very
benign oversight had been triggered by the memory of what it felt
like to live with her first husband's pathological messiness. Once
she realized that this is where her anger was coming from, she was
able to address it with H., and he reassured her that he hadn't in-
tentionally blown off their housekeeping routine. Living with the
awareness of the old relationship will take some vigilance on both
of your parts, but eventually, and we do mean eventually, if you
have really processed the whys and whats of the divorce, the first
relationship will recede so far into the background that it barely
bleeps on the radar screen of your new marriage.

Don't Be Afraid of Couples Counseling

If you run into some stumbling blocks in your new relationship, don't be afraid to seek some professional help. Anna
did this before she married B., who brought some baggage
from his first marriage and family. It can feel weird and scary
at first. You may be a veteran of couples therapy with your
ex-husband and the whole idea of spending time analyzing a
relationship might just give you the heebie-jeebies. We understand, we really do. We've been there. Try not to let those
battle scars get in the way of doing some excellent work on
this new relationship. Do not even think about seeing the
same person you saw with your ex—by all means, see some-

one new! And it doesn't have to be a long-term proposition either. You might have a few things you want to work out in the context of a safe, neutral environment and it might be helpful to go to several sessions. It's a positive, proactive thing to do, and chances are, it will help you sort out whether this is the relationship for you. Particularly if you are contemplating remarriage (or living together), premarital counseling is a terrific way to get yourselves in tune to the challenges and rewards of your particular couplehood.

Affianced Again?

So, you're totally in love, you know this is right, and you've decided to get married again. Since you're probably not the starry-eyed thing you were the first time around, it's likely that this proposal moment has a different romance to it. Maybe your story will be like Miranda's: she and her now-fiancé, G., had a very tumultuous relationship, and spent a lot of time soul-searching, with Miranda feeling a good deal of doubt about her readiness to commit again. One night, they were having dinner with friends when they were asked, "So when are you two going to get married?!" Miranda and G. looked at each other nervously but excitedly, and replied in unison, "Soon!" She likes to summarize their story as, "He asked me a hundred times and I finally said yes."

And after teasing Sarah that she'd have to be the one to propose marriage, H. did one night get down on bended knee and pop the question in their kitchen when he was making dinner (the tuna was overgrilled, but they were overjoyed). In all likelihood, the moment won't be a complete surprise, as you'll probably have progressed from oblique innuendo to more frank talks about "commitment" and "forever."

Special Butterflies in Your Stomach:
News and Nerves

You start spreading the word, and very soon, everybody's atwitter with your news. So why do you feel oddly nervous? Several of the reaffianced and remarried women we spoke to reported feeling more nervous about the second time than they were about the first. As our friend Miranda confessed, "I still feel nervous about getting remarried. It's very real and I'm not going to pretend that I don't feel nervous. You always think, it went wrong the first time!" Realize that your nerves, unless they are serious panic attacks of the variety Carrie Bradshaw experiences in the bridal shop on an episode of *Sex and the City* (she got hives when trying on a wedding dress), are probably only a function of your hard-won self-awareness and your determination to get it right this time.

One of the things that surprised Sarah was the variety of reactions she got when she told people. There was the overelation reaction, commonly occurring among the newly-marrieds; the relief reaction, usually from her elders, which seemed to imply "Thank god you finally got married because you must have been miserable as a single person"; the mild shock of the matchmaking colleague who set them up; and then the surprise of some girlfriends who had been privy to her waffling and wonderings over the two years before the engagement. This kind of reaction can be one of the harder ones to deal with. Sarah found that the best way to cope with her mystified friends was to show them that she, too, found the news pretty amazing. In other words, you can say, "Yep, I've come a long way, haven't I?" and if they still doubt you, don't worry about it. They'll soon adjust to the new reality. In general, people are going to be genuinely happy for you, so relax and enjoy being a topic of light gossip and commotion.

Finally, at the risk of insulting your intelligence or your sense of decorum, we advise you not to talk about remarrying your new flame with friends or family until your divorce is final. Beyond being a faux pas, it could have negative repercussions on your legal proceedings if you and your ex have a contentious situation.

Informing Your Ex-Husband

Yes, you really should tell your ex. It's not totally necessary, but it's a polite thing to do. Try to inform him sooner rather than later, so that he doesn't hear the news from someone else at a party, read about it in the paper, or run into you and your husband on the subway. You could call him on his cell phone (if he has one) or write him a note by regular mail if you don't like the thought of an interactive dialogue. And, as we've counseled you before, only use email as a last resort. Your happy news may not be happy news to him, and it's just not pleasant to picture him forwarding it with some snide comment to his cronies. You certainly don't have to invite the man to your wedding, unless you remain exceedingly close and he has a fabulous relationship with your groom-to-be. Inviting the ex-spouse is not unheard of, it's just not customary, especially when you don't have any children or other ties to bind you.

When You Do Decide to Say "I Do" Again...

"Second marriages are for fun!" says our friend Miranda's Aunt Abigail. Indeed, the great thing is that after all of the soul-searching, the second time around you have license to focus on yourself and your partner and not worry so much about the outside world. You're not so distracted by conventions and expectations, and it can feel wonderfully liberating. Maybe you don't even need a period of being engaged. You're a grown-up woman, after all; you've already had a husband, and maybe you just feel like running down to City Hall. Indeed, Sarah felt some weird discomfort at the term "fiancé" for H. Somehow, proud as she was to announce their important new status, every time she introduced him as such, she winced a bit. It sounded exaggerated like "*fee-un-say*." It sounded so young and so old-fashioned at the same time . . . but what else was there? My plus-one? Husband-to-be? Main man? As cloyingly formal as it is, the term seems to work better than anything else.

Nuptials—Take Two

As soon as you've told your adoring fans that you're getting married, be aware that you may get a round of twenty questions about just where, when, and how you're going to tie the knot. Deflect all inquiries from these well-intentioned well-wishers if you don't know the details yet. Just tell them to stay tuned. What's most important, of course, is taking the time to do it the way *you* and your fiancé want to. Though you might want to consult a book or two for some ideas, there's no need to follow any strict second-wedding etiquette. Instead, what's probably among your big priorities is the need to make it different from the first time. Most of our interviewees were very clear on this one thing: avoiding déjà vu, which, put in a more positive way, means also that you can have whatever you didn't have for your first wedding.

Many women who had traditional weddings the first time around envision something more intimate for the next time. For example, Elizabeth envisions "a private, small ceremony somewhere exotic like Greece or Tahiti. I would definitely downplay the big wedding thing, it would be much more about *us*." Our friend Caitlin, still living a block from her ex, simply fantasizes about getting remarried "somewhere far away."

Nancy, under pressure from her parents and her beau's parents to get married, decided a stealth and semi-spontaneous approach was the best. She and her boyfriend, who had just had a baby together, registered for domestic partnership and then opted to get married during a Caribbean vacation: "We picked a beach, didn't tell anyone we were doing it, and no one knew. We waited a while to tell people; we waited to tell our parents until we could see them in person. Partly, we just wanted to prove that being married didn't make a big difference in how people perceived us."

Propriety and Precedent

Though it's terrific that people are so keen on offering advice and ideas, try not to let yourself get overly caught up in someone else's conception of what's "appropriate" or what's "in good taste." Just be thankful that it's the twenty-first century and you're not subject to the standards of forty years ago, when Emily Post wrote about "When a Divorcée Remarries" in her famous book *Emily Post's Etiquette*. "The bride may not wear a veil or orange blossoms (signifying virginity) and she should not wear white. The dress should be a simple street-length gown worn with a hat (for modesty) in any style she prefers." Even the recently updated *Amy Vanderbilt Complete Book of Etiquette* seems a bit crusty for today's world, but it does suggest that standards and customs have loosened up: "What the bride wears at her second wedding depends on her age, the season, the time of day the wedding is to be held, and the formality of the occasion . . . The second-time bride may carry a very simple bouquet . . . She does not wear a veil, but if she likes the idea of wearing something on her head she may wear flowers, a bow, or a simple hat of some kind."

The message we can take from the etiquette mavens past and present seems to be this: if your first wedding was a big and traditional affair, it may make sense for your second wedding to be a more modest, more relaxed affair. Amy Vanderbilt goes on to suggest that one should dispense with the formalities like receiving lines, big bridal parties, engraved invitations, the rehearsal dinner, an all-white cake, formal processional (i.e., "Here Comes the Bride" music) or recessional (i.e., Mendelssohn). She also makes a point to suggest that it's not in good taste to register for wedding gifts, unless you eloped or had a small wedding the first time around. People *will* ask you where you're registered, though, so if you're a pragmatist, you might buck protocol here. Everything else ultimately seems like fair game, including wearing white if it pleases you.

It might very well be the first time for your fiancé, a situation which might also influence the style and size of your wedding. Men think about matrimonial splendor, too, maybe not as often or in as much detail as your average woman does, but it's good to consider their dreams if they have them. This was the case for several of the women we spoke to, who, even though they had fairly big traditional weddings the first time around decided, for their fiancé's sake, to have grand celebrations the second time around too. As Valerie recalls, "At first I wasn't going to wear a wedding dress. When I went shopping, everything looked so bride-y, but then I realized my fiancé really wanted me to wear something fairly traditional, so I found a beautiful compromise: a white strapless two-piece."

Chances are that if you had an extravagant fête the first time around, you probably don't feel like another one anyway. Sarah and her husband H. contemplated a few scenarios before settling on getting married in New York City. Though on the surface of things, there were some resemblances to her first wedding, which was also in the city and in a church, the mood and mode were really quite different. For one thing, she didn't feel she should ask her parents to help financially, so they were doing it themselves, as many second-timers do. It was about half the size of the first; summer instead of winter; a cocktail party took the place of a rehearsal dinner; and champagne and cake on the church rooftop followed the ceremony instead of a full sit-down meal.

This is not to say that the planning second time around doesn't have its tough spots. For example, when it comes to the church choreography, the encore bride might not want to be "given away." Somehow, as incredibly close as Sarah is to her father, the symbolism suggested by this didn't feel right. She thought about striding purposefully alone, but that seemed kind of lonely or bridesmaid-like (plus she worried people might think her father wasn't alive, or that they were estranged). In the end, what felt most right was to walk with her groom, arm in arm, partners joining each other. But when you reach the point of considering your ceremony, if your father is still alive and you are close, don't let propriety or even precedent get in the way. The most important thing is to do what feels right to you and your groom. The whole "giving away" concept is rather nineteenth century anyway. Think of it instead as being escorted, and then you're free to choose who does what.

Maybe you feel like throwing a bash worthy of your triumphant happiness. If this is the way you feel, and the kind of thing you both want, then this is not the time for false modesty. Go for it, like our friend Maeve did. In her first marriage, she had eloped to the beach. When she got married the second time, she wanted to do it up exuberantly: "This time, we had a church wedding, and I wore a big old white gown. It was very traditional. It was the time of our lives. I was forty-two, and I remember thinking, I'm too old for this dress, but who cares? He burst into tears when he saw me." Again, don't worry about age-appropriateness, and heck, even Amy Vanderbilt says white is all right.

Despite how different you make the event, don't be surprised if you feel some smidgen of discomfort at certain points of the process, particularly if you do have a sizable wedding. For example, Valerie said most of the 150 people on her invite list were her husband's relatives and friends because "somehow to invite so many of mine made me feel like a hypocrite." And as Erin, currently in the middle of planning her second wedding, volunteered, "I don't want to seat people from my first wedding with people at the second who don't even know I was divorced, in case they start comparing notes." Along these same lines, although seven years had passed between Sarah's two weddings, she felt weird receiving wedding presents from the same group of people who'd attended her first. The important thing to realize, of course, is that people are so happy for you that they want to commemorate and celebrate with you. Chances are, the last thing they're thinking about is your first wedding. You could institute a "no gifts" policy statement, but you risk looking like a big party pooper.

Ms. Doubtfire—The Name Thing

Names are so personal, so full of history and heritage, that it's hard to suggest any firm pros and cons in the area of whether or not to adopt your second husband's name. You may dislike the inherent sexism involved in taking his name. Or you may be very fond of your family name, especially if you've always used it and built up some professional equity with it. On the other hand, maybe your fiancé's last name has a particularly mellifluous ring to it with yours, and that's reason enough for you. Maybe you're thinking of having kids (or even already have one) and you feel it's just easier to have that same common denominator. It's not necessarily a statement of traditionalism to take his name—women still do it all the time. But we will say that if you're like Sarah and you only recently changed your name back to your original surname, chances are you don't want to go through that colossal administrative hassle again.

A Triumph of Hope over Experience, or A Fine Predicament

Samuel Johnson once called remarriage the "triumph of hope over experience" which is a nice way of thinking about it, but we also don't mean to suggest that getting remarried is the *summum bonum*, the only way to be happy as a couple or happy in life. Rather, as Anne Roiphe recently subtitled her new book, marriage is "a fine predicament." It's not perfect, and it's not for everyone, but many of us are willing to take another chance at it.

CHAPTER TEN

When Life Hands You Limes, Make Mojitos

After the final no there comes a yes
And on that yes the future world depends.

—Wallace Stevens,

"The Well Dressed Man with a Beard"

I f you're still in the throes of the disappointment and sadness of it all, you probably have a hard time relating to our enthusiasm for the fringe benefits of divorce. That's understandable. It takes time to move through the thickets of the tragedy, time to wander through the morass and muck of a marriage gone wrong. Our hope, though, is that this chapter will inspire those of you who are still meandering your way through the wilderness and serve as a lantern of sorts, illuminating the path before you until you see light at the edge of the forest. We promise, despite all indications otherwise, that you *will* emerge from this experience with a deeper sense of your own power in the world and a renewed sense of vitality and joy. If, on the other hand, you're pretty well out of the woods, we think you'll recognize yourself in many of the voices of the brave women whose nuggets of new-found wisdom we present in this final chapter.

Mojitos

Ingredients:
   2–3 oz. of light rum
   1 lime, halved
   2 tsp. sugar
   Small handful of mint
   Soda water

Preparation:
Place sugar, mint, and splash of soda water in a pint glass. Use fork to lightly press mint and dissolve sugar until it smells of spearmint gum. Squeeze both halves of lime into the glass, leaving one hull in the mixture. Add rum, stir, and fill with ice. Top with soda water and garnish with mint sprig.

Hello Darkness, My Good Friend

As we've emphasized throughout the book, to take advantage of the truly amazing and transformative upside of divorce, you need to take time to learn what went wrong and what your role was in the demise of the relationship. The more you face the divorce and its lessons for you, with the help of loved ones and perhaps a counselor, the quicker and more fully you'll heal and move forward in your life. You'll suffer as you grope through the brambles and knotty trails of your soul—the sadness, profound disappointment, bitterness, anger, and loneliness—but we guarantee that you'll emerge wiser and more peaceful for it. In Delia's words, "I had to have really crappy feelings and spend some time with them, and now I feel so much happier." The process of making sense of what happened may take some time, possibly several years, but slowly you'll gain some satisfying clarity and heartfelt conviction about how you want to lead your life going forward.

Finally Living for *You*

If you face your demons head-on, you're likely to start experiencing the upside to the divorce fairly quickly. One of the most important benefits reported by many of the women in this book was the experience of rediscovering who they were, what they wanted out of life, and how to be the mistresses of their own destiny. We heard this sentiment time and again in our interviews. Divorcées felt themselves finally coming into their own and hitting their stride as individuals, uncovering their most essential core and living in a way that was true to that core.

For Isabel, leaving her husband meant coming out as a lesbian, so she relates, "It gave me the freedom to be who I really am and find my true love." While Isabel "came out" in a literal sense, many other women felt that they "came out" as themselves, as more authentic versions of themselves, after the divorce. Delia remarked, "I finally permitted myself to pursue what I really wanted all along. I feel like I'm grown up now. I lived my life trying to please, and there's some way in which I'm not doing that anymore." Elizabeth expressed her post-marital development in a similar fashion: "I feel more mature, more confident in myself, more secure in knowing what I need and being okay with that, living for myself. I'm much more solid in *me*."

Like many women we interviewed, Gina felt like she had really lost herself in her marriage: "I no longer knew who Gina was and was living totally in E.'s world." Getting divorced meant finding her own identity again and building a very different kind of life. One incident captures her transformation well. After splitting from E., she took all the jewelry he had given her, including her wedding ring, sold it to a jewelry store and bought a pair of small diamond earrings for herself. Then one day she was strolling down the street and walking by the store and spotted the wedding ring, which was very distinctive, in the display window. In that moment, she had a kind of out-of-body experience, where she felt she was looking at an older version of herself represented by the ring. In comparing the woman staring at the ring to the woman who used to wear the ring, she realized that she had grown to live so much more fully and authentically since the divorce.

The Power of One

Becoming a single person again after having merged your identity and lifestyle with someone else puts you in touch with your autonomy in a profound way, and this new autonomy can become quite inspiring and fulfilling.

Rachel, who had followed her ex around the country and put his career before hers for many years, found herself fiercely dedicated to her art and determined to pursue it with everything she had. Sydney came to see she had led her married years "in W.'s shadow" and discovered her own professional ambition after they separated, taking on leadership roles in business school in a way she never would have dreamed of before. And, after living with her ex for over ten years, Megan realized that she loved living alone, arranging a place based on her preferences alone, making her own very healthy dinners and exercising at whatever hour and in whatever fashion she desired.

This newfound sense of agency and independence can have an existential thread running through it, whereby you realize "we're all born alone and die alone," in Greta's words. Greta reported that before the divorce, she used to find this sentiment extremely depressing, but living on her own gave her an ultimately empowering feeling of "Wow, it's all up to me, I am doing all these adult things on my own." Divorce had a similar effect on Cindy, who said, "I became really strong because I learned that I have control

over my own happiness, that I can't sit and complain and say someone else made me unhappy. I learned that if you take charge of your
own life, anything is possible. I started my own business, I'm buying my own house. It was empowering to realize that I can do
everything by myself and bring about my own happiness."

The *Carpe Diem* Effect

As with any life-altering event, divorce can also inspire you to
stop beating around the proverbial bush and go after your true
passions. Delia, for instance, finally decided to attend graduate
school in American history after years of postponing it. Gina trav-
eled to places she'd always wanted to go. Similarly, Dawn finally
allowed herself to pursue the high-powered career she'd always
wanted after years of her ex trying to dissuade her from doing so.
One of the unexpected gifts of divorce, then, is that you learn to
be true to yourself, in many cases because you suffered the costs
of not being true to yourself in your marriage. Seemingly out of
nowhere, a fierce and palpable sense of self arises in you, and you
can't imagine how you went around in the world without it—and
then you realize that it was lying dormant in you all along.

At Home on the Emotional Range

Besides seizing the day, the tragedy of divorce can also allow you
to savor the deliciousness of living with more zest than you ever
have. Because you've been so phenomenally down at times, you
can find yourself ecstatic when you do experience joy, and appre-
ciative of it in a way you perhaps weren't before. You feel joy but
also a kind of meta-joy at how joyous you can be. Joy and pain,
sunshine and rain, these things go together and have more meaning in relation to each other. Going to the darkest depths of your
soul and emerging intact gives you access to the brightest and
most radiant parts of yourself. As Leslie said, "I appreciate the
times I'm happy much more, and there are more times that I'm
truly, deeply happy." The experience of divorce, if you don't fight

the panoply of feelings twirling and swirling within you, gives you immense emotional depth and range. And while post-divorce life may not always find you blissed out, you are likely to feel consistently *vital*, alive to the world in all its pleasures and pains.

I Am Divorcée, Hear Me Roar

Many divorcées describe emerging from the experience with a feeling that they are winners of an emotional "survivor" test and that they can now live through anything. Like any harrowing experience in life that demands all your mettle and moxie, divorce will bring out internal reservoirs of strength you may have never known existed, and you'll find this new strength changes you down deep and makes you bolder in lots of areas of life.

In Mehta's words, "What I gained from the divorce was the sense that I could do anything on my own . . . and I could handle whatever came my way." Janine remarks about herself, "I'm a much stronger person. It was the hardest thing I have ever had to do in my entire life . . . and I learned you will survive, you won't die, your heart will mend." Dawn too comments, "I feel like I can do just about anything now. I have a strength I didn't have before, and I am deeply proud of myself for doing what I did [walking away from an emotionally abusive husband]." Dawn still has an image that she got from a therapist she saw during the divorce that sustains her in difficult times: she pictures herself on an island by herself with only one tree, and no matter what the weather is (what's going on in her life), if she just stands her ground firmly on the island and holds on to the tree, she'll be okay.

A New Humility

Along with a heightened sense of their own powerfulness, divorcées also report gaining a new sense of the limits of their power and the importance of compassion, forgiveness, and acceptance. These two lessons may seem contradictory, but in fact they are not. Hardship often gives you a new perspective on what real strength is made of and on what you can control (yourself) and what you can't (others, external events).

Several divorcées talked about becoming less judgmental and more understanding of others. Sydney explains: "I had been so hard on myself my whole life, it made me hard on others. Then, I went through all these things that went wrong for me, and I became much more open-minded and accepting. I now tell my family, who are very judgmental and made me judgmental in the first place, that it's okay to make mistakes, in fact sometimes it's a good thing to make a mistake."

In a similar vein, Leslie describes the divorce as a huge identity shift for her that dramatically changed her outlook. "It took away the idea that I had a charmed life. It made me far more empathic toward others. When you've had the feeling, oh my God, my life is falling apart, it's humbling and makes you more accepting of others who are having a hard time." Leslie also talks about the importance of forgiving both yourself and the other person: "Forgiveness is a much better place to be than filled with guilt or anger. And the mistakes people make, they don't do it on purpose. People are doing the best they can do, including you."

Gina, too, talks about becoming a "kinder, gentler friend" than she was before the divorce. "I'm much more compassionate. I don't just give harsh advice like I used to; I'm softer, not such a tough cookie. I understand how hard it is to change." Laura echoes many of the precious sentiments with, "I really like who I've become because of the divorce. I've become this very nice person because of it."

As you heal and grow into your new life, you'll likely find that the divorce has this uncanny way of unearthing both the warrior and the saint in you, of making you both braver and kinder than you ever thought you could be.

Learning Who Your True Peeps Are

Another benefit of divorce is that it can strengthen your ties of friendship and family even while it tests them. There's nothing like misfortune to help you find out who your real friends and most important loved ones are. Many divorcées talk about the divorce reinforcing and deepening certain friendships and relations with family members while simultaneously diminishing or eliminating other connections. The people who see you through the misery and heartache, and love you despite all your temporary insanity, are likely to be the people you can trust your whole life.

Kay especially experienced an interesting rejiggering in her friendships. She felt she learned who she could turn to when she was down, who could accept the new person she was becoming, and who couldn't. She reconnected with some of her oldest friends, lost other friends, and also gained critical new friends who fit well with her post-divorce self. While this reorganizing of your support system can sometimes be painful, especially if you lose or can no longer connect with a friend or relative, you also emerge from the divorce with a clearer and deeper sense of who your most essential and trusted peeps are.

Gleaning the Wisdom of the Ages

Divorce can also give you the kind of perspective on life that is usually reserved for sage village elders. Think of yourself as precocious. Sometimes, as in *Spinal Tap*, it's "a little too much f——ing perspective," but ultimately these lessons can serve you well your whole life and give you a leg up on the people who might not catch on until they're in a retirement home.

"Time heals all wounds" sounds like an empty platitude until you've suffered a serious wound and had it heal quite remarkably with time. And, when you're suffering, "this too shall pass" can ring like a Pollyanna-ish attempt to cheer you up. But divorce will teach you the resounding and reassuring truth of these clichés. Leslie says the best advice anyone gave her was to remember it would get better and she would not feel awful forever. As our friend Angela often says, "Just hold on for the ride, and one day you'll be able to get off." Valerie was lucky enough to have this long-range perspective during the middle of her divorce. She comments, "Overall, even though it was so unfortunate the whole time, even at my lowest point I had the foresight to say, 'I wish it could be three months from now,' because I knew I'd be even better by then."

Long after the divorce is over, you'll likely find yourself going back to the memory of the dreadfully difficult days and realizing you've survived and even gone on to thrive. Holding on to this knowledge can give you a more Zen approach to life, whereby you can put bad days or unfortunate events into perspective and realize their insignificance in the greater scheme of your life.

A Delicate Etching on the Soul

Without exception, every woman we spoke to felt the divorce had made her wiser, bolder, and ultimately happier. Our respondents would preface these sentiments with, "It was the most painful/horrible/disillusioning experience of my life," but they all felt that despite the trauma, they were grateful to have gone through it and grown in the ways they had. They all articulated a profound sense of "I would not be the person I am today"—a person they are proud to be—without the experience (several women said these exact words). People regretted or felt guilty about a lot of things—the wedding, their contribution to the downfall of the marriage, "losing years"—but no one regretted the overall experience. Each person had a strong sense that it had shaped them in ways central to their being.

Our friend Delia put it this way: "I feel like there's an enormous upside to it. It was excruciatingly painful, I worried that it meant I'd wasted my twenties . . . But in my case, every single door has opened. I really feel like I'm better off." Laura also expressed the funny mixture of feelings common among our respondents: "I'm so thankful it happened because I would not be the person I am today without it. It's strange, I'm so embarrassed about the divorce and yet so thankful for it too. I wish it had never happened and yet I don't wish it didn't happen. I would not be as strong or thoughtful or wise as I am today." Elizabeth said simply, "I regret putting my friends and family through the wedding and the debacle of our marriage, but I don't regret the experience at all. It taught me so much."

However, especially as the years pass, you may find yourself identifying less and less as a "divorcée" and thinking about the circumstances of the divorce less and less. You will likely go weeks and months without receiving a mental visit from your ex. You'll meet new people and they will have no idea you were divorced, and your old friends will stop thinking about you that way. In fact, it can sometimes be almost creepy how normal your life can become after such a huge debacle. Life goes on, you discover, and all the trauma and drama fade away; after a while, the divorce is only a tiny, imperceptible dot on the horizon of your life.

The experience, though, will live on in you in subtle and often invisible ways. It will become so fully integrated into your being, so much a part of you that it's not even noteworthy. It lives in your cells and tissues. It's in your voice, gestures, and smiles. Leslie described it this way: "The divorce is part of who I am in a quiet way like where you grew up and who your parents are. It's not like your job, something that you might change, but more like your hometown or your dog—who you are in a deep way. It's essential to who you are, and you wouldn't be the same without it. I would never want to go through it again, but I would never take the experience away. I really like the ways I've changed."

As time passes, then, the divorce becomes a delicate etching on your soul—something that has changed you forever in mostly wonderful ways, in unexpected ways, and in ways imperceptible to anyone but you. You have absorbed its lessons so deeply and thoroughly that they manifest themselves only as a precocious wisdom and vital radiance that shines out brightly from within.

Books for Consultation & Consolation

If you picked up our book at the bookstore, chances are you know that the shelves are groaning with resources for the divorcing person. A simple Web search will also yield thousands of entries. However, not all of them are that useful, especially for the young divorcing woman without children. The list below is not at all exhaustive but it does represent the books we found most helpful, inspiring, and generally edifying.

Just the Facts, Ma'am: Quick Reference

The Complete Idiot's Guide to Surviving Divorce (2nd edition), by Pamela Weintraub, Terry Hillman, Elayne J. Kesselman. New York: Alpha Books, 1999.

We like the upbeat tone of this book. It offers soup-to-nuts guidance on all topics, with lots of definitions of tricky legal terms and reliable information. If you aren't finding exactly what you need in our book, pick up a copy of this one.

The Unofficial Guide to Divorce, by Sharon Naylor. New York: John Wiley & Sons, 1998.

This guide provides a balanced overview of the logistics of the legal process in jargon-free language, including a particularly thorough treatment of negotiation and financial issues.

Truly Helpful Self-Help

Crazy Time: Surviving Divorce and Building a New Life, Revised Edition, by Abigail Trafford. New York: HarperPerennial, 1992.

This is a classic in the genre of self-help. Even though it's starting to show its age a bit, it charts the emotional journey with wisdom and a wonderfully intimate tone.

Divorce Hangover: A Successful Strategy to End the Emotional Aftermath of Divorce, by Anne Newton Walther, M.S. San Francisco: Tapestries Publishing, 2001.

The concept of a "hangover" works very well as an organizing principle for this book's advice and wisdom. It's very readable, with lots of bullets, numbered lists, and assignments to help you recover.

The New Creative Divorce: How to Create a Happier, More Rewarding Life During—and After—Your Divorce, Mel Krantzler, Ph.D. and Pat Krantzler, M.A. Massachusetts: Adams Media Corporation, 1999.

Written by two divorced people who married each other, this book helps you see how you can turn your personal pain into positive growth. This book's heart is totally in the right place.

Too Good to Leave, Too Bad to Stay: A Step-by-Step Guide to Helping You Decide Whether to Stay In or Get Out of Your Relationship, by Mira Kirshenbaum. New York: Plume (reprint edition), 1997.

If you are unclear about whether to stay in your marriage or get out, this book is for you. Written with an authoritative, no-nonsense tone, the diagnostic questions will help you get clarity.

Pop-Sociology/Psychology

The Starter Marriage and the Future of Matrimony, by Pamela Paul. New York: Villard, 2002.

The first book to study our demographic, this is fairly serious and statistic-filled nonfiction. But Paul also interviewed about sixty divorced people—men and women—and their voices run through her examination of the "starter marriage" phenomenon and provide some character and color.

The Unexpected Legacy of Divorce: The 25-Year Landmark Study, by Judith Wallerstein, Julia Lewis, and Sandra Blakeslee. New York: Hyperion, 2000.

A longitudinal study and bestseller, this book can be pretty absorbing reading if you are a child of divorce. Wallerstein studies the effects of divorce on adult children, finding that many of them have trouble with conflict and commitment to a partner.

Memoir

Breaking Apart: A Memoir of Divorce, by Wendy Swallow. New York: Hyperion, 2001.

The story of one woman's decision to leave a marriage after ten years and two children, this book might not speak directly to you, but there's a good deal of wisdom and perspective here.

Generation Ex: Tales from the Second Wives Club, by Karen Karbo. New York: Bloomsbury, 2001.

Though Karbo writes about ex-spousal relationships sustained because of children, the book is a highly entertaining read even for the childless divorcée. It's a memoir that really reads like an absorbing and witty novel.

Split: Stories from a Generation Raised on Divorce, edited by Ava Chin. New York: McGraw-Hill, 2002.

A collection of articles and stories by writers of our generation who grew up with divorce among their parents, this book aims to be "a support group between the covers of a book," and some of the pieces are indeed moving and well written.

Women on Divorce: A Bedside Companion, edited by Penny Kaganoff and Susan Spano. New York: Harcourt Brace, 1995.

A literary anthology of women writers on divorce, this book includes elegant articles by writers like Ellen Gilchrist, Anne Roiphe, and Daphne Merkin.

Financial Advice

The Courage to Be Rich: Creating a Life of Material and Spiritual Abundance, by Suze Orman. New York: Riverhead Books, 1999, 2002.

Almost anything by Suze Orman is bound to be solid stuff. Though her advice is not specific to the divorcée, this one is a particular favorite of ours. She manages to be really practical and philosophical at the same time.

Suddenly Single: Money Skills for Divorcées and Widows, by Kerry Hannon. New York: Wiley, 1998.

This brief and straightforward guide addresses the essentials of good finances and includes coverage of insurance, investments, and budgeting.

Somewhat Random but Actually
Quite Relevant Literature

Fault Lines: Stories of Divorce, collected and edited by Caitlin Shetterly. New York: Berkley Publishing Group, 2001.

This is an anthology of short stories that have the theme of divorce in common. The anthology includes pieces by some literary heavy hitters, such as Russell Banks, Ann Beattie, Raymond Carver, John Cheever, Lorrie Moore, Alice Munro, and John Updike. While the stories don't address the topic head-on, they explore the inner worlds of complicated characters and give you a chance to muse on the subject in a metaphorical way.

Letters to a Young Poet, Rainer Maria Rilke, M. D. Herter Norton (translator), Franz Xaver Kappus. New York: W.W. Norton & Company, Reissue edition, 1994.

This slender book is filled with ten sweepingly emotional letters from the poet to a student in 1903. It beautifully explores the relationship between intimacy and independence in romantic love and encourages you to dig deep within yourself to find what is true for you and create a life based on that.

Self-Reliance and Other Essays, Ralph Waldo Emerson. New York: Dover, Unabridged edition, 1993.

Although written in sometimes dense nineteenth-century American English, Emerson's essay on self-reliance cannot help but inspire you to find your unique strengths and make the most of them against all odds.

Acknowledgments

First and foremost, we would like to express enormous gratitude to the many women who spoke to us about their divorces with such generosity and honesty, enabling us to build this book girlfriend by girlfriend.

We would also like to thank our agent, Maria Massie, whose confidence in our project and calm support nurtured us in the early stages and helped us find our home at Broadway Books with Ann Campbell, our editor. Ann's amazing editorial talents, reflected on every page of the book, made revising the manuscript remarkably easy and satisfying.

To our friend Elizabeth Pearson, who helped us get the book off the ground on a crucial morning in Palm Springs, we owe much of the book's initial momentum. For lending expert advice at various stages of the process, we are grateful to Heather Byer, Jessica Green, Lynn Harris, Katie Orenstein, Pamela Paul, Maura and Merry Phelan, and Betsey Schmidt. A big thank-you goes out to Maggie Peters for the fabulous photo shoot and for giving us so much of her time and talent.

For their enthusiasm and interest along the way, Sarah would like to thank Sarah Banks, Lucy Barzun, Alexandra Frangos, Tom and Caroline Grauman, Lisa and Dan Haines, Eliot Hoyt, Ellen Hufbauer, Allyson Mendenhall, Mariana Mensch, Sarah Ries, Juliet Siler, Serita Winthrop, and Alexis Walker. For carrying her through many a rough patch, Sarah is especially grateful to her family. To Kay, boundless thanks for making the collaborative writing process as fun and inspiring as could be. Finally, Sarah would like to thank Greg for his unfailing good humor, camaraderie, and steadfast love.

Kay would like to extend a huge thanks to Sarah for originally conceiving of the idea for the book, inviting her to coauthor it and being such a wonderful, conscientious collaborator. Kay would also like to thank her peeps in San Francisco for providing feedback on matters great and small and for yelping with joy every time the book moved an inch closer to becoming a reality: Stephanie Ashe, Ethan Balogh, Jane Benitz, Kelly Close, Marites Cristobal, Jane Dickstein, Stacy Katz, Kasama Lee, Amy Marr, Jennifer Paperman, Jason Patent, Colette Plum, Loren Pogir, Page Sargisson, Vindi Singh, Lindsay Swain, and Stacy Wenzel. Finally, Kay would like to acknowledge her more farflung family and friends, who cheered her on from across a continent and, in some cases, an ocean: the Berner family, Cecilia Burgin, Jessica Green, Ingeborg Hoesterey, Kenworth and Cynthia Moffett, Andrea Piperakis Sanders, Alex Sapirstein, and Betsey Schmidt.

Index

abuse
after the separation, 86–87,
144–145
emotional, 26–27, 31, 112,
144–145
in a fault-based divorce, 132
as one of criteria for a lawyer,
112
physical, 86–87, 112, 132
safety measures, 86–87
Academy of Family Mediators, 121
adultery
diplomacy concerning, 178
legal aspects, 132–133
others' reaction to your, 177, 178
alcoholism. See substance abuse
American Academy of Matrimonial
Lawyers, 113
anger
and the grieving process, 41–42,
148
management of, 101–102
misplaced, 227
of others about the divorce,
68–69
assets. See possessions
attorney. See lawyer; legal aspects

bank accounts, 95–96, 226
belongings. See possessions
biological clock, 222–223
blind dates, 166–167, 201–202

boyfriend
"better than nothing" relationship, 210
former male friend as, 202–203
go slowly with, 196–197
his insecurities about your ex,
213–214
insta-marriage, 190–191, 196
legal aspects, 230
moving in with, 80–81
"negativity bias," 212–213
and old mutual friends, 172
residue of the divorce with,
211–215
budget, how to create, 103–105

children
delay in motherhood, 21
your biological clock, 222–223
commitment, fear of, 211–212,
219–221
communication
about division of possessions, 91
about money, 226
about new address, 83
about your remarriage, 229–230
calling your ex, 46–47
closure with an uninteresting
date, 199–200, 202
discussing your ex, 176–177,
178, 207–209
"elevator speech," 167–168

flirting, 200–201
ground rules for, 149
improvement after the divorce,
    149
intermittent with ex, in tribute,
    154
role in the failure of marriage,
    30–31
shifting from "we" to "I," 75
telling friends and family, 57–59
telling miscellaneous others,
    72–73, 137, 162, 167–168
telling people at work, 70–71
telling your date you are di-
    vorced, 207–209
while dating, 197, 198
with your husband about want-
    ing divorce, 110–111
with your lawyer, 117, 118
community property, legal aspects, 87
coping mechanisms
    change of scenery, 181
    exercise, 42, 181
    to overcome embarrassment, 165
    support system, 59–64,
        180–181, 243
    wisdom of the ages, 243–244
    work, 50–51
    See also counseling; self-
        realization
counseling
    couples or premarital, 227–228
    marriage, 37
    post-divorce, 63–64, 140, 191
court appearance, 132
credit cards, 96–98, 146
cultural aspects
    cohabitation, 11
    high divorce rate, 21–22, 163
    perception of divorce, 160–161,
        171
    societal pressure for marriage,
        10–12, 17–18, 19

dating
    avoid inadvertent stalking,
        196–197

avoid oversharing, 198
be yourself, 198
boy mania, 189–190
closure with an uninteresting
    person, 199–200, 202
in the early phase, 185–191
experimental, 192–194
fear of never meeting the right
    person, 209–210, 221
flirting, 200–201
four brilliant insights, 186
insta-marriage, 190–191
lack of interest in, 187–188
"negativity bias" while, 212–213
online, 204–205
as a process of elimination, 196
setups, 166–167, 201–202
and sex. See sexual activity
subtle communication while,
    197
telling your date you are di-
    vorced, 207–209
tips, 196–201
where to meet men, 64,
    201–206, 221
your "type," 194–195, 205
decision-making
    to begin divorce proceedings,
        108–111
    to have children, 21
    to hire a lawyer, 88, 112–113,
        127
    to move out, 78–79, 88, 131
    your name, 72, 235
decree of divorce, 134–135
depression, 24
    medication for, 49
    and need for a lawyer, 112
    sleep patterns with, 48–49
desperation, 209–210, 221
divorce
    children of, 2
    costs, 119, 120, 129. See also
        lawyer, costs
    do-it-yourself (pro se), 124–128
    "drive-through," 128
    fault-based, 132–134

integration into identity, 244–245
legal process of, 111–134
"no-fault," 130–132, 133
others' perceptions of, 160–161,
170–171, 183, 208
others' reaction to, 62, 65–69,
168–170
positive attitude about, 52–55
"quickie," 128–129
relationship with ex after, 74
social context for, 9, 21
statistics, 8, 217
when to begin proceedings,
108–111
your perception of, 161–165,
183, 208–209
yours *vs.* your mother's, 20–22
your synopsis of the, 167–168
divorce clinic, 120
divorce shower, 181–182
do-it-yourself divorce, 124–128
Dominican Republic, 128–129
"drive-through divorce," 128
drugs. *See* substance abuse

economics. *See* financial aspects
"the elevator speech," 167–168
email, 141–142, 154, 230
emotional aspects
anger. *See* anger
desperation, 209–210, 221
embarrassment, 163, 164, 165
fear. *See* fear
feeling comfortable with,
240–241
feelings expressed by your ex,
143–149
"getting over" your ex, 158
grieving process, 36–47, 135,
148–150
of insta-marriage, 191
joy. *See* joy
of mediation, 122–123
of moving in with a new flame,
80–81
of receipt of divorce papers,
134–135

sadness. *See* sadness
self-doubt, 40–41
of starting divorce proceedings,
108–111
when your ex finds someone
else, 151, 152, 156–157
in the workplace, 70
your inner adolescent, 39–40
ex, encounters with your
avoid calling, 46–47
in the beginning, 137–152
boundaries, 143
change, 150–152
communication about your remarriage, 230
emailing, 141–142, 154, 230
and your family, 74
grieving together, 148–150
with his new flame, 151–152,
174
minimize quibbles, 139–140
and moral capital, 138–139
and moving in with your new
flame, 80–81
and mutual friends, 173–174
no contact policy, 152–154
odd behavior by, 142–148
preparation for meetings with,
139
sleeping together after separation, 148
your memories, 157–159,
182–183, 226, 244
your need for revenge, 140–141
exercise, 42, 181

family
how to tell them, 57–59
importance of, 42
loans from, 106
losing the in-laws, 73–75
pressure to marry from the,
14–16
reactions to the divorce, 65–69
renewal of relationships with, 3,
61–62
fault, legal aspects, 132–134

fear
 about divorce, 171
 of commitment, 211–212,
  219–221
 of communication with your ex,
  141
 and the grieving process, 37–38
 of never meeting the right person, 209–210, 221
 of the outside world, 14, 206
films, 10
financial aspects
 budget, how to create, 103–105
 community property, 87
 cost of a lawyer, 113, 115, 117,
  118, 119
 cost of the divorce, 119, 120,
  129
 debt, 87, 97–98, 112
 direct-deposit paycheck, 96
 division of finances, 87, 88, 98,
  99–100
 equitable distribution, 87
 establishing credit in your name,
  97
 housing, 106
 inheritance, 87, 88
 interest on investments, 88
 inventory, 99–100
 joint bank accounts, 95–96, 226
 joint credit and debit cards,
  96–98, 146
 of remarriage, 225–226
 single income limitations, 77,
  81, 102–107
 your own bank account, 96
flirting, 200–201
friends
 compassion toward, 242
 the ex, 149, 154–156
 girlfriends, 53–54, 152, 189,
  206–207
 help on moving day, 82–83
 how to tell them, 57–59
 to listen to you, 42
 male, as accidental boyfriends,
  202–203

 mutual, 62, 172–180
 new, 62–63, 180–181
 pressure for marriage from, 17,
  18
 reactions to the divorce, 65,
  67–69
 real and true, 242–243
 renewal of relationships with, 3,
  53–54, 60–61
 setups by, 166–167, 201–202
 for temporary housing, 79, 106
future, vision of the, 34–35, 54, 215,
 219

generational aspects
 perception of marriage and divorce, 161
 pressures for marriage, 10, 18–19
 your divorce *vs.* your mother's,
  20–22
gossip, 177
grieving process, 36–47, 135,
 148–150
guilt
 about wedding gifts, 164
 and the grieving process, 44–45
 leaver's, 100–101, 111

health
 advantages of pets, 64
 exercise, 42, 181
 sleep patterns, 48–49
 spaciness, 49
 weight changes, 47–48
holidays, 182–183
housing
 budget considerations, 106
 cohabitation with a new flame,
  80–81
 cohabitation with the ex, 79–80
 decision to move out, 78–79,
  88, 131
 making the old home new,
  84–85
 new home, 81–84
 temporary arrangements, 79,
  106

husband, ex. *See* ex, encounters with
your

ideology, 26, 65–66, 243
in-laws, 73–75
insomnia, 48–49
insta-marriage, 190–191, 196
Internet. *See* email; websites
interviewees for the book, 5–6
inventory, how to create, 99–100

journal, 54, 100, 139
joy
appreciation of, 240
and freedom, 45–46
of others about the divorce, 69
at receipt of divorce papers,
134–135

lawyer
alternatives to. *See* divorce, do-
it-yourself; mediation
communication with, 117, 118
costs, 113, 115, 117, 118, 119
how to find, 113–114
key questions for, 114–115
preparation for first meeting,
114–116
retainer agreement, 116–117
when to hire, 88, 112–113, 127
leaver's guilt, 100–101, 111
legal aspects
decree of divorce, 134
"discovery," 100
division of finances, 98, 99–100
division of property, 87–89
divorce process, 108–109,
111–134
documentation, 90, 99, 102,
129, 134, 142
of having less entanglement,
22–23
of a new flame, 230
prenuptial agreements, 226
pro se filing for divorce,
124–128
restraining orders, 86–87, 145

retainer agreement, 116–117
separation agreement, 110, 131
See also lawyer
legal centers, 127–128
loneliness, 42–43, 46–47, 237
love
continued belief in, 165
first and only, 13–14
idealism and myths, 16–17, 218
not the only criterion, 219

marital assets. *See* possessions
marriage
alternatives to "forever,"
219–221
common reasons for, 10–19
common reasons for failure of,
8, 24–31
continued belief in, 165
debriefing the, 148–150,
223–224, 237
grieving process for a, 36–47,
135, 148–150
insta-marriage, 190–191, 196
mementos of the, 92–95
memories of the, 157–159,
182–183, 226, 244
new perspective on, 218–223,
229, 235
outgrowing each other, 24–26
roles in, 29–30
the second. *See* remarriage
statistics, 217
marriage counseling, 37
media, wedding mania in the, 10
mediation, 120–124
mediator, questions to ask the, 124
memories, 157–159, 182–183, 226,
244
mental aspects
right attitude, 51–55
spaciness, 49
Mr. Right, 192, 219
mojitos, 237
money. *See* financial aspects
motherhood, 21, 222–223
moving. *See* housing

name change
    after remarriage, 235
    need for decree of divorce, 134
    return to family name, 71–72,
        126
"negativity bias," 212–213
Nevada, 128
"no-fault" divorce, 130–132, 133

online dating, 204–205

paralegals, 127–128
petition for divorce, 129–130
pets, 64, 88, 91–92
physical activity, 42, 181
possessions, division of shared
    with an abusive ex, 86–87
    communication about, 91
    emotional aspects, 76, 77
    leaver's guilt, 100–101
    legal aspects, 87–89
    mementos of the marriage,
        92–95
    pets, 88, 91–92
    tips, 89–90
    wedding gifts, 164
    wedding ring, 92–94
post-marital friendship (PMF), 149,
    154–156
premarital counseling, 227–228
prenuptial agreements, 226
pro se, 124–128
public registration of fault, 132

"quickie divorce," 128–129

rage. See anger
rebellion, marriage as, 15
relationships. See boyfriend; remar-
    riage
religious aspects, 26, 65
remarriage
    ambivalence toward, 219–221
    avoiding bigamy, 127
    faith in the possibility, 221–222
    financial aspects, 225–226
    name change, 235

new perspective on marriage,
    218–223, 229, 235
    others' reactions to, 229–230
    preparation for, 223–228
    statistics, 217
    telling others, 229–230
    telling your ex, 230
    wedding ceremony, 231–235
    and your biological clock,
        222–223
residence. See housing
resources
    books, 246–250
    for do-it-yourself divorce,
        126–127
    lawyer referral, 113–114
    online. See websites
restraining order, 86–87, 145
revenge
    your ex's desire for, 148
    your desire for, 140–141
ring, wedding, 92–94, 238–239

sadness
    and the grieving process, 37–38,
        135, 148
    of others about the divorce, 68
    at receipt of divorce papers, 135
safety aspects, 86–87, 198–199, 204
self-realization
    and compassion, 55, 241–242
    discovering what you want in a
        relationship, 218–219,
        224–225
    discovering your personal style,
        83, 239
    entitlement to, 22, 238
    finances and self-reliance, 107
    integration of the divorce,
        244–245
    new routines, 51–52, 64, 239
    outgrowing each other, 24–26
    overcoming embarrassment,
        165
    pampering yourself, 52, 54–55,
        83–84, 94, 102
    perspective on life, 243–244

rediscovering your inner adolescent, 39–40
shifting from "we" to "I," 75
through being alone, 35–36, 43, 107, 239–240, 241
the transformation, 237–244
separation
mandatory period of, 131, 133
trial, 36–37, 40, 89
separation agreement, 110, 131
setups, 166–167, 201–202
sexual activity
exploration phase, 189–190
safe sex or no sex, 198–199
waiting period, 197
singledom
at ease with, 222, 225, 238–244
initial reactions to, 33–47
social occasions, 165–171
transition to, 180–181
sleep patterns, 48–49
social life
importance of, 206
meeting people, 64, 166, 186, 188, 207. *See also* dating
mutual friends, 62, 172–180
transition to singleton, 180–181
social occasions, 165–171, 173–174
software, for do-it-yourself divorce, 127

substance abuse, 28–29, 132
support system, 59–64, 180–181
See also family; friends

websites
Academy of Family Mediators, 121
American Academy of Matrimonial Lawyers, 113
American Bar Association, 130
completecase.com, 126
do-it-yourself divorce, 126–128
online dating, 204–205
"quickie divorce," 128
We the People, 127–128
wedding ceremonies
attending, 165–166
your second, 231–235
wedding gifts, 164, 232, 234
wedding ring, 92–94, 238–239
weight change, 47–48
work and career
as coping mechanism, 50–51
direct-deposit paychecks, 96
generational aspects, 20–21
how to tell coworkers, 70–71
single income from, 106
time off, 71
worldview, 26, 65–66

© Margaret Peters

About the Authors

KAY MOFFETT (right) is a San Francisco-based Web editor and corporate writer and SARAH TOUBORG is an executive editor at Prentice Hall in New Jersey. The authors met while pursuing undergraduate degrees at Harvard. Both women were divorced by their early thirties. Sarah remarried in 2002.